D1391458

C·O·U·N·T·R·Y
C·R·A·F·T·S

CHANCELLOR
PRESS

EDITORIAL

Editorial Director, Family Circle Books — Carol A. Guasti
Associate Editor — Kim E. Gayton
Project Editor — Leslie Gilbert Elman
Copy Editor — Laura Crocker
Book Design — Bessen, Tully & Lee
Cover Photo — Carin Riley
Illustrations — Lauren Jarrett
Editorial Production Coordinator — Celeste Bantz
Editorial Assistant — Sherieann Holder
Typesetting — Alison Chandler, Maureen Harrington, Cheryl Aden
Indexer — Candace Gylgayton

MARKETING

Director, Family Circle Books & Licensing — Margaret Chan-Yip
Direct Marketing Manager — Jill E. Schiffman
Associate Business Manager — Carrie Meyerhoff
Administrative Assistant — Laura Berkowitz

First published in 1991 by The Family Circle, Inc.

This 1992 edition published by
Chancellor Press
Michelin House
81 Fulham Road
London SW3 6RB

ISBN 1 85152 224 7

Produced by Mandarin Offset

Printed in Hong Kong

T·A·B·L·E OF
C·O·N·T·E·N·T·S

W·E·L·C·O·M·E T·O
C·O·U·N·T·R·Y C·R·A·F·T·S

Country crafts celebrates a way of living that is uniquely American. The making of crafts embraces both nostalgia and practicality—in a world of trendy styles and high-tech proliferation, it speaks of enduring family values. And just as our ancestors found time for crafting after chores were done, so today we turn to crafts in our leisure time as a way to express our creativity, our individuality, and our love of family and friends.

Spring, summer, autumn or winter—the seasons dictated both the lives and livelihoods of our forebearers. Often the color, patterns, inspiration and even the materials used in country crafting were taken from nature. The classic crafting techniques found in this book reflect both country style and seasonality.

Ranging in difficulty from elementary to advanced, the craft projects include quilting, embroidery, cross stitch, doll making, wood working, rug hooking and of course, knitting and crocheting. Complete how-to's and patterns are provided for every project. We hope this book becomes your gateway to bringing country crafts into your home, and reaping the rewards of a shared sense of history, of following in the tradition of making things by hand. Each time you craft something, you are creating a link from the present to the future, for your children and their children to treasure. Each craft you create is a unique expression of you—your involvement, your commitment, your love.

ING

Everything seems fresh and new. The air feels softer and smells fragrant. Flowers begin to appear, children run out to play *without* their heavy winter coats…and you know it's springtime in the country.

Spring is a time of renewal and rebirth, babies and brides. Bring the beauty of this season into your home with crisp linens and froths of lace. Crochet a beautiful bedspread, make a bedroom set from linen handkerchiefs, or drape a dressing table in muslin.

There is something about spring that is essentially feminine—so we devote a section to "her." There are dainties to inspire the most romantic side of any woman: pillows of ribbons and lace, a floral chintz kitty, an elegant pierced paper lamp shade.

We also offer "everlasting" fabric flowers to craft, a basketful of Easter surprises (just look and see what the Easter Bunny can bring this year!) and a gathering of our favorite needle arts to beautify your home or give to a special someone.

In the country, spring is one of the busiest times of the year. Everyone works to ready the home and farm for the seasons ahead. All the activity and planning for the months to come make spring in the country a season full of promise and joy.

L · I · N · E · N
AND LACE

Crisp and
white, the look of linen and lace adds a graceful touch
to every decor. It's no wonder these have been favored
crafting materials for generations.

HANDKERCHIEF & LACE BEDROOM SET

What makes it country? A clean, light, feminine look created with soft fabric and bits of lace.

Average: For those with some experience in sewing.

General Materials:
Same-size square handkerchiefs (we used 10- or 10½-inch square white women's handkerchiefs with plain edges; men's plain white handkerchiefs bought by the dozen, colored bandannas, or mismatched handkerchiefs can be used if they have plain edges and are the same size); matching thread; 1½-inch-wide white polyester lace with 2 straight edges; cardboard square slightly larger than handkerchiefs.

General Directions:
The handkerchiefs are joined with strips of lace side by side into rows as wide as necessary. The rows are sewn together to make the "fabric" as long as needed.

1. *Estimating Number of Handkerchiefs Needed:* When possible, the number of 10-inch handkerchiefs needed for a project is indicated. In other cases, add 1½ inches to the size of the handkerchiefs to get the size of the assembling unit. Measure the item you wish to cover. Where applicable, subtract 3 inches from the length and width for the border lace that will be attached to the outside edges of the assembly. Divide the resulting measurements by the size of the assembling unit. This tells you how many handkerchiefs you need for a particular project, and how many rows to assemble.

2. Wash the handkerchiefs to shrink them. Press them with a steam iron.

3. *Adjusting Handkerchief Size:* For the projects to square up properly, with corners matching, the handkerchiefs have to be perfect squares. Measure all four sides of each handkerchief. Cut a square cardboard template the size of the smallest side of the smallest handkerchief. Place each handkerchief on the template, turn under the excess fabric, and press it in place.

4. *Making Rows:* Place the first two handkerchiefs on the sewing machine side by side and about 1½ inches apart. Set a narrow zigzag stitch to about 6 stitches per inch; practice on a scrap of fabric. Cut a 5-yard length of lace. Place the lace in the space between the handkerchiefs so the lace's long edges overlap the adjacent handkerchief edges slightly. All top edges should be flush and even. Stitch along each long lace edge to join the handkerchiefs. Cut off the lace flush at the bottom edge. Repeat along the opposite side of one of the handkerchiefs. Continue adding lace and handkerchiefs to the row until it is as wide as needed.

5. *Joining Rows:* Lap a length of lace between the rows, and join them in the same way the handkerchiefs were joined in Step 4.

6. *Finishing Edges:* When indicated, sew a single strip of lace all around the outside edges of the assembly, mitering the corners.

*Sweet spring,
full of sweet days and roses.*
— George Herbert

BEDSPREAD
(photo, page 4; for queen-size bed)

Materials:
General Materials *(page 5)*: 49 handkerchiefs, and 34 yards of lace.

Directions:
Assemble the bedspread following General Directions, Steps 2 to 5 *(page 5)*. The bedspread is seven handkerchiefs-to-a-row wide, and seven rows long. It drops to cover a few inches of the box spring, and is spread flat under the shams. Make the bedspread floor length if you don't wish to make the matching dust ruffle. Make the bedspread longer, to cover the bed pillows with an 8-inch tuck, if you don't wish to make the matching pillow shams. Finish the assembled bedspread following General Directions, Step 6.

DUST RUFFLE

Materials:
General Materials *(page 5)*; 1 white flat bed sheet.

Directions:
Measure the box spring; add two times the depth of the box spring to the width, and one time the depth to the length. Cut a platform piece from the bed sheet to these measurements. Following General Directions, Steps 1 to 4 *(page 5)*, make a row of handkerchiefs for each drop edge. Depending on the height of the bed, you may need to add more than one row of handkerchiefs to each drop edge for a floor-length dust ruffle. Join handkerchief rows, if necessary, following General Directions, Step 5. Stitch a strip of lace along the upper edge of each top handkerchief row, and along the lower edge of each bottom row. Find the centers of all three drop edges, and pin mark them. Do the same for the handkerchief rows. Matching the marks, join the handkerchief rows to the drop edges, layering the upper lace edges over the fabric, and pleating any excess handkerchief at each end of the drops.

The nicest thing
about the promise of spring
is that sooner or later
she'll have to keep it.
— Mark Beltaire

PILLOW SHAMS WITH FRENCH BACK
(photo, page 4; 22 inches square, plus lace edge)

Materials for Two Shams:
General Materials *(page 5)*: 8 handkerchiefs, and 8 yards of lace; two 24-inch square European pillows; 1 yard of 45-inch-wide white cotton-blend fabric.

Directions:
1. Sham Front: Following General Directions, Steps 2 to 5 *(page 5)*, make two rows of two handkerchiefs each, and join the rows to make a sham front. Finish the sham front following General Directions, Step 6. Repeat to make a second sham front.

2. Sham Back: Cut the cotton fabric in half lengthwise to make two 22½ x 36-inch pieces. Cut a 14-inch length from each piece, and then a 16-inch length. Place the same-size pieces together, and mark the sets "large" and "small." You will need one large and one small piece for each sham's French back.

3. On all four back pieces, hem one 22½-inch edge ¼ inch, then 2 inches. Turn under the other edges ⅛ inch, and press.

4. Assembling: Turn one sham front wrong side up. Place one large and one small sham back piece right side up over the sham front so the pressed edges of the back pieces align with the handkerchief edges, not the lace edges; adjust the pressed edges so the back pieces fit. Overlap the hemmed back piece edges about 4 inches at the center back. Pin the sham back pieces to the handkerchief edges all around, and topstitch. Insert one of the pillows through the opening in the back. Repeat for the second pillow sham.

NECK ROLL
(photo, page 4; about 33 inches long, plus ruffle)

Materials:
General Materials *(page 5)*: 6 handkerchiefs, and 4 yards of lace; 1 yard of white cotton-blend fabric; synthetic batting; 2-inch-wide ruffled lace for roll ends; 1 yard of 1-inch-wide white grosgrain ribbon.

Directions:
1. Neck Roll Cover: Following General Directions, Steps 2 to 5 *(page 5)*, make two rows of three handkerchiefs each, and join the rows to make a rectangle. Sew a strip of 1½-inch lace to each long edge. Sew a strip of ruffled lace to each short end. Lap one long lace edge over the opposite long edge to make a tube, and stitch.

2. Pillow: Cut a 23 x 33-inch cotton fabric rectangle. Fold the rectangle in half lengthwise, right sides together. Stitch a ½-inch seam along the long edge and one short end. Turn the pillowcase right side out. Roll up the batting, and stuff the pillowcase with it. Slipstitch the open short end of the pillowcase closed *(see Stitch Guide, page 214)*.

3. Center the pillow inside the neck roll cover. Cut the ribbon in half. Wrap one ribbon length around the neck roll cover at one end of the pillow, and tie a bow. Repeat at the other end of the pillow.

TABLE OVERCLOTH
(photo, page 4; about 48 inches square, to fit a 24- to 30-inch-diameter table)

Materials:
General Materials *(page 5)*: 16 handkerchiefs, and 13 yards of lace.

Directions:
Following General Directions, Steps 2 to 5 *(page 5)*, make four rows of four handkerchiefs each, and join the rows to make a square. Finish the overcloth following General Directions, Step 6.

LAMP SHADE SKIRT
(photo, page 4)

Materials:
General Materials *(page 5)*: 2 handkerchiefs, and 3½ yards of lace; 1½ yards of ruffled lace; 1½ yards of shirring tape.

Directions:
1. Cutting: Prepare the handkerchiefs following General Directions, Step 2 *(page 5)*. Cut the handkerchiefs in quarters into 5-inch squares.

2. Sewing: Following General Directions, Step 4, make one row of seven handkerchief quarters, with embroidered corners, if any, at the lower left. Sew a strip of lace to one short end of the row.

3. Stitch a strip of 1½-inch-wide lace along the upper and lower edges of the row. Sew the ruffled lace to the bottom edge of the lower lace strip. Sew the shirring tape along the top of the row, on the wrong side, flush with the bottom edge of the upper lace strip; stop ½ inch from the short ends of the row. Using a ½-inch seam allowance, stitch the short ends of the row to make a ring, being careful not to stitch over the cords in the shirring tape. Place the skirt over the lamp shade, and pull up the cords until the skirt fits the shade's top edge. Knot the cords to secure the skirt.

C O U N T R Y   W A Y S

• Washing Lace •

Lace, especially antique lace, must be cleaned very carefully.

Fill a large, wide-mouthed jar halfway with soapy water. Put the lace in the jar, and shake the jar gently. Pour out the soapy water, and fill the jar halfway with fresh water. Shake the jar gently to rinse the lace.

If the lace is stained, soak it in a mixture of one part lemon juice, one part water, and a pinch of salt. Rinse the lace with fresh water.

Dry the lace by pinning it carefully to a board covered with a thick white towel; colored towels may leave visible traces of fuzz on the lace.

TASSELED BEDSPREAD
(72 x 96 inches)

What makes it country? An heirloom-quality design that makes this bedspread a treasured gift for newlyweds.

Challenging: Requires more experience in crocheting.

Materials:
DMC Brilliant Crochet Cotton (218-yard ball): 42 balls of White; size 6 steel crochet hook, OR ANY SIZE HOOK TO OBTAIN GAUGE BELOW; 5-inch cardboard square.
Gauge: Each Motif = 6½ inches, measured diagonally from corner to corner.
Note: *The bedspread is made up of 216 motifs. As each motif is made, it is crocheted to the adjacent motifs at the corners through the back loops only of each stitch. After each row of motifs is crocheted, the adjacent motif sides are sewn together through the back loops only before crocheting the next row so the bedspread does not stretch out of shape.*

Directions:
1. First Motif: Starting at the center, ch 12. Join with sl st to form a ring. **Rnd 1:** Ch 4, 4 dc in same ch as joining, drop loop from hook, insert hook in 4th ch of first ch-4 and draw dropped loop through — **beginning popcorn st made;** ch 4, * skip 1 ch, 5 dc in next ch, drop loop from hook, insert hook in first dc of the 5-dc group and draw dropped loop through — **popcorn st made;** ch 4; rep from * 4 more times. Join with sl st to top of first popcorn st — 6 popcorn sts made. **Rnd 2:** Ch 3, 4 dc in first ch of ch-4 made in previous rnd, drop loop from hook, insert hook in top of first ch-3 and draw dropped loop through — **beginning popcorn st made;** * ch 4, skip 1 ch, popcorn st in next ch, ch 4, work popcorn st in 2nd ch of ch-4; rep from * 4 more times, ending with ch 4, sk 1 ch, popcorn st in next ch, ch 4. Join to top of first popcorn st — 12 popcorn sts made. **Rnd 3:** Ch 3, 1 dc in first ch-4 lp, * ch 4, 2 dc in next ch-4 lp, ch 2, 2 dc in next ch-4 lp; rep from * 4 more times, ending with ch 4, 2 dc in next ch-4 lp, ch 2. Join to top of first ch-3 — 12 loops made. **Rnd 4:** Ch 3, 1 dc in next dc, * ch 5, 1 dc in each of next 2 dc, ch 4, 1 dc in each of next 2 dc; rep from * 4 more times, ending with ch 5, 1 dc in each of next 2 dc, ch 4. Join to top of first ch-3. **Rnd 5:** Ch 3, 1 dc in next dc, * ch 3, 1 sc in center ch of ch-5, ch 3, 1 dc in each of next 2 dc, ch 5, 1 dc in each of next 2 dc; rep from * 4 more times, ending with ch 3, sc in center ch of ch-5, ch 3, 1 dc in each of next 2 dc, ch 5. Join to top of first ch-3. **Rnd 6:** Ch 3, 1 dc in next dc, * ch 7, 1 dc in each of next 2 dc, ch 3, 2 dc in center ch of ch-5, ch 3**, 1 dc in each of next 2 dc*; rep from * to * 4 more times, then rep from * to ** once. Join to top of first ch-3. **Rnd 7:** Ch 3, 1 dc in next dc, * ch 3, 1 sc in center of ch-7, ch 3, 1 dc in each of next 2 dc, ch 2, 2 dc in ch-3 lp, 1 dc in each of next 2 dc, 2 dc in next ch-3 lp, ch 2**, 1 dc in each of next 2 dc*; rep from * to * 4 more times, then from * to ** once. Join to top of first ch-3. **Rnd 8:** Ch 3, 1 dc in next dc, * ch 3, 1 dc in each of next 2 dc, ch 2, 2 dc in ch-2 lp, 1 dc in each of next 6 dc, 2 dc in next ch-2 lp, ch 2**, 1 dc in each of next 2 dc*; rep from * to * 4 more times, then rep from * to ** once. Join to top of first ch-3. **Rnd 9:** Ch 3, holding back last loop of each dc, work 1 dc in each of next 3 dc, yarn over hook and draw through 4 loops; * ch 5, 2 dc in ch-2 lp, 1 dc in each of next 4 dc, ch 2, skip 2 dc, 1 dc in each of next 4 dc, 2 dc in ch-2 lp, ch 5**; holding back last loop of each dc, work 1 dc in each of next 4 dc, yarn over hook and draw through 5 loops*; rep from * to * 4 more times, then rep from * to ** once. Join to top of first ch-3.

(Continued on page 10)

If a thing is old,
it is a sign that it was fit to live.
The guarantee of continuity
is quality.
—Eddie Rickenbacker

Rnd 10: Sl st in each ch to 4th ch of first ch-5, ch 3, 1 dc in last ch of ch-5; * 1 dc in each of next 3 dc, ch 2, skip 2 dc, 1 dc in next dc, 2 dc in ch-2 lp, 1 dc in next dc, ch 2, skip 2 dc, 1 dc in each of next 3 dc, 1 dc in each of next 2 ch of ch-5, ch 9**; in next ch-5 work 1 dc in each of last 2 ch*; rep from * to * 4 more times, then rep from * to ** once. Join to top of first ch-3. Fasten off.

2. *One-Sided Joining, Second Motif* (see Fig. I, 1, *page 11*)**:** Work as for First Motif until Rnd 9 has been completed. ***Rnd 10:*** Follow Rnd 10 of First Motif up to but not including first ch 9. ***Now join First and Second Motifs on one side as follows:*** Ch 4, sl st in center ch of ch-9 on First Motif; ch 4, working on Second Motif only, in next ch-5 work 1 dc in each of last 2 ch, 1 dc in each of next 3 dc, ch 2, skip 2 dc, 1 dc in next dc, 2 dc in ch-2 lp, 1 dc in next dc, ch 2, skip 2 dc, 1 dc in each of next 3 dc, 1 dc in each of next 2 ch of ch-5; ch 4, sl st in center ch of ch-9 on First Motif, ch 4 to complete joining on one side. In next ch-5 of Second Motif work 1 dc in each of last 2 ch. Continue to work on Second Motif only as follows: Starting at * on Rnd 10 of First Motif, complete the other 4 sides.

3. *Two-Sided Joining, Third Motif:* Work as for First Motif until Rnd 9 has been completed. ***Rnd 10:*** Follow Rnd 10 of First Motif up to but not including ch 9. ***Now join Third Motif to First and Second Motifs as follows:*** Ch 4, sc in center joining ch of First and Second Motifs, ch 3, sl st in sc just made—***picot st made;*** ch 4, working on Third Motif only, in next ch-5 work 1 dc in each of last 2 ch, 1 dc in each of next 3 dc, ch 2, skip 2 dc, 1 dc in next dc, 2 dc in ch-2 lp, 1 dc in next dc, ch 2, skip 2 dc, 1 dc in each of next 3 dc, 1 dc in each of next 2 ch of ch-5; ch 4, sl st in center ch of ch-9 on Second Motif, ch 4 to complete joining of Third and Second Motifs. In next ch-5 of Third Motif work 1 dc in each of last 2 ch. Continue to work on Third Motif only starting at * on Rnd 10 of First Motif up to but not including ch-9 on sixth side of Third Motif. ***Now join Third and First Motifs as follows:*** Ch 4, sl st in center ch of ch-9 on First Motif, ch 4. Join to top of first ch-3 on Third Motif. Continue to join the remaining Motifs following One-Sided, Two-Sided, or Four-Sided Joining (*see* Fig. I, 1). After each row of Motifs is crocheted, sew the adjacent Motif sides together through the back lps only of each st before crocheting the next row of Motifs.

4. *Four-Sided Joining, Occurs First at 23rd Motif:* Work as for First Motif until Rnd 9 has been completed. ***Rnd 10:*** Follow Rnd 10 of First Motif up to but not including ch-9. ***Now join 23rd and Sixth Motifs as follows:*** Ch 4, sl st in center ch of ch-9 on Sixth Motif; ch 4, working on second side of 23rd Motif only, * in next ch-5 work 1 dc in each of last 2 ch, 1 dc in each of next 3 dc, ch 2, skip 2 dc, 1 dc in next dc, 2 dc in ch-2 lp, 1 dc in next dc, ch 2, skip 2 dc, 1 dc in each of next 3 dc, 1 dc in each of next 2 ch of ch-5*, ch 4, sc in center joining ch of Fourth and Sixth Motifs, ch 3, sl st in sc just made—***picot st formed;*** ch 4, working on third side of 23rd Motif only, rep from * to * once, ch 4, sc in center joining ch of Third and Fourth Motifs, picot st; ch 4, working on fourth side of 23rd Motif only, rep from * to * once, ch 4, sc in center joining ch of 22nd and Third Motifs, picot st; ch 4, working on fifth side of 23rd Motif only, rep from * to * once, ch 4, sl st in center ch of ch-9 on 22nd Motif; ch 4, working on sixth side of 23rd Motif only, rep from * to * once. Join to top of first ch-3. Fasten off.

5. *Fringe:* Wind the thread 20 times around the cardboard square. Cut the thread at one edge of the square to make twenty 10-inch-long strands. Hold the strands together, and fold them in half to form a loop. Insert the hook from the back to the front in the first ch-9 sp on one side of the bedspread, and draw the loop through. Draw the loose ends of the strands through the loop, and pull tightly to knot the fringe. Continue tying fringes to the side and bottom edges of the bedspread following Fig. I, 1. Leave the top edge of the bedspread free. Trim the fringes evenly.

C O U N T R Y   W A Y S

• *Lace* •

This fine handiwork has been in existence for centuries. Lace always has been difficult to make, very costly, and highly prized. While the most costly laces were, and still are, made by hand, machine-made lace has been available since the mid-1700's. In fact, the technology used to make lace by machine has existed since about 1590.

From Alençon to Valenciennes, the varieties of lace seem endless. Most laces are named for the cities in which they first were produced, and come from France, Italy, Belgium, Ireland, Spain and the Middle East. Laces vary in the methods and materials used to produce them, and in their patterns and styles.

FIG. I, 1 TASSELED BEDSPREAD HEXAGON MOTIF JOINING DIAGRAM

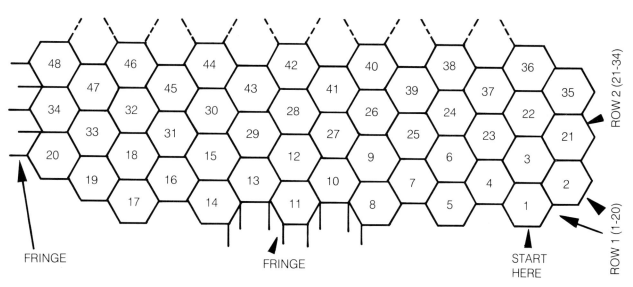

COUNTRY WAYS

• Muslin •

This cotton fabric was named for the Turkish city of Mosul, but most of the muslins known in Europe and America came from India.

Sometimes the fabric was dyed or printed, but most muslin was, and still is, bleached or left its natural color. It is distinguished by its texture, which ranges from fine to coarse, and its weave, which sometimes includes jacquard-style patterns.

Muslin fabric usually was stiffened. Depending on its stiffness, muslin was used for curtains, bed linens or garments. The stiffest muslin sometimes was known as "mourning" or "widow's" muslin. It was used to make widow's caps, collars and cuffs. Today, muslin often is treated with stiffener, and most patterns recommend washing the fabric before using it.

In early trading records, some muslins were referred to as "calicuts" because they came from the Indian port of Calicut. This makes charting the history of muslin rather difficult, because brightly printed calico fabric also takes its name from Calicut. In fact, the plain-weave fabric we know as muslin still is called "calico" in England.

It has long been an axiom of mine that the little things are infinitely the most important.
— Sir Arthur Conan Doyle

RUFFLES AND ROSES VANITY SET

What makes it country? Using ingenuity to create a pretty dressing area from simple sheets. What a lovely way to pamper yourself!

Average: For those with some experience in sewing and crafting.

DRESSING TABLE

Materials:

3 solid color twin-size flat bed sheets; 6 yards each of 1- and 1½-inch-wide coordinating color double-faced satin ribbon; matching threads; 1½ yards of coordinating floral print fabric for table top (enough to cover Mirror Frame also); 17½ x 38 inches of ¾-inch-thick particle board; four 25¾-inch-long screw-on table legs; 17½ x 38 inches of ¼-inch-thick glass with safety edges; synthetic batting; pinking shears; sewing needle; kitchen string; staple gun.

Directions:

1. Table: Fasten the table legs to the particle board. Cover the board with the batting, and staple the batting edges about 8 inches under the table.

2. Skirt Lining: Press one of the bed sheets, and spread it over the table so the sheet edges touch the floor all around. Staple the sheet to the board edge. Using the pinking shears, cut off the bottom edges of the sheet just above the floor. Cut away the excess fold at each corner, leaving a straight vertical slit.

3. Skirt: Open the hems of the remaining two sheets, press them, and cut six 31½-inch lengths across the full width; set aside the remaining sheet fabric. At each bottom edge, turn up ½ inch, then 3 inches, and stitch a hem. At each top edge, turn under 1 inch and press. Place a length of kitchen string inside along the fold and, at the center of the panel, stitch through the string for ½ inch. Stitch a casing ½ inch from the top fold without catching in the string. Gather the fabric on each panel; gather the table side panels to 17½ inches. On the longer panels, stitch the strings to the panel edges 9½ inches to each side of the centers to hold the gathers; on the shorter panels, stitch 8¾ inches from the centers. Staple two of the longer panels across the table front, stapling the center of each panel to the table just under the string. Continue stapling toward each panel end, arranging the gathers evenly. Repeat on the table back. Staple the shorter panels to the table sides.

(Continued on page 14)

4. *Ruffles:* From the remaining sheet fabric, cut six 2-inch-wide strips across the full width with the pinking shears. Fold each strip in half lengthwise, and press. Open each strip, and lay a length of kitchen string inside along the fold. Using a wide zigzag machine stitch, sew over the string without catching it in the stitches. Gather the strips to match the skirt panels, and stitch the string ends. Hand-sew the ruffles to the skirt panels, over the staples, with the top edge of the ruffles about ¾ inch above the table.

5. Using the pinking shears, cut a floral print rectangle the same size as the glass. Spread the floral print rectangle over the table top, under the glass.

6. *Roses:* Cut two 30-inch lengths of 1½-inch-wide ribbon for the large roses, and six 22-inch lengths of 1-inch-wide ribbon for the small roses. For each length, closely fold over one end six times and sew the bottom edges together *(see* Fig. I, 2A)*;* do not cut the thread. Fold the ribbon downward diagonally *(see* Fig. I, 2B) and wind it around the center, sewing the bottom edge *(see* Fig. I, 2C)*.* Finish the wind and, at the left side *(see* Fig. I, 2D)*,* repeat the folding and winding. Repeat until the ribbon is used up, making the last "petals" looser. Cut a 1½-yard length of 1½-inch-wide ribbon, and tie it into a bow with 18-inch-long streamers. Stitch the center of the bow. Hand-sew the bow to one front table corner along with one large and three small roses. Repeat at the other front corner.

RUFFLES AND ROSES VANITY SET   RIBBON ROSES

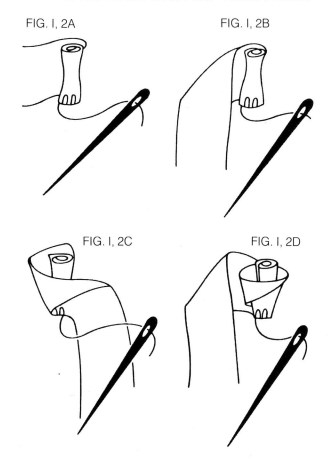

FIG. I, 2A

FIG. I, 2B

FIG. I, 2C

FIG. I, 2D

MIRROR FRAME
(photo, page 13)

Materials:
27 x 30 inches each of floral print fabric and synthetic batting remaining from Dressing Table *(page 12)*; ¼ yard of same color bed sheet fabric used for Dressing Table; 1 yard of same 1½-inch-wide and 2 yards of same 1-inch-wide double-faced satin ribbon used for Dressing Table; matching threads; 22 x 25 inches of plywood or particle board with a centered 13½ x 16½-inch cutout; 15 x 18-inch mirror; 4 mirror holders; kitchen string; pinking shears; sewing needle; staple gun.

Directions:
1. Wrap the batting over the plywood or particle board frame, and staple the batting edges to the back of the frame. Cut an X in the batting that connects the corners of the frame's center cutout. Pull the center batting to the back of the frame and staple it, trimming away the excess. Cover the frame with the floral print fabric in the same way.
2. Using the pinking shears, cut 180 inches of 2-inch-wide strips and 120 inches of 1¼-inch-wide strips from the bed sheet fabric. Make ruffles with the strips and kitchen string following Dressing Table, Step 4 *(page 14)*. Pull up the ruffles to half their length. Using the photo on page 13 as a placement guide, hand-sew the ruffles to the frame, turning under the raw ends.
3. Attach the mirror and mirror holders to the back of the frame.
4. Following Dressing Table, Step 6, make one large and three small ribbon roses. Hand-sew the roses to the center top of the frame *(see photo)*.

STOOL
(photo, page 13)

Materials:
¾ yard of same floral print fabric, and 1¼ yards of 48-inch-wide same color bed sheet fabric used in Dressing Table *(page 12)*; matching thread; clean joint-compound bucket; 14-inch-diameter circle of ½-inch-thick plywood; 14-inch-diameter circle of 2-inch-thick foam; synthetic batting; three ½-inch-long wood screws; sewing needle; pinking shears; kitchen string; staple gun.

Directions:
1. Drill three evenly spaced holes in the bucket bottom, and screw the bottom to the plywood. Turn the bucket plywood side up.
2. Place the foam circle and several rounds of batting over the plywood. Wrap a large piece of batting over the entire top and staple the batting piece to the plywood edges, trimming away the excess. Lay the floral print fabric over the batting and staple the fabric to the plywood in the same way, pulling the fabric gently until it is smooth and fairly taut. Trim away the excess floral fabric.
3. Using the pinking shears, cut two 18½-inch lengths from the bed sheet fabric across the full width. Following Dressing Table, Step 3 *(page 12)*, make two skirt panels. Gather each panel to 24 inches, and staple it to the plywood edge. Cut two 48 x 2-inch strips from the bed sheet fabric with the pinking shears. Make a ruffle following Dressing Table, Step 4 *(page 14)*, and hand-sew it around the stool.

*The first day of spring
was once the time for taking
the young virgins into the fields,
there in dalliance
to set an example of fertility
for Nature to follow.
Now we just set the clock
an hour ahead
and change the oil in the crankcase.*
— E. B. White

E·S·P·E·C·I·A·L·L·Y
FOR HER

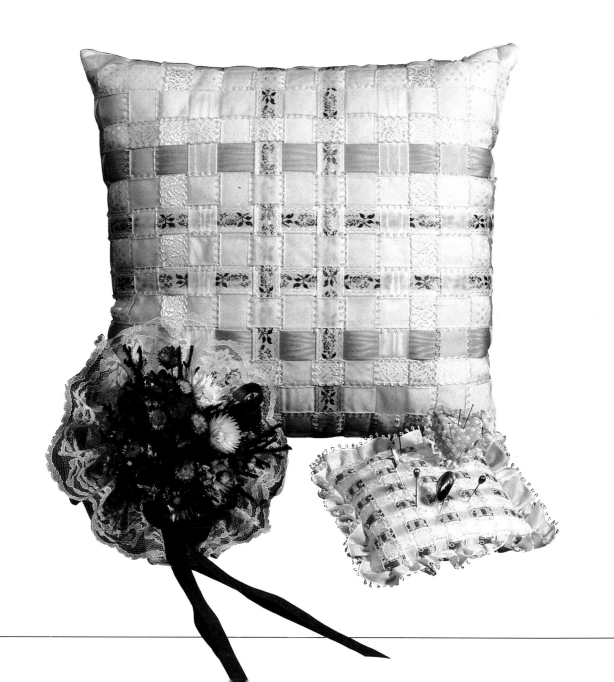

M

other, daughter,
sister, best friend or a bride-to-be—make one of these
lovely projects to touch the heart of a special woman.

COUNTRY WAYS

• *Decorating with Lace* •

Lace always has been a prized possession. In the past, even bits of lace weren't discarded. After an item had outlived its usefulness, the lace used to decorate it was clipped off and saved for another purpose. Lace has been used primarily for fashion, but certain varieties of lace have been used to trim household items.

Although decorating styles have changed drastically over the centuries, lace has remained a popular home decorating material. Today, no matter what your country preference, lace can fit into your decor.

For a Victorian look, use lace antimacassars on chairs and sofas, and tacked over velvet-covered pillows. Crocheted lace tablecloths are lovely for the dining room, or on a fabric-covered night table.

To create Colonial or Americana country, use simple-patterned lace for curtains, and as table runners and dresser scarves.

If you decorate in French country style, tack lace edging on open kitchen shelves. Filet crochet lace is just right for curtains.

If you like the simple look of Southwestern or Shaker style, top the heavy pine furniture that characterizes these styles with lace. Mix and match a few lace dresser scarves for an interesting look. Even if your living areas are too rough-hewn for anything dainty, bring out lace in the bedroom, where a feminine influence is never out of place.

WOVEN RIBBON PILLOW
(14¹⁄₂ inches square)

Average: For those with some experience in crafting.

Materials:
16-inch square of white satin; matching thread; 1-inch-wide ribbons: 4½ yards of white picot, 2¾ yards of white moire, 1⅞ yards each of white dot, white floral jacquard and colored jacquard, and 1 yard of pink; 16-inch square of lightweight fusible interfacing; 14-inch square pillow form, or synthetic stuffing; pressing cloth.

Directions:
1. *Cutting:* Cut the following 16-inch ribbon lengths: ten of white picot (3), six of white moire (1), four each of white dot (2), white jacquard (4) and colored jacquard (6), and two of pink (5). The numbers in parenthesis refer to the order in which the ribbons will be laid out.
2. *Weaving:* With the fusible side up, place the fusible interfacing on an ironing board. Place the ribbons horizontally across the interfacing, matching their top edges and pinning them into the ironing board, in this order: 1, 2, 3, 4, 5, 3, 6, 3, 6, 3, 5, 4, 3, 2, 1. For the vertical layout, pin the ribbons in this order: 1, 2, 3, 4, 1, 3, 6, 3, 6, 3, 1, 4, 3, 2, 1, weaving the vertical ribbons over and under the horizontal ribbons, and leaving about a ¹⁄₁₆ inch space between the ribbons. Pin the ribbons at their bottom ends, keeping their side edges parallel. Using the pressing cloth and an iron set on steam, fuse the ribbons in place.
3. *Assembling:* With right sides together and edges matching, pin the woven ribbon pillow front to the satin square. Taking a seam deep enough to catch the outside edge of the outside ribbons, stitch around three sides and four corners. Turn the pillow right side out, and stuff it. Turn in the open edges, and slipstitch the opening closed *(see Stitch Guide, page 214).*

WOVEN RIBBON PIN CUSHION

(photo, page 16; 5½ inches square)

Average: For those with some experience in crafting.

Materials:

6½-inch square of white satin; matching thread; 1⅜ yards each of ½-inch-wide pink ribbon and ⅜-inch-wide white floral jacquard ribbon; 2⅔ yards of ⅜-inch-wide white picot ribbon; 1⅜ yards of 1-inch-wide white picot ribbon; 6½-inch square of non-woven fusible interfacing; synthetic stuffing.

Directions:

1. Cut the pink, white jacquard and ⅜-inch-wide picot ribbons into 6½-inch lengths. Following Woven Ribbon Pillow, Step 2 *(page 17)*, pin seven pink and six white jacquard ribbons vertically to the interfacing. Then weave the ⅜-inch-wide picot ribbons horizontally through the vertical ribbons, and fuse all the ribbons in place.

2. Stitch together the ends of the 1-inch-wide picot ribbon. Fold and mark the ribbon in quarters. Stitch a gathering line along one long edge of the ribbon, and a second gathering line ¼ inch from the first gathering line. With right sides together, pin the ribbon to the woven ribbon cushion front, matching the quarter marks to the corners, and pull up the gathers to fit. Stitch a ½-inch seam. With right sides together, stitch the satin square to the woven ribbon cushion front along the previous stitching around three sides and four corners. Turn the cushion right side out, and stuff it. Turn in the open edges, and slipstitch the opening closed *(see Stitch Guide, page 214)*.

POTPOURRI NOSEGAY

(photo, page 16)

Easy: Achievable by anyone.

Materials:

Two yards of ⅝-inch-wide burgundy velvet ribbon; cone-shaped plastic flower holder with lace edging; floral wire; green floral tape; variety of blue, burgundy and white dried flowers *(see photo)*; potpourri *(directions, page 114)*.

Directions:

Arrange the flowers in a pleasing bouquet, and wrap their stems with floral wire. Insert the bouquet and the potpourri into the flower holder, and wrap the protruding stems with floral tape. Make ribbon bows, and decorate the nosegay with them.

COUNTRY WAYS

• Mother's Day •

Contrary to the popular belief that Mother's Day was fabricated by greeting card companies to boost their sales, the holiday actually has a more heartfelt history. The celebration of Mother's Day generally is credited to Anna M. Jarvis, who lived in Pennsylvania at the turn of the century.

Anna Jarvis began holding an annual service in memory of her mother the year after her mother died, on May 9, 1905. She encouraged other sons and daughters to do the same.

The idea of an annual celebration devoted to mothers everywhere became Anna Jarvis' personal crusade. She wrote thousands of letters to politicians and other influential people asking for the holiday to be recognized officially. Finally, in 1913, the United States Congress voted to support the idea. Mother's Day is celebrated every year on the second Sunday in May.

Be she fairer than the day,
Or the flow'ry meads in May,
If she not be so to me,
What care I how fair she be?
—George Wither

PIERCED PAPER LAMP SHADE

Challenging: For those with more experience in crafting.

Materials:

5 x 12 x 7-inch hexagon chimney lamp shade frame; lamp shade paper; tracing paper; sheet of Saral transfer paper; 3 yards of ¼-inch-wide dark brown velvet ribbon; 1¾ yards of ¾-inch-wide beige grosgrain ribbon; lamp shade piercer (available at some craft stores); X-acto® knife with #11 blade; 12-inch square of plate glass; stylus; white glue; gum eraser; scissors; 3 dozen clothespins; thick towel; paper for pattern.

Directions:

1. Trace the full size designs in Figs. I, 3A and B *(pages 20-21)* onto paper. Place the lamp shade frame on the lamp shade paper, trace the outline of each panel onto the paper and cut it out. Center the design in Fig. I, 3A on one of the paper panels. Place the transfer paper, shiny side down, between the design tracing and the paper panel. Using the stylus, trace the design onto the paper panel. Repeat with the design in Fig. I, 3B on the second panel. Continue to transfer the designs,

alternating them, on the remaining paper panels.

2. Place one paper panel on the towel on a flat surface. Using the lamp shade piercer, punch holes through the dots in the traced design, pushing the piercer deeply and evenly through the paper into the towel. Repeat on the other paper panels.

3. Place one paper panel on the plate glass. Using the X-acto knife, cut along each solid design line in a continuous motion without removing the blade from the paper; turn the paper on the glass rather than lift the blade off the paper. Do not connect the breaks in the design lines. To avoid ragged edges, be sure the blade cuts through the paper completely. Remove any remaining tracing lines gently with the eraser, being careful not to crease the paper. Brush away the eraser shavings. Repeat with the other paper panels.

4. Holding one panel with its front facing you, push the cut petals and leaves away from you. Turn over the panel. Mold the cut pieces gently between your fingers to give depth to the design. Place a thin line of glue around the inside edges of the panel. Place the panel, glue side down, on a sheet of tracing paper. Avoid flattening the molded pieces, or leaving excess tracing paper that will cause visible wrinkles when the lamp is turned on. When the glue is dry, trim the tracing paper around the panel. Repeat with the remaining panels.

5. Working in alternate spaces in the lamp shade frame with one panel at a time, apply glue around the edges of the panel and place it on the frame. Hold the panel in place with the clothespins; keep the clothespins close together, overlapping them at an angle to hold the panel on the frame firmly. Place clothespins on all sides of the panel. Repeat with two more panels, and let the glue dry. Remove the clothespins. Repeat with the remaining three panels, pinning them in place at the top and bottom of the frame.

6. Draw a light pencil line around the outside bottom of the lamp shade slightly less than ¼ inch from the bottom edge. Repeat around the top. Cut a length of grosgrain ribbon to extend around the bottom of the shade. Glue one long edge of the ribbon to the shade along the line. Dot glue along the opposite edge of the ribbon, and turn the edge to the inside of the shade. Repeat at the top of the shade.

7. Cut six 7-inch lengths of velvet ribbon. Glue one length over a side seam where the panels meet. Press the ribbon in place smoothly. Repeat with the remaining lengths. Glue the remaining velvet ribbon, stretching it to fit, to the top of the shade at the bottom edge of the grosgrain ribbon *(see photo)*. Overlap the short ends of the velvet ribbon about ¼ inch, and cut the end on the bias. Repeat at the bottom of the shade.

FIG. I, 3A   PIERCED PAPER LAMP SHADE

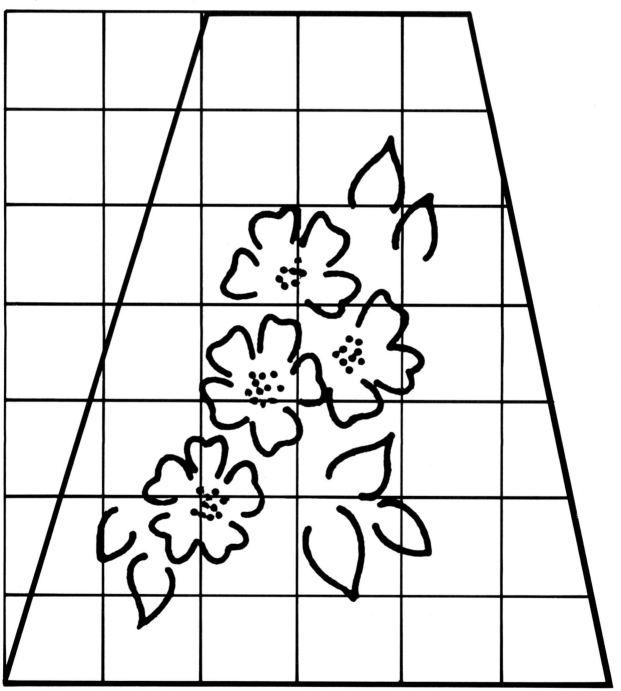

FULL SIZE PATTERN

FIG. I, 3B PIERCED PAPER LAMP SHADE

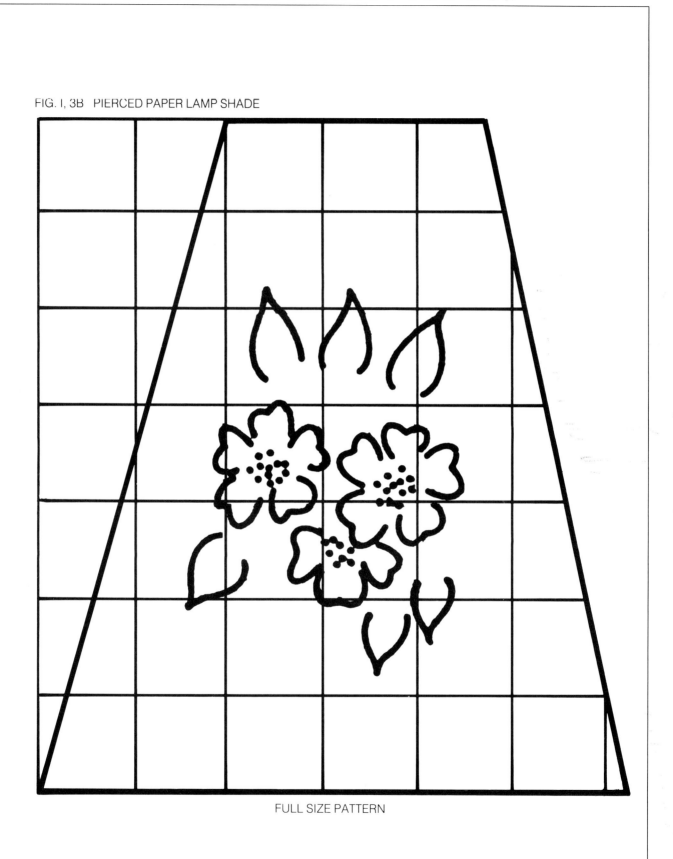

FULL SIZE PATTERN

PRETTY KITTY
(11 x 18 inches)

This chintz cat makes a lovely pillow, or you can fill it with sand and use it as a whimsical doorstop. What makes it country? A simple yet recognizable silhouette.

Average: For those with some experience in sewing.

Materials:
⅝ yard of 48-inch-wide floral chintz; matching thread; synthetic stuffing; Dark Brown embroidery floss; embroidery needle; two ½-inch-diameter eyes; 1 yard of ¾-inch-wide pink picot-edged grosgrain ribbon; buttontwist thread; paper for pattern.

Directions (¼-inch seams allowed):
1. Cutting: Enlarge the pattern in Fig. I, 4 onto paper, following the directions on page 215. From the chintz, cut a pair each of Cat and Tail pieces, and one Base.

2. Face: Using two strands of floss in the needle, embroider the nose in satin stitch and the mouth in backstitch on one Cat piece *(see Fig. I, 4 and Stitch Guide, page 214)*.

3. Assembling: Stitch the Cat pieces right sides together, leaving the bottom edges open. With the side seams matching the center marks on the Base and right sides together, pin and sew the Cat to the Base, leaving about 3 inches open for turning. Turn the Cat right side out, and topstitch across the bottom of each ear *(see dotted lines on Cat pattern piece in Fig. I, 4)*. Stuff the Cat. Turn in the open edges, and slipstitch the opening closed *(see Stitch Guide)*.

4. Tail: Sew the Tail pieces right sides together, leaving the straight ends open. Turn the Tail right side out, and stuff it. Turn in the open ends, and slipstitch them to the Cat side seam *(see line on Cat pattern piece in Fig. I, 4)*. Tack all but the last 4 inches of the Tail to the Base seam.

5. Finishing: Sew on the eyes. Tie the ribbon in a bow around the Cat's neck. Using the buttontwist thread, stitch on 6-inch-long whiskers *(see photo)*.

FIG. I, 4   PRETTY KITTY   1 SQ. = 2″

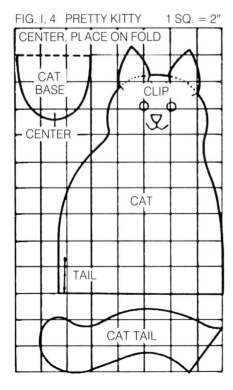

A thing of beauty is a joy for ever:
Its loveliness increases; it will never
Pass into nothingness.
—John Keats

STENCILED SHAKER BOXES

Easy: Achievable by anyone.

Materials:

General Materials for Stenciled Picnic Basket & Napkins *(page 80)*; round Shaker-style wooden boxes: 10-inch-diameter, 12-inch-diameter and 13-inch-diameter; Country Colors Heartland acrylic paints: Light Village Green, Light Roseberry, Light Stoneware Blue, and Light Pink Blossom; satin water-based varnish and sealer; 3 stencil brushes; 2-inch foam brushes; bond paper; sandpaper; tack cloth; 1-inch-wide masking tape; compass; ruler.

Directions:

1. Cutting the Stencils: Using the compass, draw a ¾-inch-radius circle and a ½-inch-radius circle on the bond paper. Using the ruler, draw four ⅜ x 1-inch rectangles centered at right angles to each other to form a basketweave pattern *(see small box in photo)*. Following Stenciled Picnic Basket & Napkins General Directions, Step 1 *(page 80)*, cut a separate stencil for each circle and the basketweave pattern.

2. Preparing the Boxes: Sand the boxes and lids lightly in the direction of the wood grain. Wipe off all the sawdust with the tack cloth.

3. Small Box: Using a foam brush, paint the box Light Village Green. Let the paint dry for 1 hour. Tape the basketweave stencil to the center top of the box lid with masking tape. Following Stenciled Picnic Basket & Napkins General Directions, Step 2, stencil the box lid top and outside edges, and the box sides in Light Roseberry *(see photo)*.

4. Medium-size Box: Paint the box Light Roseberry, and let the paint dry for 1 hour. Tape the stencil of the large circle to the top of the box lid, and stencil the circle in Light Village Green. Repeat randomly across the lid top and outside edges, and the box sides. When the green paint is dry, stencil a Light Stoneware Blue small circle overlapping each large circle. Use a different dry stencil brush for each color. Clean the stencils and brushes following Stenciled Picnic Basket & Napkins General Directions, Step 3.

5. Large Box: Paint the box Light Stoneware Blue. When the paint is dry, use the masking tape to create stripes on the top and outside edges of the box lid. Tape stripes on the box sides to match the lid *(see photo)*. Using a foam brush, paint the untaped areas Light Pink Blossom. Let the paint dry; remove the tape.

6. Finishing: Let the paints dry for at least 1 hour. Brush a coat of varnish and sealer on each box.

POTPOURRI SACHET

Easy: Achievable by anyone.

Materials:

8 x 11 inches of fabric; matching thread; 20 inches of ¾- to 1-inch-wide ribbon or satin cording; additional satin cording *(optional)*; 9 inches of lace trim *(optional)*; potpourri *(directions, page 114)*.

Directions (¼-inch seams allowed):

1. Cut the fabric in half to measure 4 x 11 inches. Sew the halves right sides together along the sides and bottom, curving the corners; leave the top open. Fold down the top 3 inches to the wrong side. Turn the pouch right side out.

2. Trims (optional): Stitch cording along the sides and bottom of the pouch. Or sew lace trim on the inside or outside of the open top edge.

3. Fill the pouch with the potpourri, and tie a bow with the ribbon or cording to close the sachet.

F·L·O·W·E·R·S
EVERLASTING

Craft fabric
flowers that will "bloom" forever. Whether your
country leanings are toward Americana, Victorian or
even Southwestern style, flowers are the perfect
complement to any room.

EVERLASTING BLOOMS

*What makes it country? One of Nature's most perfect
decorative accessories, crafted from lovely fabrics.*

Easy: Achievable by anyone.

General Directions:

1. Patterns: Trace the patterns for the full size petals
and leaves on pages 27 and 30. The solid pattern lines
are the cutting lines; the broken lines are the details.
Place the pattern pieces on the fabric with the arrows
on the lengthwise grain.

2. Fabric Yardage: Make a sample of each type of
flower to become familiar with the technique, and to
estimate yardage requirements. Decide how many
flowers you will make of each type, and figure yardage
based on the width of the fabric.

3. Sizing Fabric: Cut a 12 x 18-inch fabric rectangle,
and place it on a sheet of brown or other plain paper.
Spray the fabric thoroughly with two coats of clear
acrylic spray varnish. Let the fabric dry completely
between coats.

4. Floral Wire: Use covered wire as a support for the
petals and leaves. Use wire cutters to cut stem wire to
the desired lengths.

5. Gluing: Use tacky white craft glue to assemble the
flowers. When attaching covered wire to the petals and
leaves, apply the glue to the wire, not to the fabric, and
use a short piece of stem wire to spread the glue on the
covered wire.

6. Wrapping: Except when directed otherwise, use
masking tape to wrap stamen bunches and petal wires
together, and use green floral tape to attach the flower
to a stem wire. Then wrap the stem wire, and any other
exposed wire, with the floral tape. To wrap with floral
tape, hold the tape at a slant at the flower base and
press the tape in place. Wrap the tape around the stem
spirally, stretching the tape as you wind to keep it taut
and smooth. Attach the leaves to the stem as you wrap.

(Continued on page 26)

> **There is material enough
> in a single flower
> for the ornament of a score
> of cathedrals.**
> —John Ruskin

Lavender Lace Asters and Peonies (directions, page 26)

LAVENDER LACE ASTERS

(photo, page 24)

Materials:

1¾-inch-wide lavender lace hem facing; matching thread; sewing needle; pearl pep stamens (available at craft supply stores); 3 to 5 purchased fabric or paper leaves per flower; No. 19 stem wire; wire cutters; green floral tape; masking tape; purple wide felt-tip marker; small watercolor paintbrush; rubbing alcohol; cotton balls.

Directions:

1. For each aster, cut an 18-inch length and a 12-inch length of lace. Following the lace's design, cut off about ⅜ inch from one long edge of the 12-inch length. Using the thread and sewing needle, make a row of gathering stitches ⅛ inch from the opposite long edge. Draw up the stitches tightly, and tack the short ends of the lace together to form a ruffled circle. Color the inside of the circle with the purple marker. Touch the colored area with the watercolor brush dipped in the alcohol to blend the color. Without trimming the 18-inch length, repeat the gathering, place the large circle around the small circle, and tack the short ends of the large circle together. Fasten about 20 stamens into a bunch with floral tape, and insert the bunch into the center of the small circle.

2. Place a length of stem wire beside the stamen stems, and wrap them together with masking tape. Wrap a cotton ball around the base of the aster, and wrap the cotton ball with floral tape. Continue winding the floral tape down the stem, attaching three to five leaves as you wrap.

PEONIES

(photo, page 24)

Materials:

Organdy in three shades of pink, or white organdy and rose pink fabric dye; green taffeta lining fabric; yellow pep stamens (available at craft supply stores); No. 30 pink covered wire; No. 30 green covered wire; No. 16 stem wire; wire cutters; green floral tape; masking tape; clear acrylic spray varnish; green fine-point permanent felt-tip pen; tacky white glue; paper for pattern.

Directions:

1. Dyeing White Organdy: Cut the organdy into ½-yard strips. Following the fabric dye manufacturer's directions, dye the strips three shades of pink by leaving some strips in the dye longer to turn them darker shades. Let the organdy strips dry thoroughly before using them.

2. Sizing Fabric: Size the organdy following General Directions, Step 3 *(page 25).*

3. Cutting: Trace the pattern pieces in FIG. I, 5 onto paper. Place the pattern pieces on the fabric following General Directions, Step 1. Use the lightest pink organdy for the large petals, and the darkest pink organdy for the small petals. For each large peony, cut 24 single petals of each size; they will be assembled into 12 sets each of small, medium-size and large double petals. For each peony bud, cut 20 or 24 single small or medium-size petals, to be assembled into 10 or 12 sets of double petals. Stretch the edges of each petal to ripple them.

4. Double Petals: Cut 3-inch lengths of pink covered wire. For each double petal, coat 1 inch at one end of a wire length with glue. Sandwich the coated end between two same-size petals, leaving the uncoated wire end extending beyond the petals. Let the glue dry.

5. Calyx and Leaves: For each large peony or peony bud, cut a calyx and three to six leaves from the green taffeta. Stretch the edges of each leaf to ripple them. Using the green pen, sketch the veins on each leaf indicated by the broken lines on the pattern piece. Cut 3½-inch lengths of green covered wire. Glue a wire to the center back of each leaf, letting the excess wire extend below the leaf. Tape the leaf stems together in groups of three.

6. Large Peony: Fasten 24 stamens into a bunch with floral tape to form a center; leave some floral tape free at the bottom. Arrange 12 small double petals evenly around the center, and twist the wires together. Repeat with 12 medium-size and 12 large double petals. Twist all the wires together, and cover them with masking tape. Place a length of stem wire beside the twisted petal wires, and wrap them together with masking tape. Take the floral tape left hanging free at the bottom of the stamens, and wrap it around the stem wire where the tape and stem meet. Cut an X in the center of the calyx, and insert the stem through the opening. Push the calyx up to the flower base, and glue it in place. Wrap the entire stem with floral tape, attaching the leaves as you wrap.

7. Peony Bud: Gather and twist together the wires of 10 or 12 small or medium-size double petals; omit the center stamens. Cover the wires with masking tape. Finish assembling the bud following Step 6.

FIG. I, 5   EVERLASTING BLOOMS   PEONY   1 SQ. = ½"

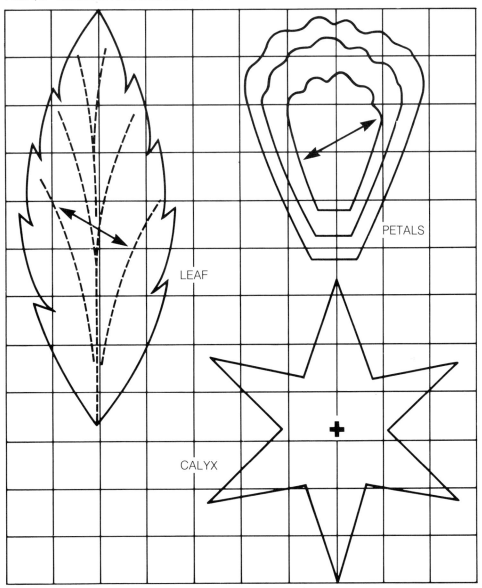

LEAF

PETALS

CALYX

FULL SIZE PATTERN

Each flower is a soul
opening out to nature.
—Gerard de Nerval

AZALEAS
(photo, page 29)

Materials:
White organdy; dark green satin fabric; rose pink, fuchsia, coral and tangerine fabric dyes; small yellow stamens (available at craft supply stores); No. 26 white covered wire; No. 26 green covered wire; No. 16 stem wire; wire cutters; green floral tape; masking tape; clear acrylic spray varnish; green fine-point permanent felt-tip pen; tacky white glue; watercolor paintbrush; paper toweling; iron; paper for pattern.

Directions:
1. Dyeing Fabric: Each azalea flower is made of six 5-petal florets. All the petals for one flower can be cut from an 8 x 18-inch piece of dyed organdy. Following the fabric dye manufacturer's directions, dye the organdy the color and shade desired; the longer the organdy stays in the dye, the darker the shade will be. At the same time, dye lengths of white covered wire to match. Remove the organdy and wire from the dye, and rinse them in cool water. Roll the organdy and wire in paper toweling, and iron them dry. The dyeing and ironing should take only a few minutes per flower.
2. Cutting: Trace the azalea petal and leaf pattern pieces in FIG. I, 6 *(page 30)* onto paper. Place the pattern pieces on the fabric following General Directions, Step 1 *(page 25)*. For each azalea flower, cut 30 petals from the same piece of dyed organdy.
3. Petals: Using the watercolor brush, paint the edge of each petal with diluted glue. While the glue is still tacky, roll the lower side edge of the petal between your thumbs and forefingers toward you, stretching the fabric slightly as you roll *(see photo)*; the rolled side is the top side of the petal. Continue around the petal. Let the petal dry. Center and glue 1 inch of a 3-inch length of matching dyed wire to the underside of the petal.
4. Florets: Fasten 10 stamens into a bunch with masking tape to form a center. Arrange five petals evenly around the center, and twist the wires together. Wrap the wires with floral tape to make one floret. Make six florets for each azalea flower.
5. Leaves: Size the satin fabric following General Directions, Step 3. For each azalea flower, cut seven leaves from the sized satin. Glue a 3-inch length of green covered wire to the center back of each leaf, and let the glue dry. Using the green pen, sketch the veins on each leaf indicated by the broken lines on the pattern piece.
6. Assembling: Attach six florets to the top 2 inches of a length of stem wire. Wrap the entire stem with floral tape, attaching the leaves as you wrap.

COSMOS
(photo, page 29)

Materials:
White organdy; purple and marine blue fabric dyes; 2 purchased small green velvet leaves per flower; No. 26 white covered wire; No. 26 green covered wire; No. 19 stem wire; wire cutters; green floral tape; yellow floral tape; tacky white glue; watercolor paintbrush; paper toweling; iron; paper for pattern.

Directions:
1. Dyeing Fabric: Mixing the purple and marine blue fabric dyes together in equal proportions, dye the organdy and lengths of white covered wire a pale lavender blue following Azaleas, Step 1.
2. Cutting: Trace the azalea petal pattern piece in FIG. I, 6 *(page 30)* onto paper. Place the pattern piece on the dyed organdy following General Directions, Step 1 *(page 25)*. For each cosmos, cut five petals.
3. Petals: Prepare the petals following Azaleas, Step 3.
4. Stamen: Cut a 2- or 3-inch length of green covered wire, and make a small hook at one end. Wrap a 3-inch length of yellow floral tape around the hook, molding the tape into a small ball.
5. Assembling: Arrange five petals evenly around the stamen, and twist the wires together. Wrap the wires with green floral tape. Attach the flower to a length of stem wire with green floral tape, and continue winding the floral tape down the stem, attaching two leaves as you wrap.

COUNTRY WAYS

• Making Arrangements •

Flower arranging styles are as numerous and varied as flowers themselves are. Victorians preferred small, carefully arranged nosegays called "posies." In a 19th century American farmhouse, a bunch of wildflowers was common. In the South, lavish bouquets of blossoms from the garden were — and still are — the fashion in flower arrangements.

In arranging everlasting flowers, choose any style you like. Make a mixed bouquet, or stick to one or two types of flowers. Use an opaque container to hide the wire stems. A block of floral foam will hold the stems in place.

We used baskets and copper pots for our containers, but china, pottery, or even a clay pot would look wonderful, too.

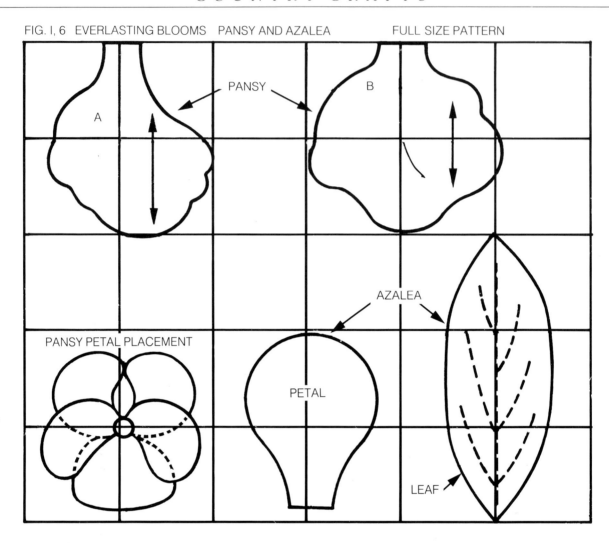

FIG. I, 6 EVERLASTING BLOOMS PANSY AND AZALEA FULL SIZE PATTERN

PANSY

A

B

AZALEA

PANSY PETAL PLACEMENT

PETAL

LEAF

As the sun colors flowers,
so thus art colors life.
—Anonymous

VELVETEEN PANSIES

Materials:

Velveteen in 2 or 3 shades of violet; dried split peas; 3 purchased leaves per flower; No. 24 green covered wire; No. 16 stem wire; wire cutters; green floral tape; masking tape; cadmium yellow and cadmium orange acrylic paints; clear acrylic spray varnish; small stiff paintbrush; 2-inch-wide paintbrush; purple wide felt-tip marker; tacky white glue; tracing paper; carbon paper; stylus or dry ballpoint pen; thin cardboard for pattern.

Directions:

1. Stamen: Soak the split peas in water until they are soft. Insert the end of a 4-inch length of covered wire into glue, and then into the flat side of a softened split pea. Paint the pea yellow or orange, and let the paint dry overnight.

2. Sizing Fabric: Size the velveteen on the wrong side following General Directions, Step 3 *(page 25)*. Using the 2-inch-wide paintbrush, paint the sized velveteen with glue. Let the glue dry.

3. Cutting: Trace the pansy pattern pieces in Fig. I, 6 onto tracing paper. Using the carbon paper and stylus or dry ballpoint pen, trace the pattern pieces onto the cardboard and cut them out. Place the pattern pieces on the velveteen following General Directions, Step 1. For each pansy, cut two A petals, turn over the pattern, and cut two more petals. Cut one B petal.

4. Petals: Define the center and edges of each petal with the purple marker. Using the small stiff paintbrush, highlight each petal by stroking from the center outward with yellow and orange paint *(see photo)*. Glue a 3-inch length of covered wire to the center back of each petal.

5. Assembling: Following the placement diagram in Fig. I, 6, arrange the petals around the stamen and twist the wires together. Place a length of stem wire beside the twisted petal wires, and wrap them together with masking tape. Wrap the stem wire with floral tape, attaching three leaves as you wrap.

MARIGOLDS

Materials:

4½ yards of seam tape per flower, in shades of yellow, gold and orange; matching threads; matching color crepe paper; sewing needle *(optional)*; 2-inch-diameter Styrofoam® ball (makes 2 flowers); 5 to 6 purchased leaves per flower; No. 16 stem wire; wire cutters; green floral tape; waxed dental floss; short straight pins; tacky white glue.

Directions:

1. Flower Head: Cut the Styrofoam ball in half. Center a 6-inch square of crepe paper over the rounded side of one half, and twist the corners of the paper together on the flat side. Tie the twist with dental floss. Cut the seam tape into 1½-yard lengths. Make a row of gathering stitches along one long edge of each length. Pull up the gathers to about one third the original length, leaving the thread ends loose to adjust the gathers. Beginning at the outside edge of the ball, attach the tape ruffles to the ball with glue-dipped straight pins in rows ½ inch apart. Work the ruffles back and forth toward the rounded center top, and then toward the uncovered outside edge. It will take about three lengths of ruffles to cover the flower head.

2. Assembling: Make a hook at one end of a length of stem wire. Untie the floss on the crepe paper. Insert the wire into the center top of the flower, and pull the wire through the flower, leaving the hook about halfway in the ball. Wrap the twisted paper and stem wire with floral tape, attaching five to six leaves as you wrap.

E · A · S · T · E · R
PARADE

Easter means baskets and bunnies! Create your own beautiful baskets with découpage blossoms, stitch up a cuddly stuffed bunny and, for a special baby, a bunny crib quilt and toy.

BEAUTIFUL EASTER BASKET

Easy: Achievable by anyone.

Materials:

Unpainted basket with handle; ½ yard of 54-inch-wide floral chintz; acrylic paint: 1 bottle and 1 spray can in same color to coordinate with chintz; Mod Podge®; Stiffy® Fabric Stiffener; FolkArt® Clear Cote Hi Shine Brilliant Glaze (available at craft supply stores); paintbrushes; hot glue gun; soft cloth.

Directions:

1. Spray paint the basket. Use a paintbrush and the bottled acrylic paint to paint the rim and handle.
2. Set aside ¼ yard of the chintz for a bow. Cut out floral designs from the remaining chintz.
3. Brush Mod Podge over the backs of the chintz cutouts, and arrange the cutouts on the basket *(see photo)*. Dampen the cloth in warm water, squeeze it well, and wipe the cutouts with firm motions. When the cutouts are dry, apply Mod Podge over them.
4. From the ¼ yard of chintz, cut an 8 x 54-inch, 8 x 27-inch, 8 x 23-inch, and 8 x 3-inch strip. Work the fabric stiffener into the strips. Fold each strip's long edges so they overlap in the middle. Hang the strips until they are almost dry.
5. When the strips are almost dry, fold the short ends of the 27-inch strip to the middle, and overlap them. Gather the strip in the middle, and open the bow loops. Repeat with the 23-inch strip. Place the two bows together, and place the 54-inch strip underneath them for a streamer. Wrap the 3-inch strip around the center of the double bow and streamer. Cut fish tail ends on the streamer. Using the photo as a placement guide, glue the bow and streamer to the basket handle.
6. When all the chintz is dry, spray the entire basket, including the bow and streamer, with two or more coats of glaze, letting the glaze dry between coats.

COUNTRY WAYS

• Easter Eggs •

The egg, a symbol of life, has long been associated with the Easter season and its promise of rebirth. It is believed the tradition of coloring eggs began as a way to represent the flowers that would bloom soon after Easter.

In old England, children were given hard-boiled eggs at Easter time. It became a custom to roll the eggs down a hill. The last egg to break brought good luck to the child who rolled it.

One of the most charming Easter egg customs is for the head of the household to divide a colored cooked egg among the members of the family so every person gets a piece. If one of the family members ever gets lost or goes astray, thinking about the people with whom he shared the egg will make them think of him — and their thoughts will guide him home.

---

*Faith is the bird
that feels the light
and sings when the dawn
is still dark.*
— Rabindranath Tagore

EASTER BUNNY PALS

Average: For those with some experience in sewing.

SMALL BUNNY
(about 8 inches tall)

Materials:

9 x 18 inches of fleecy fabric; 1-inch-diameter matching color pompon; scrap of white fleece or felt for bib, or 9-inch square of felt in color desired for overalls, or 8 inches of 1½-inch-wide ruffled eyelet lace for apron *(optional)*; matching sewing threads; 14 inches of ribbon for neck bow *(optional)*; 2 small black beads and strong black thread, or scrap of blue felt, glue, and white thread or typewriter white-out for eyes; synthetic stuffing; scrap of Pink embroidery floss; embroidery needle; sewing needle *(optional)*; pink rouge; powder puff; paper for pattern.

Directions (¼-inch seams allowed):

1. *Pattern:* Enlarge the pattern in FIG. I, 7A *(page 36)* onto paper, following the directions on page 215. Cut out the pattern pieces.

2. *Cutting:* Cut a pair each of Front and Back pieces from the fleecy fabric. If you wish, cut one Bib from white fleece or felt. Or, if you wish, cut two Overall Pants pieces and one Overall Top from felt.

3. *Bunny:* Machine-stitch the Front pieces, right sides together, along CF. Repeat with the Back pieces along CB, leaving an opening for turning between the two notches. Pin the Front and Back right sides together, seams matching. Machine-stitch around all edges except the foot ends with darts. Fold one foot so the seams match, and stitch the dart edge. Repeat on the other foot. Turn the bunny right side out, and stuff it firmly. Turn in the open edges, and slipstitch the opening closed *(see Stitch Guide, page 214)*.

4. *Bead Eyes (optional; not recommended if bunny is for small child):* Thread a sewing needle with strong black thread, and knot one end of the thread. Using the photo as a placement guide, push the needle into the bunny's head at the left eye position, and out at the right eye position. Slide a small black bead onto the needle, and push the bead up against the head. Push the needle into the head under the bead, and out at the left eye position *(see FIG. I, 7B1, page 36)*. Slide another small black bead onto the needle and up against the head. Pull up the thread slightly to indent the eyes, and fasten the thread end.

5. *Nose and Mouth:* Thread the embroidery needle with the Pink floss, and knot one end of the floss. Take a stitch from behind the left eye bead, if using bead eyes, or from the left eye position if using felt eyes,

to the right nostril *(see FIG. I, 7B2)*. Keeping the floss under the needle, push the needle into the head at the left nostril, and out on the center front seam a little below the nostrils *(see FIG. I, 7B3)*. Pull up the floss slightly to form the nose. Take a stitch directly downward, and bring out the needle at one end of the mouth *(see FIG. I, 7B4)*. Take a stitch upward, bring out the needle at the other end of the mouth, and take another upward stitch *(see FIG. I, 7B4)*. Fill in the mouth with two more stitches, and fasten the floss end. Pat a little rouge onto the bunny's cheeks, nose and inner ears with the powder puff *(see photo)*.

(Continued on page 36)

Child of the pure, unclouded brow
And dreaming eyes of wonder!
Though time be fleet and I and thou
Are half a life asunder,
Thy loving smile will surely hail
The love-gift of a fairy tale.
—Lewis Carroll (Charles Dodgson)

6. *Felt Eyes:* Cut out a ½-inch-diameter circle from a scrap of blue felt, and cut the circle in half. Glue each half circle to the bunny head at an eye position *(see photo, pages 34-35)*. Add a few white straight stitches, or a stroke of typewriter white-out, to each eye for a highlight *(see photo, and Stitch Guide)*.

7. *Bib (optional):* Pin the Bib's upper edge under the bunny's chin, matching the Bib's CF fold to the bunny's CF seam. Slipstitch the Bib in place around all edges.

8. *Overalls (optional):* Machine-stitch the Overall Pants pieces, right sides together, along CF and CB. Fold the Overall Pants, matching CF to CB, and stitch the crotch seams *(see arrow on pattern piece in* FIG. I, 7A). Turn the Overall Pants right side out. Lap the top edge of the Pants ¼ inch over the lower edge of the

Overall Top, matching the Pants' CF seam to the Top's CF fold. Topstitch around the Pants waist, catching the bottom edge of the Top in front. If you wish, add decorative topstitching along the Overall Top and Pants edges *(see photo)*. Put the Overalls on the bunny. Cross the straps in the back, tuck their ends under the Pants' back top edge, and tack them in place.

9. *Apron (optional):* Wrap an 8-inch length of 1½-inch-wide ruffled eyelet lace around the bunny's waist for an apron, and sew the lace's short ends together.

10. *Finishing:* Sew the pompon to the bunny's CB seam about ½ inch above the crotch seam. If you wish, tie a 14-inch length of ribbon in a bow around the bunny's neck. Omit the pompon and bow if the bunny is wearing Overalls.

FIG. I, 7A   SMALL BUNNY   1 SQ. = 1"

CF
CB
FRONT
BACK
CF, PLACE ON FOLD
DART
DART
BIB
WAIST
CF OR CB
OVERALL PANTS
STRAPS
FOLD
CF FOLD
OVERALL TOP

FIG. I, 7B   BUNNY FACE

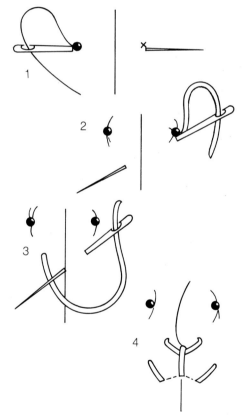

1

2

3

4

LARGE BUNNY

(photo, pages 34-35; about 11 inches tall)

Materials:

13 x 22 inches of fleecy fabric; 1-inch-diameter matching color pompon; scrap of white fleece or felt for bib *(optional)*; 9 x 12 inches of felt in color desired for jacket *(optional)*; ⅜ yard of 45-inch-wide fabric, 1½ yards of lace trim, and ½ yard of 1-inch-wide ribbon for dress *(optional)*; ½ yard of 3-inch-wide ruffled eyelet lace, and 10 inches of ½-inch-wide ribbon for pinafore *(optional)*; ¾ yard of 3¼-inch-wide eyelet lace, and artificial flowers for bonnet *(optional)*; matching threads; ribbon for neck bow *(optional)*; 2 small black beads and strong black thread, or scrap of blue felt, glue, and white thread or typewriter white-out for eyes; synthetic stuffing; scrap of Pink embroidery floss; embroidery needle; sewing needle *(optional)*; pink rouge; powder puff; paper for pattern.

Directions:

1. Pattern: Enlarge the pattern in FIG. I, 7C onto paper, following the directions on page 215. Cut out the pattern pieces.

2. Cutting: Cut a pair each of Front and Back pieces from the fleecy fabric. If you wish, cut one Bib from white fleece or felt. If you wish, cut one Jacket from felt. Or, if you wish, use the Jacket pattern piece to cut one dress bodice from fabric; the CF opening on the pattern piece is the center back of the bodice.

3. Bunny: Make the large bunny following Small Bunny, Steps 3 to 6 *(pages 34-36)*; if you are making felt eyes, cut a ⅝-inch-diameter circle.

4. Bib (optional): Attach the Bib following Small Bunny, Step 7.

5. Jacket (optional): Fold the Jacket at the shoulders *(see dotted line on pattern piece in FIG. I, 7C)*. Sew the Jacket front to the back at the underarms *(see arrows on pattern piece)*.

6. Dress (optional): Fold the dress bodice at the shoulders *(see dotted line on Jacket pattern in FIG. I, 7C)*. Sew the bodice front to the back at the underarms *(see arrows on Jacket pattern)*. Cut off ½ inch from the bodice's bottom edge. Cut a 10 x 35-inch rectangle for the dress skirt. Sew the skirt's short ends right sides together, stopping 2½ inches from the top edge. Turn under the skirt's bottom edge ¼ inch, and stitch. Sew a gathering row ¼ inch and ½ inch from the skirt's top edge. Pin the skirt to the bodice, matching the center back raw edges. Pull up the skirt gathers to fit the bodice, and sew the skirt to the bodice. Turn under the center back raw edges ¼ inch, and stitch. Repeat on the sleeves' bottom edges. Sew lace trim to the neck, and

to the bottom of the sleeves and skirt *(see photo, pages 34-35)*. Put the dress on the bunny, and slipstitch the back opening closed. Tie the ribbon around the waist.

7. Pinafore (optional): Cut a 10-inch length of 3-inch-wide ruffled eyelet lace. Sew the lace's short ends right sides together to make a skirt. Cut a 4-inch length of the ruffled lace for a bib, and cut off the bound edge so the bib lies flat. Sew a narrow hem along each short end of the bib. Slide the bib's raw bottom edge under the skirt's bound top edge, matching center fronts, and topstitch the skirt to the bib. Put the pinafore on the bunny. Tie the ribbon in a bow around the waist.

8. Bonnet (optional): Sew the short ends of the eyelet lace right sides together. Turn under the lace's raw edge ½ inch, and sew two gathering rows along the folded edge. Place the lace around the bunny's ears, and draw up the gathers to fit *(see photo)*. Knot the ends of the gathering threads, and trim off the excess thread. Tack one or two artificial flowers to the bonnet.

9. Finishing: Attach the pompon following Small Bunny, Step 10. If you wish, tie a length of ribbon in a bow around the bunny's neck.

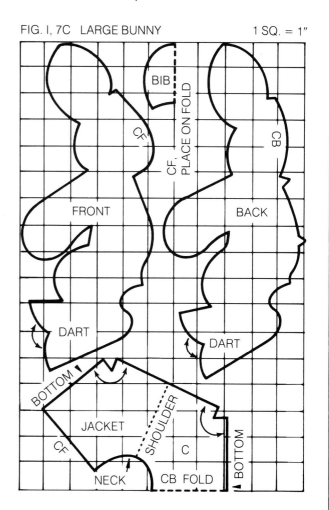

FIG. I, 7C   LARGE BUNNY   1 SQ. = 1"

BUNNY BABY SET

What makes it country? Bunnies—a favorite country pet—paired with quilting—a favorite country art.

Average: For those with some experience in quilting and sewing.

General Materials:

45-inch-wide cotton fabric: 1⅛ yards of yellow stripe, ¾ yard of red and white check, 3 yards of green and white print; matching sewing threads; dressmaker's carbon; tracing wheel; paper for patterns.

BUNNY QUILT
(44 x 51 inches)

Materials:

General Materials; 45 x 60 inches of extra-loft synthetic batting; safety pins, or quilter's pins and darner or milliner's needle; between needle *(optional)*; quilting thread *(optional)*; quilting hoop *(optional)*.

Directions (½-inch seams allowed):

1. Fabric: Wash the fabric to shrink it, and press it.
2. Pattern: Enlarge the Bunny pattern in FIG. I, 8A *(page 40)* onto paper, following the directions on page 215. Trace the full size pattern pieces in FIG. I, 8B *(page 41)* onto paper.
3. Cutting: Use the dressmaker's carbon and tracing wheel to trace the pattern pieces on the right side of the fabrics. Cut along the traced lines. **From the yellow stripe fabric,** cut a 31 x 38-inch quilt top, four 4-inch squares, and nine Ties. **From the green and white print fabric,** cut a 45 x 52-inch quilt back, two 5 x 44-inch side borders, two 5 x 37-inch top and bottom borders, nine Bunnies, and twelve Stems. **From the red and white check fabric,** cut two 4 x 38-inch side borders, two 4 x 31-inch top and bottom borders, four 5-inch squares, nine Vests, and twelve Carrots.
4. Appliqués: Using the photo as a placement guide, pin and baste the Bunnies, Carrots, Vests, Ties and Stems to the quilt top. Space the three horizontal rows of Bunnies 2 inches apart. Using matching threads, edgestitch and then satin stitch the appliqué pieces to the quilt top.
5. Borders: Sew a yellow stripe square to each end of the red and white side borders. Sew the red and white top and bottom borders to the quilt top. Sew the red and white side borders to the quilt top, matching the seam intersections precisely. Repeat for the green and white borders, first sewing the red and white squares to the side borders.

6. *Assembling:* Baste the batting to the wrong side of the quilt top, and trim the batting flush with the quilt top. Pin the quilt back to the quilt top right sides together. Stitch around three sides and four corners, leaving a 25-inch opening. Turn the quilt right side out, turn in the open edges, and slipstitch the opening closed *(see Stitch Guide, page 214)*.

7. *Quilting:* Using safety pins, pin the quilt layers together in a grid pattern. Or pin with quilter's pins, and use a darner or milliner's needle, single lengths of thread, and long stitches to baste through the quilt layers in the same way you pinned. Hand-quilt *(see Stitch Guide)*, using a between needle, quilting thread and quilting hoop, or machine-quilt in the ditch of the border and corner seams. Outline quilt ⅛ inch outside the Bunnies and Carrots. Remove the safety pins or basting threads.

C O U N T R Y   W A Y S

• *After the Baby Arrives . . . •*

Once a baby is born, there are plenty of superstitious "rules" to follow so the baby lives a long and happy life.

To ward off the "evil eye," and protect the baby from harm, put a necklace made of coral around the baby's neck, and brush the baby with a rabbit's foot.

The baby should not be allowed to look into a mirror until it is a year old, or it will die.

Cats should not be allowed in the baby's room because they "suck the breath" from a sleeping child.

Adults must never step over a crawling infant, lest they stunt its growth. Parents should not cut a baby's fingernails during its first year; they should bite off the nails, to prevent the baby from becoming a thief.

BUNNY CRIB TOY
(34 inches long)

Materials:
General Materials; 1½ yards of ⅞-inch-wide green grosgrain ribbon; 1 yard of fleecy interlining; synthetic stuffing; 4 drapery weights; 4 yellow pompons.

Directions:
1. Prepare the fabric and the pattern pieces following Bunny Quilt, Steps 1 and 2.

2. Use the dressmaker's carbon and tracing wheel to trace the pattern pieces on the right side of the fabrics. Cut along the traced lines. ***From the green and white print fabric,*** cut eight 10-inch squares, and ten 2-inch squares. ***From the red and white check fabric,*** cut ten 2 x 4-inch rectangles, and four Vests. ***From the yellow stripe fabric,*** cut four Ties. ***From the fleecy interlining,*** cut eight 10-inch squares, ten 2-inch squares, and ten 2 x 4-inch rectangles.

3. Trace a Bunny, centered, on the right side of four 10-inch green and white squares. Trace a Stem, centered, on five 2-inch green and white squares. Trace a Carrot on five 2 x 4-inch red and white rectangles.

4. Baste a same size fleece piece to the wrong side of every fabric square and rectangle near the edges. Pin the Vests and Ties to the traced Bunnies, and satin stitch them in place with matching threads.

5. Center each Bunny top square over a same size back square, fleecy sides together. Machine-straight stitch on top of the traced Bunny outlines, leaving an opening between the feet. Satin stitch over the straight stitches with green thread, leaving an opening as before. Trim the excess fabric from outside the stitching; do not clip the stitching. Do not trim the fabric at the opening.

6. Insert a drapery weight inside each Bunny at the opening, and hand-sew the weight to the fleece: Stuff the Bunnies. Machine-satin stitch across the openings, and trim the excess fabric. Tack a pompon on the back of each Bunny for a tail.

7. Repeat Steps 5 and 6 to make five Stems and five Carrots, using matching thread to satin stitch, catching ¼ inch of each lower Stem edge between the layers at the top of a Carrot, leaving an opening at one straight edge of each Carrot for stuffing, and omitting the drapery weights.

8. Arrange the Bunnies and Carrots alternately in a row, with the Carrots pointing upward, and tack the Bunnies and Carrots together. Cut the ribbon in half, and stitch the center of each half to an outside Carrot.

FIG. I, 8A BUNNY BABY SET

1 SQ. = 1″

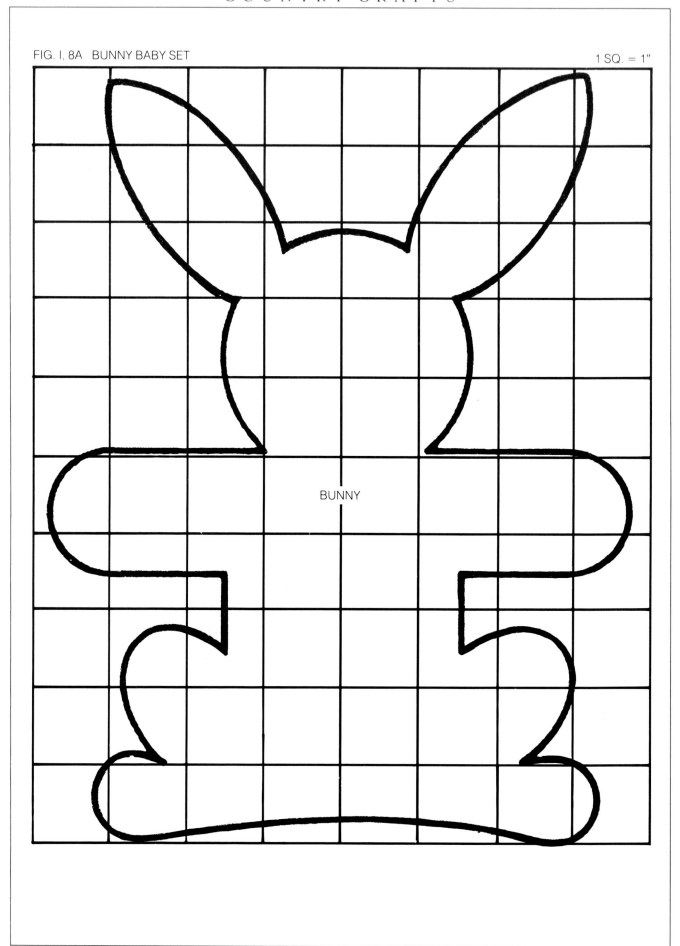

BUNNY

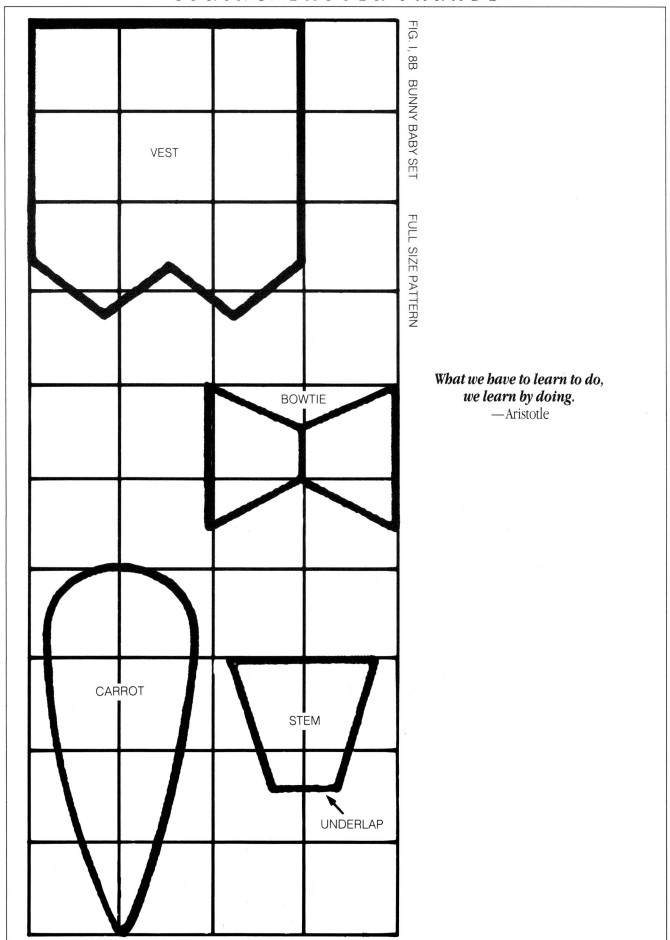

FIG. I, 8B BUNNY BABY SET

FULL SIZE PATTERN

VEST

BOWTIE

CARROT

STEM

UNDERLAP

What we have to learn to do,
we learn by doing.
—Aristotle

N·E·E·D·L·E
ARTS

D

ecorative
needlework has been considered an art form
for ages. Here, we've collected some of our favorite
country-style projects for you to stitch and enjoy.

• Needlepoint •

Needlepoint has a long and elegant history. Along with fine embroidery, it has been a craft practiced by the most genteel women.

Mary, Queen of Scots and Elizabeth I of England both worked needlepoint emblems and medallions that were cut out and sewn to velvet or brocade. In those 16th century days, most of the designs were symbolic — much like the woven tapestries of the period — with motifs ranging from mystical dragons and griffins to factual plants and animals.

In 18th century America, needlepoint designs were adapted from popular engravings. Usually they were naive renderings of landscapes and familiar scenes.

During the Victorian era, women rediscovered needlepoint through the introduction of a new style — Berlin work. Developed in Germany, Berlin work was like needlepoint except the stitcher worked the design by following a colored chart instead of a printed canvas. Berlin work also used a softer, merino wool.

Needlepoint often was used to make and decorate household items, such as fireplace screens and chair cushions, because it was so sturdy. Samples of antique needlepoint can be found in antique shops and auctions, but they are highly prized and can be quite expensive.

CAMELLIA NEEDLEPOINT COASTERS
(4½ inches square)

What makes it country? A practical item made beautiful by a floral design.

Easy: Achievable by anyone.

Materials:
28 x 7 inches of Zweigart No. 16 Orange Line canvas; 17 x 4½ inches of green felt; green sewing thread; DMC embroidery floss: 12 skeins of No. 502 Blue Green, and 1 skein of each color listed in the Symbol and Color Chart *(page 44)*; tapestry needle; sewing needle; masking tape.

Note: *The same needlepoint design is worked on all four coasters, but each coaster is stitched in a different color combination. See the Symbol and Color Chart for the four color combinations.*

Directions:
1. Canvas: Cut four 6½-inch canvas squares. Bind the edges with masking tape to prevent them from fraying. Locate the center of each square by drawing diagonal lines from corner to corner. The point at which the lines cross is the center.

2. Needlepoint: Using six strands of floss in the tapestry needle, work the design in FIG. I, 9 *(page 44)* on each canvas square in continental stitch, starting at the center of the design *(see Stitch Guide, page 214)*. Work each square in a different color combination *(see Symbol and Color Chart)*. When the design is completed, work the back ground in Blue Green to measure 4½ inches square.

3. Finishing: Trim each canvas to 5 inches square. Turn under the raw edges ¼ inch, miter the corners, and press. Cut a piece of felt slightly smaller than the square. Hand-sew the felt to the back of the square.

FIG. I, 9
CAMELLIA NEEDLEPOINT COASTERS

CENTER

CENTER

CENTER

CENTER

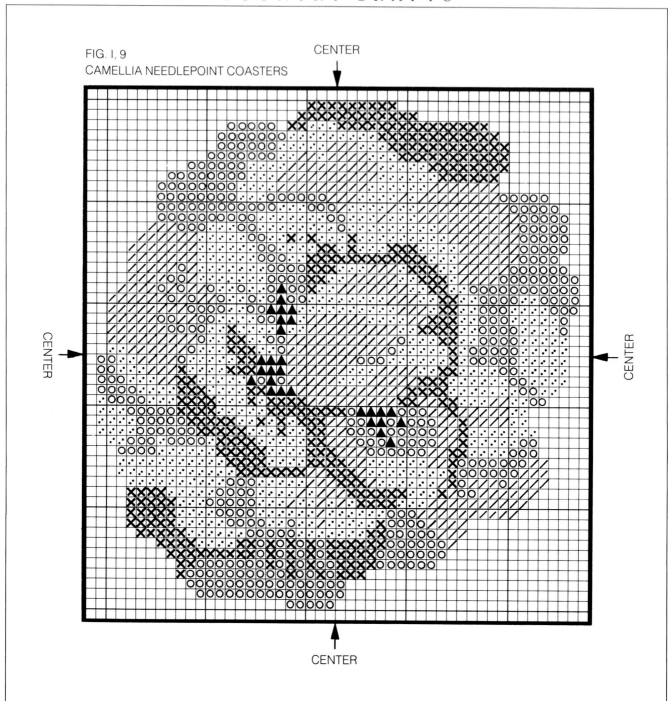

SYMBOL AND COLOR CHART

		YELLOW	PEACH	PINK	ROSE
▲	VERY DARK	783	349	816	221
⊠	DARK	725	351	309	223
⊡	MEDIUM	744	352	335	224
⊘	LIGHT	3078	353	3326	225
⦂	VERY LIGHT	746	951	818	WHITE

AMERICANA NEEDLEPOINT BOX
(finished needlepoint: about 11 x 12¼ inches)

What makes it country? A simple wooden box adorned with a colorful Americana landscape.

Average: For those with some experience in needlepoint.

Materials:
12 x 13⅓-inch wooden box with insert (available at craft supply stores); Joan Toggitt Double Mesh White 10-mesh needlepoint canvas; Paternayan Persian Yarn: 3 skeins each of Light Pink and Tan, 2 skeins each of Sky Blue and Turquoise, 1 skein each of Lemon and Dark Lemon, and small amounts of White, Pink, Dark Pink, Magenta, Burgundy, Rust, Periwinkle, Dark Blue, Sea Foam, Green, Dark Green, Olive and Black; tapestry needle; acrylic spray paint in color desired; soft cloth; scissors; masking tape; glue.

Directions:
1. Bind the edges of the canvas with masking tape to prevent fraying. Using 18-inch lengths of yarn in the needle, work the design in Fig. I, 10 *(page 46)* in continental stitch *(see Stitch Guide, page 214)*. Block the finished needlepoint following the directions on page 213. Trim the canvas to fit the box lid insert.
2. Spray a coat of acrylic paint on the box. While the paint is still wet, dampen the cloth and rub off enough paint so the wood grain shows through. Let the paint dry. Glue the needlepoint to the box lid.

FIG. I, 10 AMERICANA NEEDLEPOINT BOX

CENTER
CENTER

◪ = MAGENTA ◩ = RUST
⊟ = TAN ⊡ = LIGHT PINK
◭ = DARK BLUE ⊠ = SEA FOAM
■ = BLACK ◈ = BURGUNDY
◭ = LEMON ⊟ = TURQUOISE

◪ = DARK LEMON ◪ = SKY BLUE
◩ = PERIWINKLE ◉ = DARK GREEN
◆ = GREEN ◘ = OLIVE
⊞ = DARK PINK □ = WHITE
◇ = PINK

CROSS STITCH SHAKER BOXES

Shaker boxes are a highly practical home accessory, useful in almost any room in the house. What makes it country? Simple motifs with a colonial flavor.

Average: For those with some experience in counted cross stitch.

Materials for One Box:

DMC embroidery floss: 1 skein each of the colors listed for the design of your choice in FIGS. I, 11A to 11D *(pages 48-51)*; No. 24 tapestry needle; Shaker-style wooden box: 8 x 6½-inch oval for Blue Flower, 7-inch-diameter round for Thistle or Red Flower, and 7 x 5¾-inch oval for Fruit; white glue; narrow velvet ribbon in color desired; lace or eyelet trim; toothpick; ¼ yard of quilted fabric *(optional).*

For Fabric Lid: 14-count ivory Aida cloth: 11 x 12 inches for Blue Flower, and 11-inch square for Thistle or Fruit; embroidery hoop; foam mounting board (available at craft and needlework supply stores); masking tape; clean cloth; heavy book.

For Paper Lid: 9-inch square of perforated paper for Red Flower; paintbrush; small sharp scissors.

Directions:

1. Cross Stitch: If making a fabric lid, place the Aida cloth in the embroidery hoop. Using two strands of floss in the needle, cross stitch the design of your choice in FIGS. I, 11A to 11D centered on the Aida cloth or perforated paper *(see Stitch Guide, page 214)*. Each symbol in FIGS. I, 11A to 11D represents one cross stitch in the color indicated. The straight dark lines represent backstitches *(see Stitch Guide)*. Work the backstitches last with two strands of floss in the colors indicated. Work the straight dark lines over the thistles in backstitch with one strand of Dark Mauve *(see FIG. I, 11B)*. Press the embroidered fabric, right side down, with a steam iron to block it; do not block the embroidered paper.

2. Fabric Lid: Trace the box lid onto the foam mounting board, and cut out the circle or oval. Carefully center the embroidered fabric on the board's sticky surface, and press. Trim the fabric edge to extend about 2 inches beyond the board edge. Tape the fabric edge to the back of the board with small pieces of masking tape. Apply glue to the outside top of the box lid, and press the covered board onto the lid. Cover the board with the clean cloth and heavy book. Let the glue dry completely.

FIG. I, 11A   BLUE FLOWER CROSS STITCH

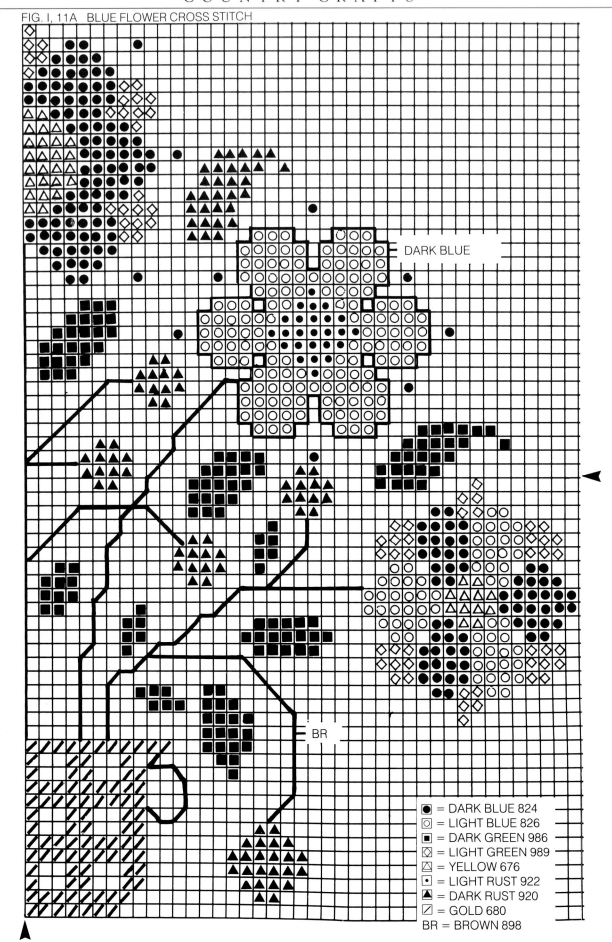

DARK BLUE

BR

- ● = DARK BLUE 824
- ⊡ = LIGHT BLUE 826
- ■ = DARK GREEN 986
- ⬙ = LIGHT GREEN 989
- △ = YELLOW 676
- ⊡ = LIGHT RUST 922
- ▲ = DARK RUST 920
- ⧄ = GOLD 680
- BR = BROWN 898

3. *Paper Lid:* Make a mixture of one part water to two parts glue. Brush the glue mixture over the outside top of the box lid. Center the embroidered paper on the lid, and press. As the glue mixture dries, smooth the paper lightly with your hands. When the glue mixture is completely dry, use the scissors to trim away the excess paper close to the lid edge.

4. *Trims:* Cut a length of ribbon long enough to go completely around the outside edge of the box lid. Using the toothpick, apply a fine line of glue around the upper outside edge of the lid, and press the ribbon over it *(see photo, page 47)*. Repeat to attach the lace or eyelet trim. Add additional trims as desired.

5. *Lining (optional):* Trace the bottom of the box twice on the quilted fabric, and cut out the circles or ovals. Cut a quilted fabric strip that is ½ inch longer than the box's girth, and 1 inch wider than the box's depth. Fold one long edge of the strip 1 inch to the wrong side, and glue. Coat the inside of the box with glue. Press the fabric strip, folded edge at the top, around the coated side of the box. Turn under the strip's excess short end ¼ inch, and glue it in place over the raw short end. Glue one circle or oval to the box bottom, and the remaining circle or oval to the inside of the box lid. Let the glue dry completely.

FIG. I, 11B THISTLE CROSS STITCH

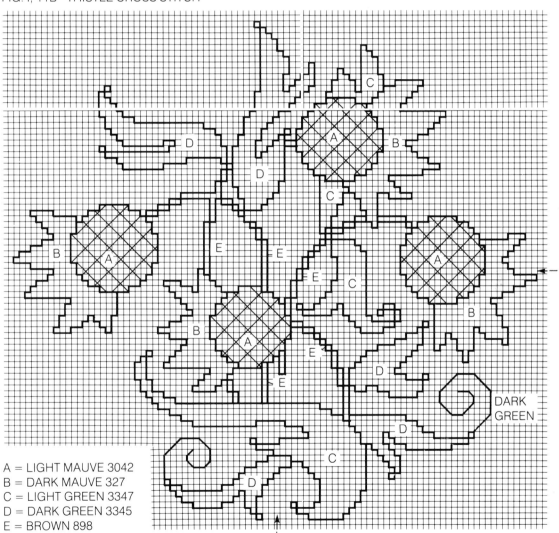

A = LIGHT MAUVE 3042
B = DARK MAUVE 327
C = LIGHT GREEN 3347
D = DARK GREEN 3345
E = BROWN 898

FIG. I, 11C FRUIT CROSS STITCH

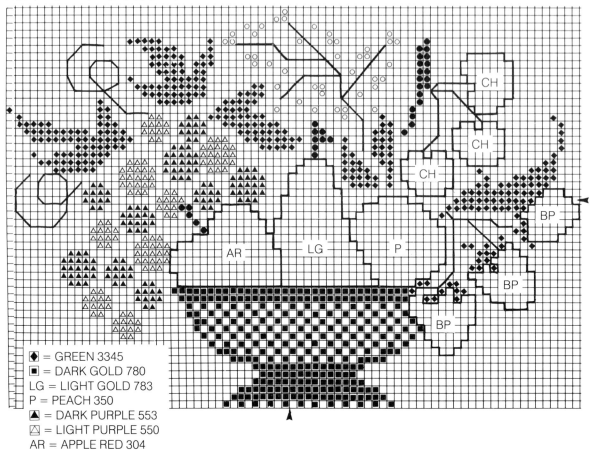

◆ = GREEN 3345
■ = DARK GOLD 780
LG = LIGHT GOLD 783
P = PEACH 350
▲ = DARK PURPLE 553
△ = LIGHT PURPLE 550
AR = APPLE RED 304
CH = CHERRY RED 814

◯ BP = BERRY PINK 321
● = BROWN 938

COUNTRY WAYS

• *Shaker Stitchery* •

It is said that Shaker women were not permitted to cross their knees while sitting. This could have made it difficult to sit and sew by hand, but the ingenious Shakers came up with a household item just for the purpose. They designed a set of two steps for a woman to place on the floor in front of her sewing chair. She would put one foot on the first step and the other foot on the second step to bring her work to a comfortable position. Often the steps contained a drawer that was used to hold sewing necessities.

FIG. I, 11D   RED FLOWER CROSS STITCH

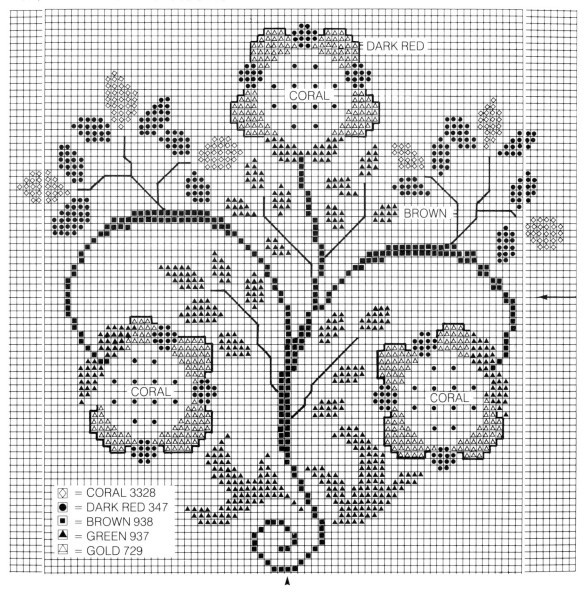

= CORAL 3328
= DARK RED 347
= BROWN 938
= GREEN 937
= GOLD 729

*Marriage is our last, best chance
to grow up.*
—Joseph Barth

WILDFLOWER EMBROIDERY

Average: For those with some experience in embroidery.

CLOVER PILLOW
(photo, page 53; 8 inches square, plus ruffle)

Materials:
¼ yard of 71-inch-wide white Zweigart Kingston linen; matching sewing thread; 1 yard of white piping, or 1 yard of ⅜-inch cotton cording; 1 yard of white ruffled lace; embroidery floss: 1 skein each of Light Pink, Dark Pink, Light Green, Dark Green and Yellow Green; No. 8 crewel needle; embroidery hoop; 8-inch square pillow form; washable fabric marker; tape; tracing paper.
Note: *The design for the Clover Pillow is slightly larger than the Clover design for the Five Flower Pillow.*

Directions:
1. *Fabric:* Cut two 9-inch linen squares, and lightly mark an 8-inch square on each. Set the squares aside.
2. *Transferring Design:* Trace the full size clover and border design in Fig. I, 12 onto tracing paper.

Tape the paper to a window pane. Center and tape one of the linen squares on top. Using the fabric marker, trace the design and dark border lines onto the linen.
3. *Embroidering:* Following Five Flower Pillow, Step 4 *(page 54)*, including the stitch and color directions for the Clover design *(page 56)*, work the design in Fig. I, 12 on the linen. When the center is completed, work the square border in open buttonhole stitch.
4. *Blocking:* Follow Five Flower Pillow, Step 5 *(page 57)*.
5. *Piping:* If making your own piping, make a 1 x 38-inch linen strip, pieced as needed, and press the seams flat. Lay the cording on the wrong side of the strip, and fold the strip over the cording, matching raw edges. Using a zipper foot, machine-stitch close to the cording. With right sides together, machine-stitch the piping to the embroidered pillow top along the 8-inch marked lines, matching the stitches of the piping. Clip the piping seam allowance at the corners.
6. *Finishing:* Pin the ruffled lace to the pillow top on top of the piping, with the lace facing inward; overlap the short ends of the lace to join them. Finish the pillow following Five Flower Pillow, Step 8 *(page 57)*.

FIG. I, 12 WILDFLOWER EMBROIDERY   CLOVER PILLOW

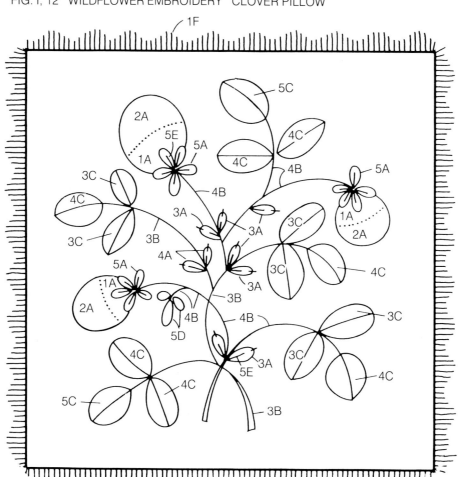

FIVE FLOWER PILLOW
(17 inches square, plus ruffle)

Materials:

1 yard of 71-inch-wide white Zweigart Kingston linen; matching sewing thread; 72 inches of pale blue piping; embroidery floss: 1 skein each of Light Pink, Dark Pink, Red, Light Yellow, Dark Yellow, Gold, Blue, Light Purple, Dark Purple, Light Green, Dark Green, Yellow Green and Medium Yellow Green; No. 8 crewel needle; embroidery hoop; 17-inch square pillow form, or synthetic stuffing; washable fabric marker; ruler; masking tape; tracing paper.

Directions:

1. *Fabric:* Cut two 18-inch linen squares, and lightly mark a 17-inch square on each. Set the squares aside.

2. *Designs:* Draw a 17-inch square on a large sheet of tracing paper. Fold the paper into quarters, drawn lines matching. At the center of one drawn line, where the fold meets the line, measure in 1 inch. Repeat on the other three sides. Using the ruler, draw diagonal lines connecting these points. Then draw lines ⅜ inch inside the diagonal lines; a diamond-shaped border will be embroidered between the double diagonal lines.

FIG. I, 13A   WILDFLOWER EMBROIDERY
FIVE FLOWER PILLOW
MOTIF PLACEMENT DIAGRAM

FIG. I, 13B
WILDFLOWER EMBROIDERY
COWSLIP

Following the placement diagram in Fig. I, 13A *(page 53)*, trace the full size flower designs in Figs. I, 13B to 13F *(pages 54-57)* onto the tracing paper.

3. *Transferring Designs:* Tape the tracing paper to a window pane. Tape one of the linen squares on top of the paper, outer lines matching. Use the fabric marker to trace the designs and diagonal lines onto the linen.

4. *Embroidering:* Separate the floss into individual strands, and use two strands of floss in the needle for all embroidery. Place the marked linen square in the embroidery hoop. First work the diamond, between the diagonal lines, in open buttonhole stitch. Work the flower designs in Figs. I, 13B to 13F using the stitches and colors indicated *(see Stitch Guide, page 214)*. Except where noted, work stems first, and leaves last.

Cowslip (Center Motif)
Colors: 1—Gold, 2—Dark Yellow, 3—Light Yellow, 4—Dark Green, 5—Medium Yellow Green, 6—Yellow Green.
Stitches: A—closed buttonhole stitch, B—stem stitch, C—satin stitch, D—straight stitch, E—lazy daisy stitch, **F**—French knot, G—open fishbone stitch.
Embroidery: Follow Fig. I, 13B. For the flowers, work the closed buttonhole stitches first, and add the straight stitches on top to define the flower petals. Work the flower centers in Gold French knots.

(Continued on page 57)

FIG. I, 13C
WILDFLOWER EMBROIDERY
WILD STRAWBERRY

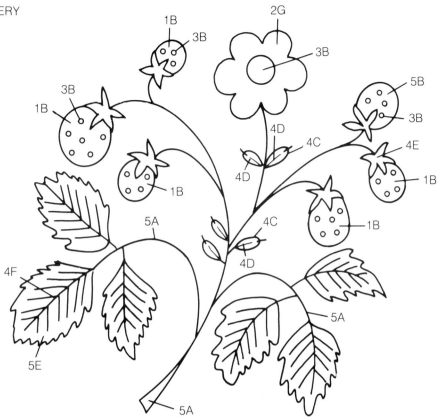

COUNTRY WAYS

• *Wildflower Wisdom* •

Wood sorrel is thought to be the true shamrock of ancient Ireland; notice its three-pointed leaves. It also is known as the "alleluia plant" because it blooms at Eastertime. Wood sorrel is edible, with a lemony tang that has led to its being called "sourgrass."

Wild strawberries and forget-me-nots have been cultivated since medieval times. Both are depicted in tapestries dating back to 1500. It was believed that gargling with strawberry juice cured throat ulcers.

Cowslips got their name from the Old English *cu* — meaning cow — and *slyppe* — meaning dung — because the flowers usually grow in naturally well-fertilized cow pastures.

Clover, especially the four-leaf variety, is a good luck plant. In olden days, four-leaf clovers were a horticultural aberration. They were so rare that finding one became symbolic of good luck. Today, botanists have developed a strain of clover that has four leaves — for folks who need good luck in a hurry.

Wild Strawberry (Top Left Motif)
Colors: 1 — Red, 2 — Light Pink, 3 — Dark Yellow, 4 — Dark Green, 5 — Yellow Green.
Stitches: A — stem stitch, B — French knot, C — lazy daisy stitch, D — straight stitch, E — satin stitch, F — open fishbone stitch, G — closed buttonhole stitch.
Embroidery: Follow Fig. I, 13C.

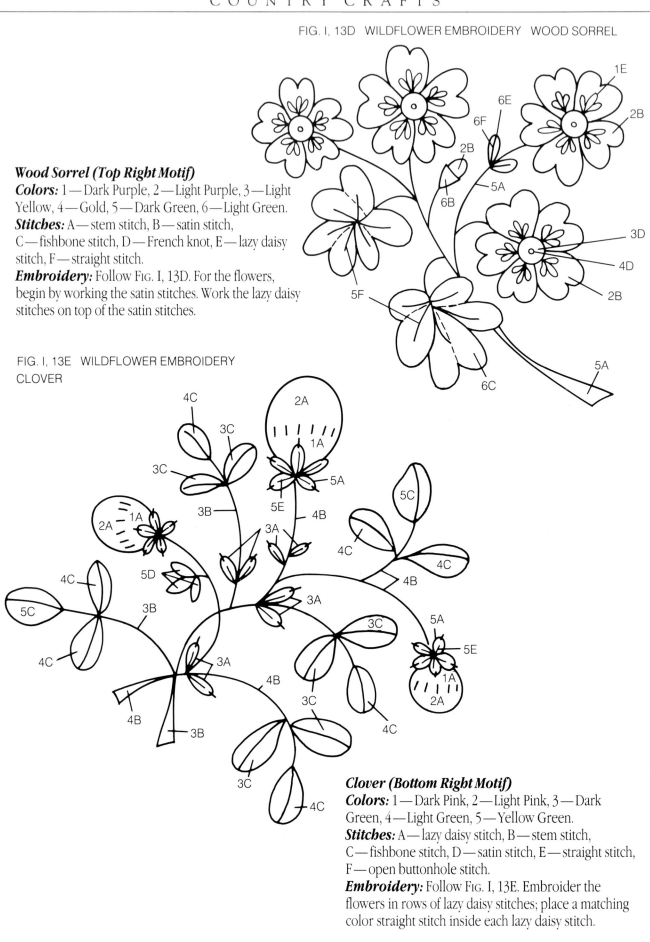

FIG. I, 13D WILDFLOWER EMBROIDERY WOOD SORREL

Wood Sorrel (Top Right Motif)

Colors: 1—Dark Purple, 2—Light Purple, 3—Light Yellow, 4—Gold, 5—Dark Green, 6—Light Green.

Stitches: A—stem stitch, B—satin stitch, C—fishbone stitch, D—French knot, E—lazy daisy stitch, F—straight stitch.

Embroidery: Follow Fig. I, 13D. For the flowers, begin by working the satin stitches. Work the lazy daisy stitches on top of the satin stitches.

FIG. I, 13E WILDFLOWER EMBROIDERY CLOVER

Clover (Bottom Right Motif)

Colors: 1—Dark Pink, 2—Light Pink, 3—Dark Green, 4—Light Green, 5—Yellow Green.

Stitches: A—lazy daisy stitch, B—stem stitch, C—fishbone stitch, D—satin stitch, E—straight stitch, F—open buttonhole stitch.

Embroidery: Follow Fig. I, 13E. Embroider the flowers in rows of lazy daisy stitches; place a matching color straight stitch inside each lazy daisy stitch.

FIG. I, 13F WILDFLOWER EMBROIDERY
FORGET-ME-NOT

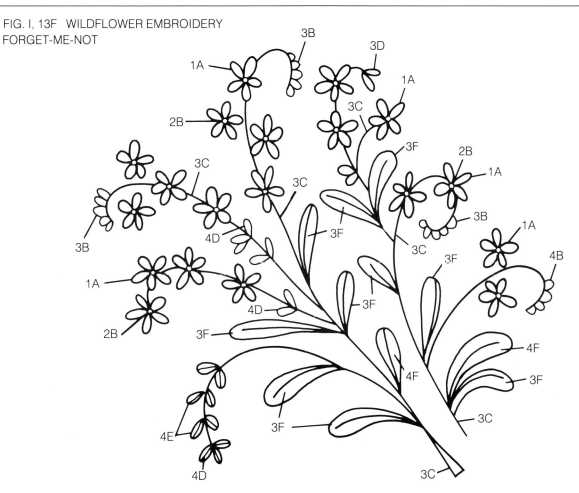

Forget-Me-Not (Bottom Left Motif)

Colors: 1 — Blue, 2 — Dark Yellow, 3 — Dark Green,
4 — Light Green.

Stitches: A — lazy daisy stitch, B — French knot,
C — stem stitch, D — single lazy daisy stitch, E —
straight stitch, F — fishbone stitch.

Embroidery: Follow Fig. I, 13F. After working the
stems, embroider the large and small leaves, then
the flowers. Work the buds last in Dark Green
French knots.

*Patience is a flower
that grows not in every garden.*
— New England saying

5. Blocking: When the embroidery is completed,
wash out the blue design tracings with cold water
following the fabric marker manufacturer's directions.
Using a damp pressing cloth, press the embroidered
linen right side down to block it.

6. Ruffle: Make a 7 x 100-inch linen strip, pieced as
needed, and press the seams flat. Fold the strip in half
lengthwise, wrong sides together, and stitch gathering
rows ½ inch and ¼ inch from the raw edges. Gather
the ruffle to about 76 inches in length, distributing the
gathers evenly.

7. Piping: Using a zipper foot and with right sides
together, machine-stitch the piping to the embroidered
pillow top along the 17-inch marked lines, matching
the stitches of the piping. Clip the piping seam
allowance at the corners for turning, if necessary.

8. Finishing: With right sides together and the ruffle
facing inward, baste the ruffle to the pillow top along
the piping edge. Pin the pillow back to the pillow top,
over the piping and ruffle, right sides together. Using a
½-inch seam allowance, stitch through all layers
around three sides and four corners. Turn the pillow
right side out, and press it. Stuff the pillow, turn in the
open edges, and slipstitch the opening closed (*see
Stitch Guide, page 214*).

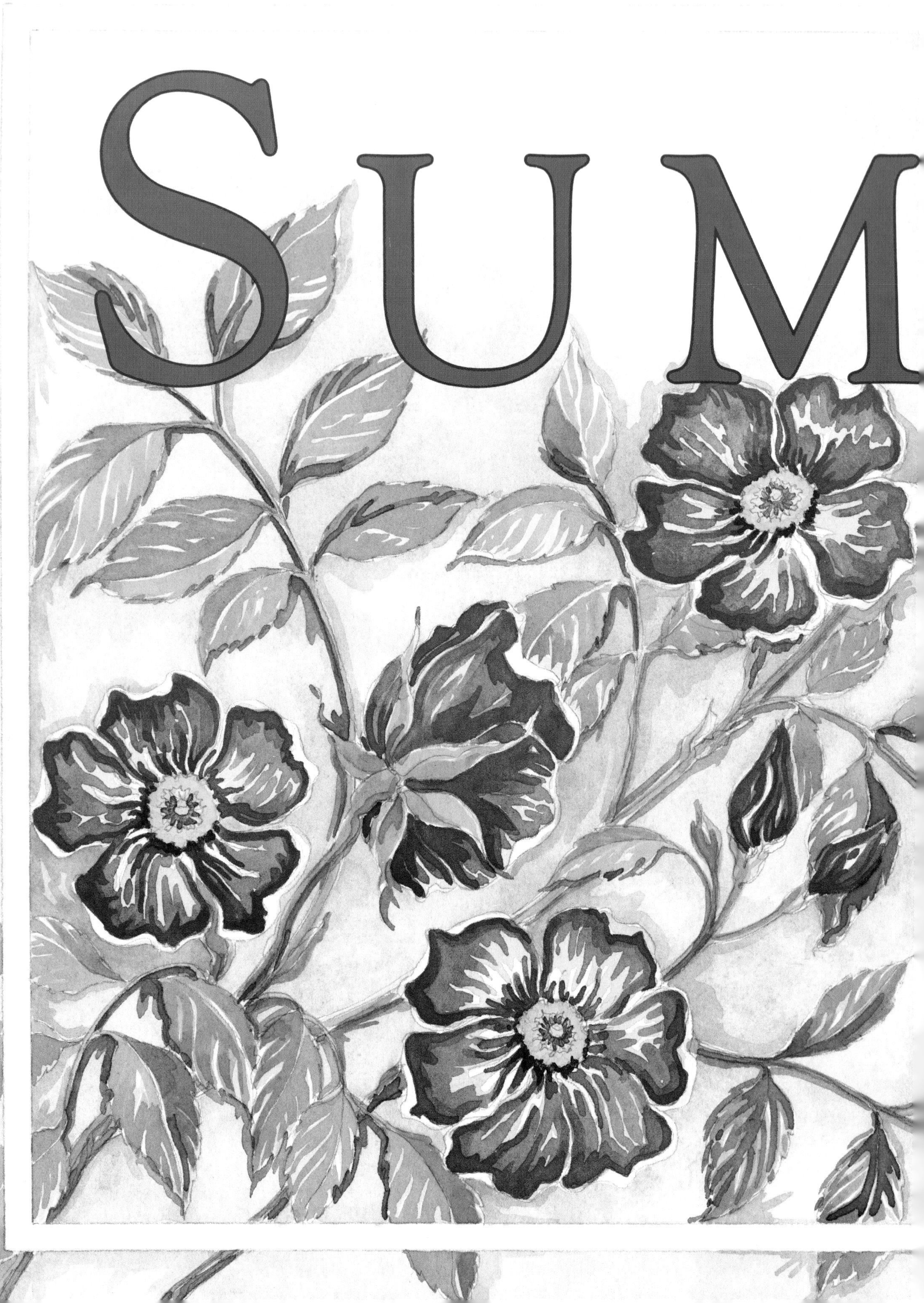
SUM

MER

Summer in the country. The warm, heavy scent of roses fills the air. The mossy softness of a river bank cools your bare feet. You can almost touch the stars at night.

It's the season for picnics in the park and backyard barbecues, Fourth of July fireworks and finding a shady spot on a sunny afternoon. Begin in your own backyard: Use paint and floral fabrics to rescue old wicker furniture. Or start from scratch and craft a redwood picnic table, classic Adirondack lawn chair, or graceful garden arbor.

For your Fourth of July picnic, or any warm-weather entertaining, our colorful, quick-stitch place mats and napkins are picnic perfect. Want to add a note of whimsy? Make our watermelon tray with matching coasters. And anyone would love our picnic basket, stenciled with summer fruits for a classic country touch.

Learn the art of rug hooking and create a beautiful floor throw for every room in your house. And because summer is the season of children, we have a selection of delightful dollies and tiny teddies to make for your favorite little one.

Comfortable and relaxed, country style embraces the rhythm of summer: long, lazy afternoons, soft twilights, and the dreamy wish that these days could last forever.

THE GREAT
O·U·T·D·O·O·R·S

Turn your backyard into a summer paradise! Build, stitch and paint your way to the perfect place for warm weather relaxing.

SUMMER PARLOR FURNISHINGS

Average: For those with some experience in crafting and sewing.

WONDERFUL WICKER FURNITURE

Materials:
White wicker furniture; floral chintz fabric scraps; white spray paint; lilac acrylic paint, or color of your choice; clear spray varnish; artist's flat paintbrush; General Materials for Stenciled Picnic Basket & Napkins *(page 80)*; stencil brush; white glue; ruler.

Directions:
1. *Preparing the Wicker:* Repair the wicker furniture, if necessary, and clean it. Spray paint the wicker, and let the paint dry thoroughly.
2. *Appliquéd Wicker:* Cut out a floral motif from a fabric scrap. Apply glue to the cutout, and to the wicker furniture where you wish to place the cutout. Press the floral cutout onto the furniture, and let the glue dry for half an hour. Spray the floral appliqué with two coats of clear varnish, letting the varnish dry between coats.
3. *Color-painted Wicker:* Using the acrylic paint and artist's paintbrush, paint alternate weaves in the wicker furniture *(see rocking chair at left in photo).*
4. *Stenciled Wicker:* Draw a diamond on paper in a size to fit the wicker furniture being stenciled *(see chair and settee in photo).* Following Stenciled Picnic Basket & Napkins General Directions, Steps 1 and 2, cut a stencil for the diamond, and stencil the diamond onto the wicker furniture with the acrylic paint and stencil brush. Clean the stencil and brush following Stenciled Picnic Basket & Napkins General Directions, Step 3.

FLORAL CHINTZ PILLOW
(16 inches square)

Materials:
½ yard of floral chintz fabric for pillow; ⅔ yard of coordinating solid color fabric, or other floral print fabric, for ruffle; matching threads; 16-inch square pillow form; 2 yards of piping.

Directions (½-inch seams allowed):
1. *Cutting:* From the pillow fabric, cut two 17-inch squares. From the ruffle fabric, cut 6-inch-wide strips and piece them as needed to measure 3 to 4 yards in length.
2. *Piping:* Pin the piping to the edges of the pillow front right sides together and raw edges even. Clip the piping seam allowance at each corner. Using a zipper foot, stitch the piping in place.
3. *Ruffle:* Stitch the short ends of the strip together to make a loop. Fold the loop in half, wrong sides together, and press. Divide the loop into quarters, and pin mark each quarter. Sew a gathering row ½ inch from the raw edge, starting and stopping at each pin. Repeat ¼ inch from the raw edge. Pin the ruffle to the pillow front right sides together and raw edges even, with a pin at each corner. Pull up the gathers to fit the pillow front. Stitch along the inner gathering row.
4. *Assembling:* Pin the pillow back to the pillow front right sides together and raw edges even. Stitch around three sides and four corners. Turn the pillow right side out, and stuff it. Turn in the open edges, and slipstitch the opening closed *(see Stitch Guide, page 214).*

***Summer afternoon — summer afternoon;
to me those have always been
the two most beautiful words
in the English language.***
—Henry James

UNDER-A-TREE PICNIC TABLE
(6 feet in diameter, and 29 inches high)

What makes it country? An ingenious design that incorporates nature, making the table both practical and beautiful.

Challenging: Requires more experience in woodworking.

Materials:
Clear heart redwood lumber *(see Notes, at right)*: one 16-foot length of 2 x 4, two 14-foot lengths of 2 x 4, and two 16-foot lengths of 2 x 12; 8d and 12d galvanized finishing nails; corrugated fasteners; sandpaper; tack cloth; crosscut saw; ripsaw; miter box; backsaw or circular saw; wood plane; rasp or sander; combination square; clamps; hammer.

Notes: *A less expensive garden grade of lumber, such as construction heart or common grade, can be used. Both are made in the same dimensions as clear heart redwood, and have the same permanence.*

The table's inner frame dimensions are for an 8- to 10-inch-diameter tree trunk. The center opening is 15 inches. You may have to vary the lengths of the A outer frame and B inner frame pieces to accommodate the tree around which you're building the table. Pick a mature tree whose growth has slowed.

> **I learned more about economics from one South Dakota dust storm than I did in all my years in college.**
> —Hubert Humphrey

CUTTING DIRECTIONS

CODE	PIECES	SIZE
A (2 x 4)	(6)	1½″ x 3½″ x 27″ Outer frame
B (2 x 4)	(6)	1½″ x 3½″ x 11″ Inner frame
C (2 x 4)	(6)	1½″ x 3½″ x 27½″ Legs
D (2 x 4)	(2)	1½″ x 3½″ x 13″ Frame braces
E (2 x 4)	(6)	1½″ x 3½″ x 19″ Knee braces
F (2 x 12)	(20)	1½″ x 11″ x 26″ Petals

Directions:

1. Following the Cutting Directions, and referring to FIG. II, 1A, cut the A, B, C, D and E pieces; all angles are 30°. Cut the D frame braces square.

2. Referring to FIG. II, 1A, assemble the A outer frame and B inner frame; the frame pieces are attached with corrugated fasteners on top and on the underside *(see FIG. II, 1A Detail)*. Leave open one A outer frame piece and, depending on the size of the tree trunk, one or two B inner frame pieces. Attach the A outer frame to the B inner frame with the D frame braces. Place the A/B/D frame assembly around the tree. Fasten the open A and B pieces to close the assembly around the tree.

3. Clamp at least three C legs in position to support the frame assembly *(see FIG. II, 1A)*. Cut one end of each E knee brace at a 45° angle, and bevel a 30° notch to fit the B inner frame corner *(see FIGS. II, 1A and 1B)*. Place one E knee brace in position, with the 45° angle against the B inner frame. With the C leg vertical, and the E knee brace placed against the leg, mark off the location of the notch on the C leg, and the cut off points on the E knee brace *(see FIG. II, 1A)*. Notch the C legs, and cut the E knee braces. Using 12d nails, nail the E knee braces to the notches in the C legs. Nail the C legs to the A outer frame *(see FIG. II, 1A Detail)*. Toenail the E knee braces to the B inner frame.

4. Following the Cutting Directions, and referring to FIG. II, 1C, cut the F petals. Lay the F petals over the frame assembly, and space them evenly to fit the tree *(see FIG. II, 1A)*; leave some space around the tree trunk for it to grow. Using 8d nails, nail the F petals to the outer and inner frames. Sand the rough edges of the table smooth, and wipe off all the sawdust with the tack cloth.

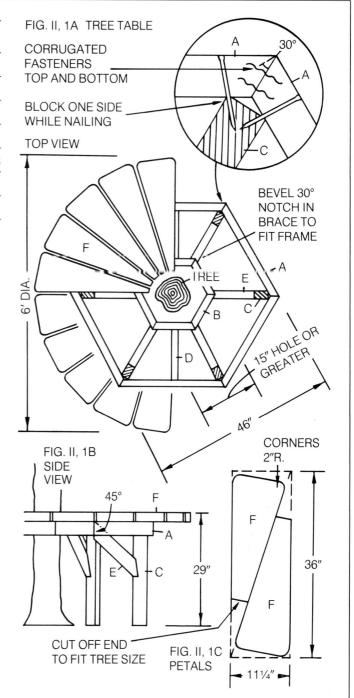

FIG. II, 1A TREE TABLE

CORRUGATED FASTENERS TOP AND BOTTOM

BLOCK ONE SIDE WHILE NAILING

TOP VIEW

30°

BEVEL 30° NOTCH IN BRACE TO FIT FRAME

6' DIA.

TREE

15″ HOLE OR GREATER

46″

FIG. II, 1B SIDE VIEW

45°

29″

CUT OFF END TO FIT TREE SIZE

CORNERS 2″R.

36″

FIG. II, 1C PETALS

11¼″

ADIRONDACK CHAIR

*An American classic named for the beautiful
Adirondack mountains in New York State. What makes
it country? It's sturdy, comfortable and attractive.*

Average: For those with some experience
in woodworking.

Materials:

Fir lumber: 6 feet of 1 x 2, 14 feet of 1 x 4, and two
12-foot lengths of 1 x 8; 4d and 6d galvanized finishing
nails; wood glue; graphite paper; stylus or dry ballpoint
pen; sandpaper; tack cloth; paint in color desired, or
wood stain; satin-finish polyurethane; paintbrushes;
crosscut saw; sabre or band saw; hammer; square;
paper for pattern.

CUTTING DIRECTIONS

CODE	PIECES	SIZE
A (1 x 8)	(2)	¾" x 7½" x 33" Legs
B (1 x 8)	(2)	¾" x 7½" x 16" Arm supports
C (1 x 2)	(1)	¾" x 1½" x 28½" Slat
D (1 x 4)	(1)	¾" x 3" x 28½" Slat
E (1 x 4)	(1)	¾" x 3" x 20½" Slat
F (1 x 4)	(1)	¾" x 3½" x 20½" Back brace
G (1 x 4)	(1)	¾" x 3" x 26½" Back brace
H (1 x 8)	(2)	¾" x 7¼" x 28" Arms
J (1 x 8)	(2)	¾" x 7" x 27" Back
K (1 x 8)	(2)	¾" x 6" x 34" Back
L (1 x 4)	(1)	¾" x 3" x 20½" Skirt
M (1 x 4)	(2)	¾" x 3½" x 20½" Slats
N (1 x 2)	(2)	¾" x 1½" x 20½" Slats

Directions:

1. Enlarge the pattern in FIG. II, 2A *(page 66)* onto
paper following the directions on page 215, and cut out
the pattern pieces. Using the graphite paper and stylus
or dry ballpoint pen, trace the pattern pieces onto the
wood pieces indicated in the Cutting Directions. Cut
out all the chair parts.
2. Using 6d nails, glue and nail the F back brace to the
A legs *(see* FIGS. II, 2B *and* 2C, *page 67)*. Glue and nail
the C slat to the A legs just in front of the B arm
supports' location *(see double dotted lines on A leg
pattern piece in* FIG. II, 2A*)*.
3. Using 6d nails, glue and nail the B arm supports to
the A legs and C slat *(see* FIGS. II, 2B *and* 2C*)*. Glue and
nail the D slat butted against the B arm supports.
4. Using 4d nails, glue and nail the G back brace to the
top back of the H arms flush at the side edges. Using 6d
nails, glue and nail the G/H arm assembly to the B arm
supports *(see* FIG. II, 2B*)*.
5. Using 6d nails, glue and nail the J and K back pieces
to the F and G back braces, with one side edge of each
J piece flush against an H arm, and the K pieces evenly
spaced in between; make sure the H arms are at a 90°
angle to the B arm supports, and the J and K back
pieces are aligned *(see* FIG. II, 2C*)*.
6. Using 6d nails, glue and nail the E slat butted against
the J and K back pieces.
7. Using 6d nails, glue and nail the M and N slats, then
the L skirt, to the A legs to complete the chair.
8. Sand the rough edges of the chair smooth, and wipe
off all the sawdust with the tack cloth. Paint or stain the
chair as desired. When the paint or stain is completely
dry, apply several coats of polyurethane, sanding lightly
between coats.

***I have spread my dreams
under your feet;
Tread softly
because you tread on my dreams.***
—William Butler Yeats

FIG. II, 2A ADIRONDACK CHAIR CUTTING DIAGRAM

1 SQ. = 3″

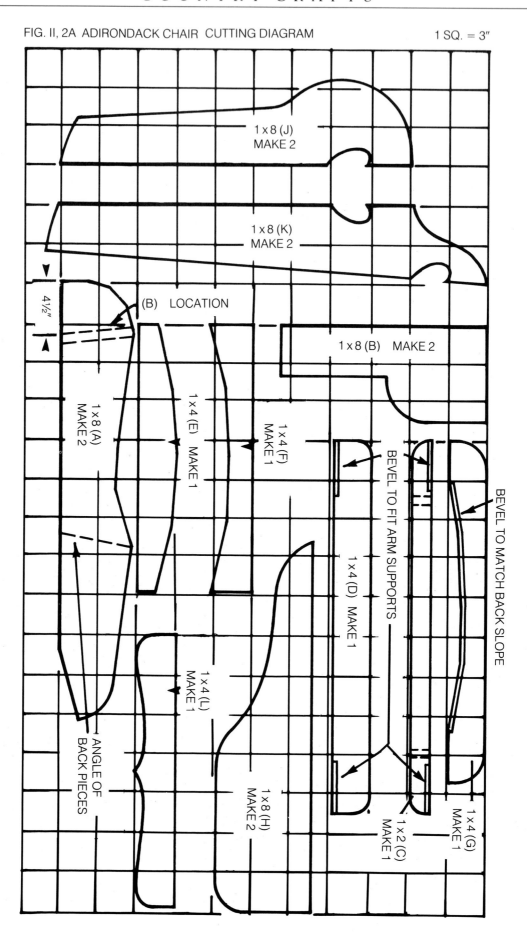

1 x 8 (J)
MAKE 2

1 x 8 (K)
MAKE 2

4½″

(B)   LOCATION

1 x 8 (B)   MAKE 2

1 x 8 (A)
MAKE 2

1 x 4 (E) MAKE 1

1 x 4 (F)
MAKE 1

BEVEL TO FIT ARM SUPPORTS

BEVEL TO MATCH BACK SLOPE

1 x 4 (D) MAKE 1

1 x 4 (L)
MAKE 1

ANGLE OF
BACK PIECES

1 x 8 (H)
MAKE 2

1 x 2 (C)
MAKE 1

1 x 4 (G)
MAKE 1

FIG. II, 2B ASSEMBLY SIDE VIEW

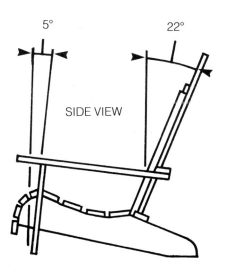

5°   22°

SIDE VIEW

COUNTRY WAYS

• The Summer "Parlor" •

Sitting outdoors on a summer afternoon can be
a delightful experience. However, busy people
sometimes overlook such a simple pleasure.
Back in 1874, a columnist for *The American
Agriculturalist* pointed out the error of our
ways. He wrote:

"We Americans, especially those of us who
live in the country, make but very little use of
our spacious summer parlor — 'all out doors.'
A wide spreading tree, a vine covered arbor,
a broad veranda or porch, an awning like a
huge umbrella, or a tent with no sides or even
an open shed is a much more comfortable
place for sewing, reading, and resting, than any
place in-doors, and often comes in handy for
ironing and other work. For the enjoyment of
the open air in any case, seats and chairs that
are not too good for rough usage or too rough
for ease are needed."

FIG. II, 2C ASSEMBLY FRONT VIEW

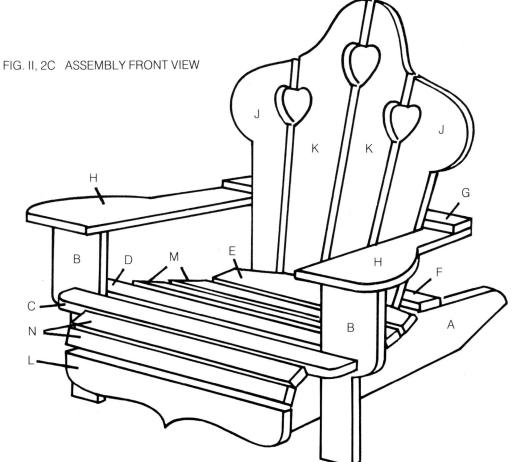

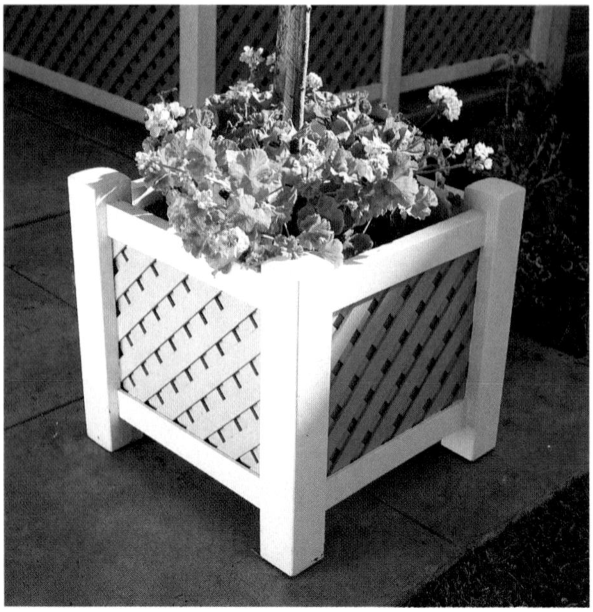

PRETTY LATTICE PLANTER

(18 x 18 x 18½ inches)

Average: For those with some experience in woodworking.

Materials:

Exterior grade plywood: ¾ x 15 x 15 inches; lumber: 12 feet of 5⁄4, and 7 feet of 3 x 4; 68 feet of ¼ x 1⅛-inch lattice; ⅜-inch brads, or staplegun with ⅜-inch staples; 2-inch Phillips head drywall screws; waterproof glue; wood putty; sandpaper; tack cloth; paint in color desired; paintbrush; ruler; power saw; miter box; backsaw; router with ½-inch straight bit; ½-inch wood chisel; power drill with ⅛-inch and ½-inch bits; Phillips head screwdriver or drill bit; countersink set; clamps; brown paper for pattern.

CUTTING DIRECTIONS

CODE	PIECES	SIZE
A (3 x 4)	(4)	2½" x 2½" x 18½" Posts
B (5⁄4)	(8)	1⅛" x 1½" x 14½" Rails
C (LAT)	(4)	½" x 13½" x 13½" Grids
D (PLY)	(1)	¾" x 14⅜" x 14⅜" Bottom

FIG. II, 3A PRETTY PLANTER SIDE DETAIL

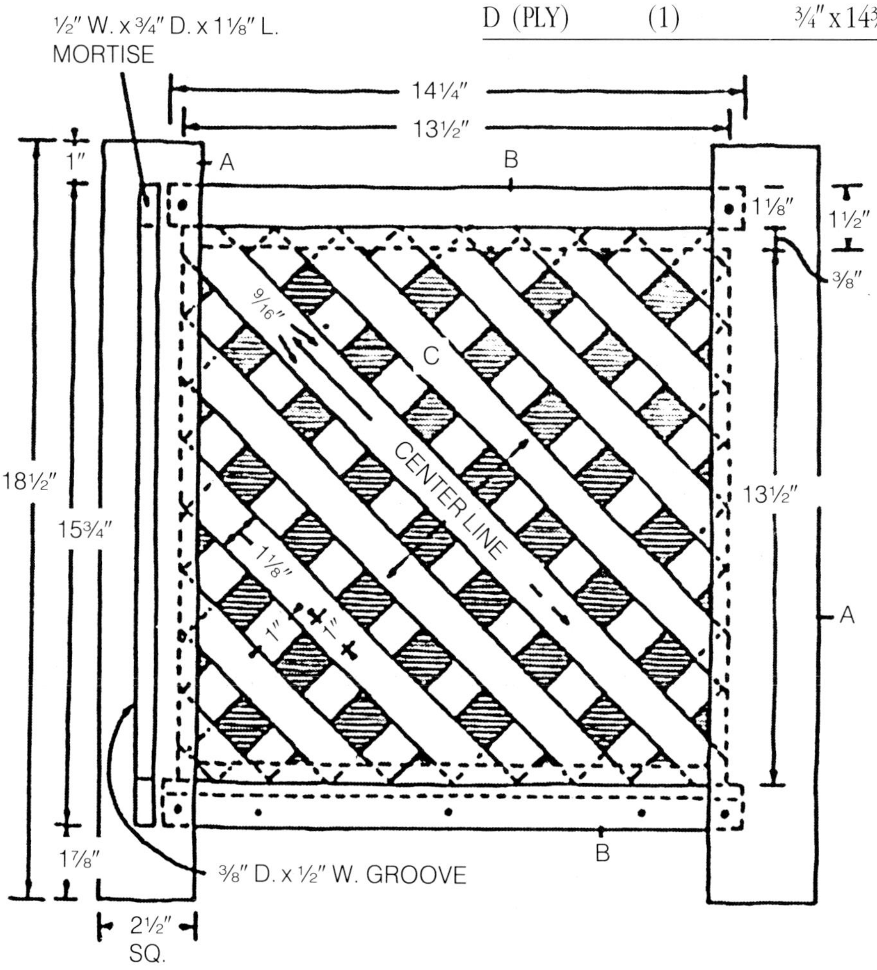

Directions:

1. Make a pattern for the C lattice grids: Draw a 13½-inch square on a piece of brown paper. Draw diagonal lines from corner to corner; these are the center lines. Using the center line that goes from upper left to lower right, draw a parallel line ⁹⁄₁₆ inch on each side of the center line; these lines mark the placement of the center lattice strip. Moving toward the lower left corner, measure 1 inch for a space, 1⅛ inch for a lattice strip, 1 inch, 1⅛ inch, and so on, to the corner. Repeat on the upper right of the center lattice strip.

2. Using the center line that goes from upper right to lower left, draw a parallel line ½ inch on each side of the center line; this pair of lines marks 1-inch square spaces. Moving toward the upper left corner, measure 1⅛ inch for a lattice strip, 1 inch for square spaces, and so on *(see* Fig. II, 3A*)*. Repeat moving toward the lower right corner. Note that the crisscrossed lattice strips

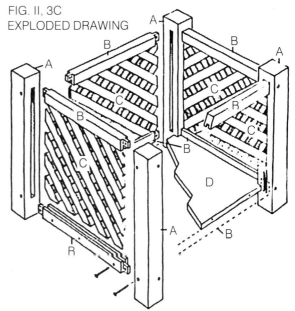

FIG. II, 3C
EXPLODED DRAWING

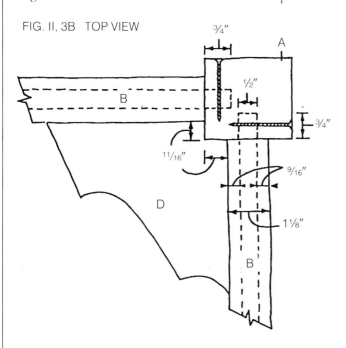

FIG. II, 3B   TOP VIEW

line up and lap at the outer edges. Darken the 1-inch squares to indicate the spaces.

3. Place the lattice on the pattern, and mark the lattice for the length of the first strip. Using the miter box, cut the lattice strip to length at a 45° angle. Repeat for all except the center lattice strip; cut the center strip so the short ends come to a point *(see* Fig. II, 3A*)*. Place the lattice strips in position on the pattern, and glue them together. Then nail or staple the lattice strips in place where they cross. Repeat to make four C lattice grids.

4. Using the power saw, rip the 3 x 4 on the 4-inch side to measure 2½ inches square. Then cut it to length for the A posts. On two adjacent sides of each A post, rout

a ½-inch-wide, ¾-inch-deep, 1⅛-inch-long mortise, centered side to side, 1 inch from the top of the post. Rout a second mortise 1⅞ inches from the bottom; the mortises are for the tenons on the B rails. Square the corners of the mortises with the chisel. Then rout a ½-inch-wide, ⅜-inch-deep groove between each pair of mortises for the C grids *(see* Figs. II, 3A *and* 3C*)*.

5. Cut the B rails to length. Rout a ½-inch-wide, ⅜-inch-deep groove in the bottom center of each B rail for a C grid. Then cut a ½ x ¾-inch tenon on both ends of each B rail *(see* Figs. II, 3B *and* 3C*)*.

6. Glue the tops and bottoms of the C grids into the grooves in the B rails, butting the grids against the rails. Let the glue set.

7. Glue the C grids into the grooves in the A posts; the tenons on the B rails will fit into the mortises in the A posts *(see* Figs. II, 3A *and* 3C*)*. Clamp the four sides of the planter together until the glue sets. Before the glue sets, measure the inside distance between the bottom B rails. Cut the D bottom to size. Notch each corner of the D bottom ¹¹⁄₁₆ x ¹¹⁄₁₆ inch *(see* Fig. II, 3B*)*. Using glue and the drywall screws, attach the D bottom between, and flush with the bottom edges of, the bottom B rails by drilling holes and countersinking the screws *(see* Fig. II, 3C*)*.

8. Anchor each B rail tenon in place in the A posts with a drywall screw *(see* Figs. II, 3B *and* 3C*)*, drilling holes and countersinking the screws.

9. Drill a few ½-inch-diameter drain holes in the bottom of the planter.

10. Sand the planter's rough edges smooth, and wipe off all the sawdust with the tack cloth. Paint the planter.

GARDEN ARBOR
(5½ x 3 x 9 feet)

Challenging: Requires more experience
in woodworking.

Materials:

Exterior grade plywood; 4 x 4 pressure-treated lumber
posts; common lumber: 1 x 1, 1 x 2, 1 x 3, 1 x 4, 1 x 6, and
2 x 4; solid crown molding; ¾-inch-thick half-round
molding *(see Cutting Directions for dimensions of
wood pieces)*; eight 3½-inch lag screws with washers;
1¼-inch and 1¾-inch No. 8 flathead wood screws; 3d,
4d, 6d and 20d galvanized finishing nails; 1¼-inch wire
brads; 2 wrap-around hinges with ¾-inch offset;
waterproof glue; sandpaper; tack cloth; wood putty;
waterproof sealer, or wood preservative; exterior paint
in color desired; paintbrushes; felt weather stripping;
tracing paper; power saw; handsaw; sabre saw or
jigsaw; miter box; backsaw; power drill with assorted
bits; countersink set; open-end or socket wrench to fit
lag screws; brace and 1-inch-diameter bit; hammer;
screwdriver; nail set; stapler; particle mask.

Note: *Wear the particle mask when working with the
pressure-treated lumber; the sawdust is toxic.*

Directions:

1. Following the Cutting Directions, cut the A posts and
A1 tracks to length.

2. On two of the A posts, draw a line down the center
of one side. On each of the remaining two A posts,
draw lines down the centers of two adjacent sides.
Draw a line ⅜ inch on either side of each center line.
Using 1¼-inch brads, glue and nail the inside edges of
the A1 tracks to the A posts along the side lines 20
inches from the posts' bottom ends *(see Fig. II, 4A, and
Detail 1, page 73)*; check that the edge of a scrap of
1 x 2 lumber fits between each pair of A1 tracks before
nailing the tracks in place.

3. Cut the B side slats, B1 vertical slats, B2 side rails,
B3 back slats, and B4 back rail to size. Using two 1¼-
inch brads diagonally per slat, glue and nail the B side
slats to B1 vertical slats 8 inches on center; note that the
third side slat from the bottom is a B2 side rail *(see Fig.
II, 4A)*. Repeat with the B3 back slats and remaining B1
vertical slats; note that the third slat from the bottom is
the B4 back rail *(see Fig. II, 4A)*.

4. Cut the C outer window frame pieces and C1 inner
window frame pieces with mitered corners. Using 6d
nails, glue and nail four C outer frame pieces together
to form a square outer window frame. Repeat to form a
second outer window frame. Using 1¼-inch brads,
repeat with the C1 inner frame pieces.

CUTTING DIRECTIONS

CODE	PIECES	SIZE
A (4 x 4)	(4)	3½" x 3½" x 86" Posts
A1 (1 x 1)	(12)	¾" x ¾" x 64" Tracks
A2 (4 x 4)	(2)	3½" x 3½" x 31" Cross beams
A3 (1 x 3)	(4)	¾" x 2½" x 3" Seat supports
B (1 x 2)	(16)	¾" x 1½" x 24" Side slats
B1 (1 x 2)	(9)	¾" x 1½" x 64" Vertical slats
B2 (1 x 3)	(2)	¾" x 2½" x 24" Side rails
B3 (1 x 2)	(8)	¾" x 1½" x 48" Back slats
B4 (1 x 3)	(1)	¾" x 2½" x 48" Back rail
C (1 x 3)	(8)	¾" x 2½" x 14" Outer window frames
C1 (1 x 1)	(4)	¾" x ¾" x 10½" Inner window frame
D (2 x 4)	(4)	1½" x 3½" x 37¼" Rafters
E (PLY)	(1)	¾" x 21¾" x 62¾" Roof front
E1 (PLY)	(1)	¾" x 21¾" x 62¾" Roof back
F (PLY)	(2)	¾" x 34¾" x 38" Roof
G (MOLD)	(2)	1⅜" x 2¾" x 37¾" Solid crown
H (1 x 4)	(2)	¾" x 2½" x 32½" Trim
J (MOLD)	(4)	¾"half-rnd x 38⅜" Trim
J1 (MOLD)	(2)	¾"half-rnd x 35½" Trim
K (PLY)	(2)	¾" x 14¼" x 54" Seat front and back
K1 (PLY)	(2)	¾" x 14¼" x 22½" Seat sides
K2 (1 x 2)	(2)	¾" x 1½" x 52½" Seat frame
K3 (1 x 2)	(2)	¾" x 1½" x 21" Seat frame
K4 (1 x 2)	(2)	¾" x 1½" x 47½" Seat frame
K5 (1 x 3)	(4)	¾" x 2½" x 12¾" Seat frame
K6 (PLY)	(1)	¾" x 22½" x 52½" Seat bottom
L (1 x 4)	(1)	¾" x 3½" x 54" Seat top
L1 (1 x 6)	(2)	¾" x 5½" x 20½" Seat top
L2 (SCRAP)	(2)	¾" x 4" x 6" Cleat
M (PLY)	(1)	¾" x 23" x 45" Lid
M1 (1 x 3)	(1)	¾" x 2½" x 42½" Cleat
N (MOLD)	(2)	¾" half-rnd x 23⅜" Trim
N1 (MOLD)	(1)	¾" half-rnd x 45¾" Trim

5. Using 1¼-inch brads, glue and nail one C outer window frame to the C1 inner window frame with inner edges flush (see Fig. II, 4B, page 74).

6. Referring to Figs. II, 4A and 4B, cut out the B1 vertical slat and B3 back slat to make space for the window. Using glue and 1¼-inch wood screws, attach the C/C1 window frame to the B3 back slats by drilling holes and countersinking the screws. Turn over the back assembly. Using 1¼-inch brads, glue and nail the remaining C outer window frame to the C1 inner window frame. Then drill holes and countersink 1¼-inch wood screws through C into the B1 vertical slats.

7. Cut and rabbet the A2 cross beams (see Fig. II, 4A).

8. Place one front A post (with one set of tracks), and one back A post (with two sets of tracks) parallel to each other about 2 feet apart on a flat surface, with the tracks for the side assembly facing each other, and the track for the back assembly on top. Place a side assembly, with the vertical slats on top (see Fig. II, 4A), in the tracks between the A posts flush with the top and bottom of the tracks, and butted against the posts. Using 6d nails, glue and nail the side assembly in place by nailing through the tracks into the side slats. Check that all is square. Repeat for the opposite side assembly.

9. Using 4d nails, glue and nail the A2 cross beams to the top of the A posts in the side assemblies (see Figs. II, 4A, and 4C, page 75).

10. Place the side assemblies on edge about 4 feet apart on a level floor, with the tracks for the back assembly facing each other. Place the back assembly, with the vertical slats on top, in the tracks flush with the top and bottom of the tracks and butted against the posts; use a piece of wood as a brace across the top (front) of the side assemblies to keep the arbor assembly square. Using 6d nails, glue and nail the back assembly in place by nailing through the back tracks into the back slats.

11. Cut the A3 seat supports to size, with a 45° angle cut at the bottom (see Fig. II, 4A, Detail 2). Using glue and 1¾-inch wood screws, attach the A3 seat supports to the A posts 3 inches from the bottom of the posts, and flush with the posts' inside corners (see Fig. II, 4A).

12. Cut the K seat front and back, K1 seat sides, K2, K3, K4 and K5 seat frame pieces, and K6 seat bottom to size. Using glue and 1¼-inch wood screws, attach the K3 frame pieces to the K1 seat sides flush at the bottom and ¾ inch from each end (see Fig. II, 4A). Attach the K2 frame pieces to the K seat front and back flush at the bottom, and ¾ inch from each end. Attach the K4 frame pieces to the K front and back flush at the top, and 3¼ inches from each end. Drill a ⅜-inch-deep 1-inch-diameter hole, centered side to side, 2 inches from the top and 2 inches from the bottom of each K5 frame

piece. Then drill a ³⁄₁₆-inch-diameter hole in the center of each 1-inch-diameter hole (see Fig. II, 4A, Detail 3); these holes are for lag screws that will be attached later. Using glue and 1¼-inch wood screws, attach the K5 frame pieces to the K front and back flush with the top edge of K, butted against the ends of K4 at the top, and resting on and overlapping K2 by ¾ inch at the bottom (see Fig. II, 4A). Using 6d nails, glue and nail the K1 seat sides to the K front and back by nailing through K1 into the edges of K5.

13. Notch the corners of the K6 seat bottom ¾ x 2½ inches to allow clearance for the K5 frame pieces. Using 4d nails, glue and nail the K6 seat bottom to the K2 and K3 frame pieces (see Fig. II, 4A).

14. Cut the L and L1 seat top pieces and the L2 cleats to size on a flat surface. Place the L and L1 seat top pieces face down in position to form an upside-down U shape. At each short end of the L piece, draw a line 1½ inches down from the long upper edge. Make sure the L1 pieces are butted against and square with the L piece. Place each L2 cleat on L/L1 with a short end of L2 on one of the lines drawn on L, and a long edge of L2 flush with the inside edge of L1 (see Fig. II, 4A, and Detail 4). Using glue and 1¼-inch wood screws, fasten the L2 cleats in place. Turn over the L/L1/L2 seat top assembly. Using 4d nails, glue and nail the seat top assembly to the top edges of the K seat back and K1 seat sides, outside edges flush.

15. Cut the M lid and M1 cleat to size. Using glue and 1¼-inch wood screws, attach the M1 cleat to the underside of the M lid 2½ inches from the front edge and 1¼ inches from the side edges of M (see Fig. II, 4A). Cut the N and N1 trim pieces to size, and miter their front corners. Using 1¼-inch brads, glue and nail the N and N1 trim pieces to the front and side edges of the M lid (see Figs. II, 4A, 4B and 4C).

16. With the arbor assembly standing upright, place the seat assembly on the A3 seat supports so the seat assembly is recessed ½ inch from the A posts' outside edges. Drill a 1½-inch-deep ³⁄₁₆-inch-diameter hole into the posts through each hole drilled in the K5 seat frame pieces (see Fig. II, 4A, Detail 3). Insert a lag screw with a washer into each hole, and tighten it with the open-end or socket wrench.

17. Attach the M lid to the L seat top piece with a wrap-around hinge placed 4 inches from each lid end along the back of the lid.

18. Draw the half pattern for the E roof front, with the Palladian arch, on folded tracing paper following the dimensions in Fig. II, 4D (page 75). Trace the half pattern onto the other half of the paper, and open the paper for the full pattern. Repeat to make a separate

FIG. II, 4A GARDEN ARBOR ASSEMBLY DIAGRAM

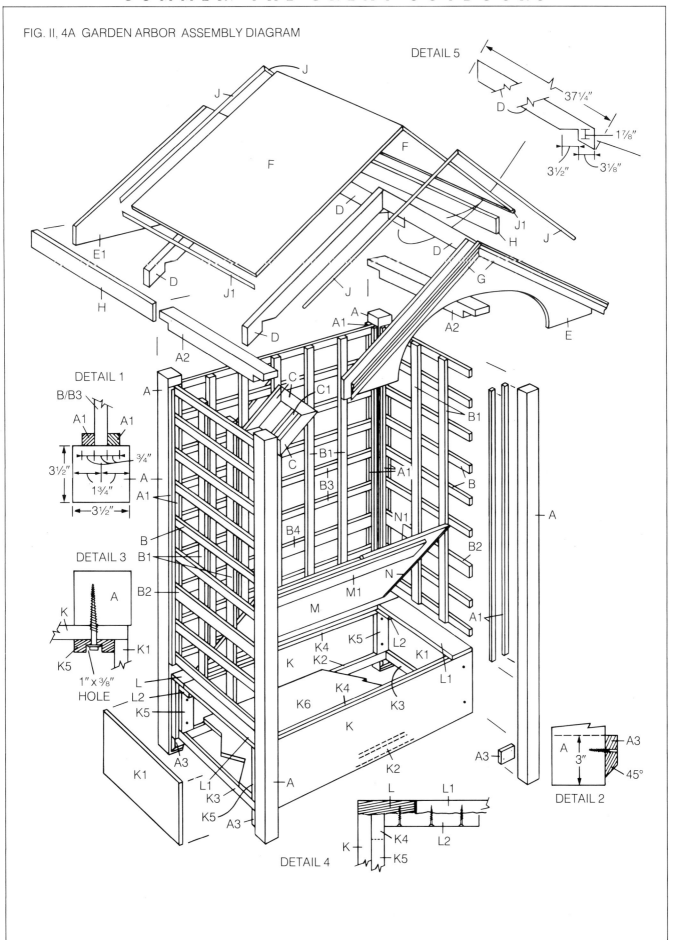

DETAIL 5

D

37¼"

1⅞"

3½" 3⅛"

DETAIL 1

B/B3

A1   A1

¾"

3½"

1¾"

3½"

A

A

A1

B

B1

DETAIL 3

K

A

K

K1

K5

K1

1" x ⅜"

HOLE

DETAIL 2

A3

A   3"   A3

45°

DETAIL 4

L   L1

K4   L2

K

K5

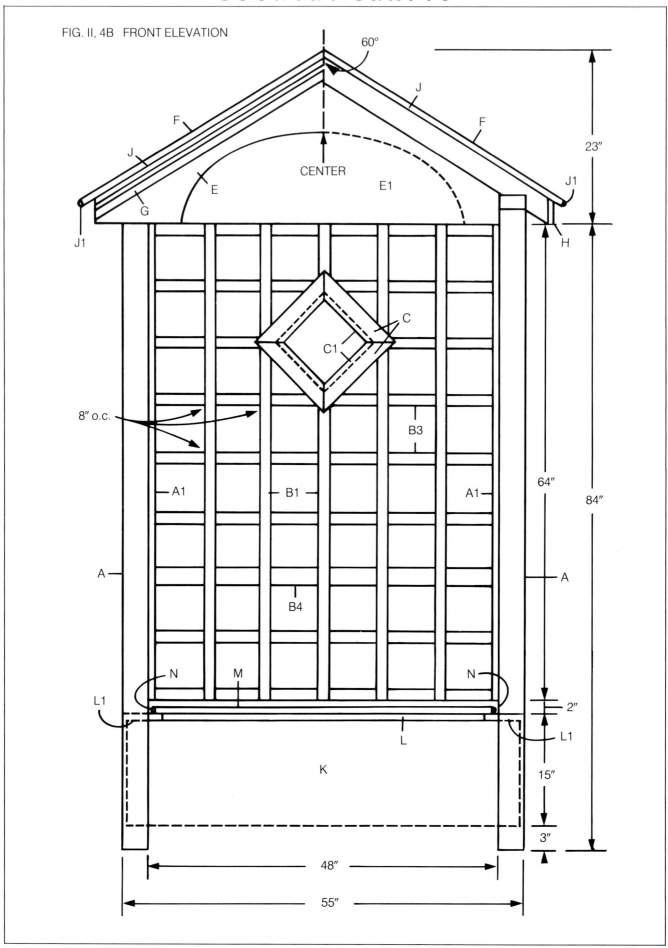

FIG. II, 4B FRONT ELEVATION

60°

23"

J

F

J1

CENTER

E

E1

G

J1

H

C

C1

B3

8" o.c.

A1

B1

A1

64"

84"

A

A

B4

N

M

N

L1

2"

L

L1

K

15"

3"

48"

55"

FIG. II, 4C   SIDE VIEW

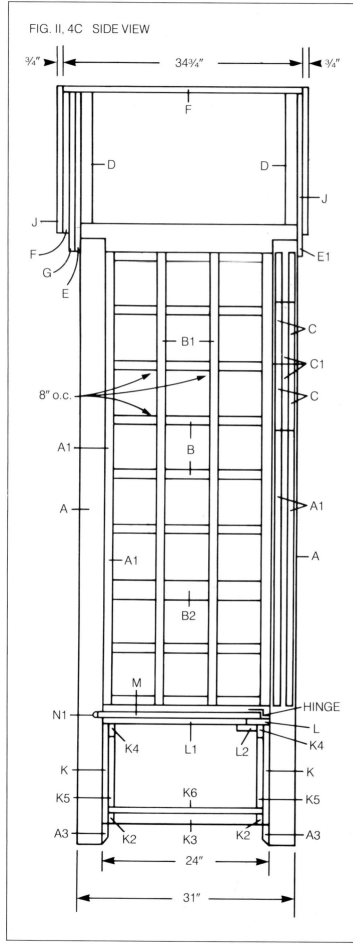

pattern for the E1 roof back without the arch. Using the patterns, cut the E roof front and E1 roof back to size.

19. Cut the D rafters to size, and notch them following the dimensions in FIG. II, 4A, Detail 5. Place two D rafters in position on a flat surface, and place the E roof front on top flush with the rafters' top and side edges. Using glue and 1¼-inch wood screws, attach the E roof front to the D rafters. Repeat with the E1 roof back on the remaining D rafters.

20. Place the D/E roof front assembly in position on top of the A2 cross beams on the arbor assembly *(see* FIGS. II, 4A *and* 4B*)*. Using 20d nails, glue and nail the D rafters to the A2 cross beams. Using 1¾-inch wood screws, fasten the E roof front to the A posts, being careful not to hit the nails attaching the rafters to the cross beams. Repeat with the D/E1 roof back assembly.

21. Cut the H trim pieces to size. Using 4d nails, glue and nail the H trim pieces to the ends of the D rafters, bottom edges flush, between the E roof front and E1 roof back *(see* FIGS. II, 4A *and* 4B*)*.

22. Cut the F roof pieces to size. Miter one end of each F roof piece 30° for the center of the roof; the opposite end of each piece is square cut.

23. Using 6d nails, glue and nail the F roof pieces to the D rafters flush with the back edges of the E1 roof back, and overlapping the E roof front *(see* FIG. II, 4C*)*.

24. Miter-cut the G solid crown molding pieces to size *(see* FIGS. II, 4A *and* 4B*)*. Using 4d nails, glue and nail the G molding pieces to the E roof front butted against the underside of the F roof pieces.

25. Cut the J and J1 trim pieces to size. Miter one end of each J trim piece 30° for the center of the roof; all other ends are 45°. Using 1¼-inch brads, glue and nail the J and J1 trim pieces to the front, back and side edges of the F roof pieces *(see* FIG. II, 4A*)*.

26. Set the nails. Fill the nail holes, and the screw holes on the window, with wood putty. When the putty is dry, sand it. Sand the rough edges of the arbor smooth. Wipe off all the sawdust with the tack cloth. Paint the arbor with the waterproof sealer or wood preservative, allowing the sealer to set for the time indicated on the package directions. Paint the arbor.

27. Staple the weather stripping around the underside edges of the seat lid. Drill a few ¾-inch-diameter holes in the seat bottom for drainage.

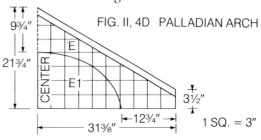

FIG. II, 4D   PALLADIAN ARCH

F·O·U·R·T·H O·F J·U·L·Y
PICNIC GEAR

The best day of the year for a picnic! Whether you go to a park or the beach, or just stay in your backyard, this day should be spent outside. To make your picnic perfect, stitch up a set of colorful al fresco dining gear.

COUNTRY WAYS

• Independence Day •

Our Fourth of July celebrations commemorate the signing of the Declaration of Independence, which demanded the American colonies' freedom from British rule. The publication of this controversial document set in motion the American Revolutionary War, which brought the United States of America into being. This, in turn, brought about the writing of the United States Constitution. Each year, we recall the struggle for freedom and our victory with picnics, parties and, of course, fireworks.

Among the signers of the Declaration of Independence were Thomas Jefferson, its author, who became our third President, and John Adams, who became our second President. The two men, one from Virginia and the other from Massachusetts, developed a love-hate relationship that endured to the end of their lives. They shared a passion for, and commitment to, achieving independence, but battled fervently over how to do it.

Jefferson and Adams are forever linked by an unusual bit of American lore. Although Adams was 8 years older than Jefferson, both men died on the same Fourth of July, exactly 50 years after signing the Declaration. Adams' last words were, "Thomas Jefferson still survives." He would never know that Jefferson had died at 50 minutes past noon, 5 hours earlier than he.

CHUCK WAGON PLACE MATS
(12 x 18 inches)

What makes it country? Denim, plus a red, white and blue color scheme.

Easy: Achievable by anyone.

Materials for Six Place Mats:
1½ yards of 45-inch-wide denim; blue and red threads; 6 red bandannas.

Directions:
1. From the denim, cut six 13 x 19-inch place mats, and six 6 x 7-inch pockets. On each pocket, trim one 6-inch end into a point that extends 2½ inches up each side edge.
2. Turn under each mat's long edges and short ends ½ inch, and stitch with blue thread. Edgestitch each mat with red thread, and stitch again with red ¼ inch inside the first red row.
3. Turn under a 2-inch hem on the straight top end of each pocket. At the other edges, turn under ⅜ inch. Edgestitch the hems with red thread, and add a red stitched square detail at the top of each pocket *(see photo)*. Pin a pocket to the lower left corner of each mat, and edgestitch the pocket's side and lower edges to the mat with blue thread.
4. Fold the bandannas, and place one in each pocket for a napkin.

There is an element of truth in every idea that lasts long enough to be called corny.
— Irving Berlin

COUNTRY WAYS

• Picnics •

The word picnic probably comes from the French word *pique-nique,* which may be derived from *piquer,* to pick. When the word first came into use in the 18th century, a picnic was a meal for which every guest contributed a dish. At some point, it became popular to hold these meals outdoors. By the 19th century, "picnic" referred to any outdoor meal.

Jane Austen often sent her characters on picnics. In her novel *Emma,* a Mrs. Elton describes her plan for the perfect picnic:

"I shall wear a large bonnet, and bring one of my little baskets hanging on my arm. There is to be no form or parade—a sort of gipsy party. We are to walk about your garden…and sit under trees…it is all to be out of doors—a table spread in the shade. Everything as natural and simple as possible."

Some readers might be more familiar with the famous picnic described by Mark Twain:

"All the different ways of getting hot and tired were gone through with, and by and by the rovers straggled back to camp fortified with responsible appetites. After the feast, there was a refreshing season of rest and chat in the shade of spreading oaks. By and by somebody shouted: "Who's ready for the cave?"

Little did Tom Sawyer and Becky Thatcher know what adventures awaited them in Injun Joe's cave…

GINGHAM BUFFET ROLLS
(12 x 21 inches)

Easy: Achievable by anyone.

Materials for Six Rolls and Napkins:
45-inch-wide red gingham: 3 yards each of 1-inch check and ⅛-inch check; matching and contrasting threads; 45-inch square of synthetic batting.

Directions:
1. *Cutting:* From the large check gingham, cut one 45-inch square, and six 18-inch square napkins. From the small check gingham, cut one 45-inch square. Then cut the following small check bias binding, pieced as needed: 13 yards of 1¼-inch-wide binding, and 17 yards of 1½-inch-wide binding.

2. *Quilting:* Place the small check square right side down on a flat surface. Place the batting and the 45-inch large check square, right side up, on top. With raw edges even, baste the three layers together. Machine-quilt diagonally across the basted square through all three layers *(see photo).* From the quilted square, cut six 12 x 21-inch place mats, and six 6 x 7-inch pockets.

3. *Ties:* Cut six 24-inch lengths of 1½-inch bias binding. For each bias strip, turn and press each long edge ⅜ inch to the wrong side, fold the strip in half lengthwise, and edgestitch along the long edges to make a tie. Stitch the center of a tie to the right edge of each place mat. Knot the ends of the ties. Use the remaining 1½-inch bias binding to bind the edges of each place mat, turning under the binding's raw end.

4. *Pockets:* Holding each pocket small check side up, turn under a 6-inch edge 1 inch, and stitch. Turn under the remaining edges ½ inch, and edgestitch the pocket to a place mat on the small check side *(see photo).*

5. *Napkins:* Bind the napkin edges with the 1¼-inch bias binding, mitering the corners and turning under the binding's raw ends. Fold each napkin and insert it, along with cutlery, into a place mat pocket. Roll up the place mat, and tie it.

We hold these truths to be self-evident; that all men are created equal; that they are endowed by their creator with certain unalienable rights; that among these are life, liberty, and the pursuit of happiness.
— Thomas Jefferson
The Declaration of Independence

WATERMELON TRAY & COASTERS
(tray: 17½ x 24 inches; coasters: 4⅜ inches in diameter)

Easy: Achievable by anyone.

Materials:
Two 18 x 24-inch sheets of Bristol board; two 18 x 24-inch sheets of poster board; newspapers; light green, dark green, cadmium red, white, and black acrylic paints; clear satin spray finish; sponge brushes; artist's paintbrushes; white glue; mat knife; stapler; scissors.

Directions:
1. Cutting: From the Bristol board, cut two 17 x 24-inch ovals with the mat knife. From the poster board, cut a 2½ x 68-inch strip, pieced by stapling, for the tray side, and two 4¼-inch-diameter circles for each coaster. From the newspapers, tear 1½-inch-wide strips for the tray, and ¾-inch-wide strips for the coasters.

2. Tray: Cut ½-inch-deep sawteeth all around one long edge of the poster board strip, and bend the teeth inward. Spread glue along the top edge of one oval, and place the strip's sawtooth edge on top so the strip's flat side is flush with the edge of the oval. Glue the

second oval on top of the first. Let the glue dry.

3. Papier Mâché: Mix 1 cup of white glue with 1¾ cups of water in a disposable pan. Dipping the newspaper strips one at a time in the glue mixture, cover the bottom and sides of the tray completely with the strips, smoothing them out with your fingers. Build about five even layers of strips. Let the papier mâché dry overnight.

4. Cover the outside of the tray with papier mâché following Step 3; let the papier mâché dry overnight.

5. Cut two large newspaper ovals to fit the inside and outside bottom of the tray. Soak the ovals with the glue mixture, and apply them to the tray to create smooth inside and outside surfaces. Let the ovals dry.

6. Coasters: Make the coasters following Steps 3 to 5.

7. Painting: Paint the inner side edge of the tray light green *(see photo)*. Mix red paint with white paint to make a melon color, and paint the inside bottom of the tray melon. Paint black seeds. Paint the outer side and bottom of the tray dark green. Paint the coasters in the same way. When the paints are dry, spray every side of the tray and coasters with three coats of clear satin finish, letting the finish dry between coats.

STENCILED PICNIC BASKET & NAPKINS

Easy: Achievable by anyone.

General Materials:

Mylar® (available at craft supply stores) or acetate sheets (available at art supply stores); black fine-point permanent felt-tip pen; craft or utility knife; cardboard, piece of glass with taped edges, or piece of acrylic (available at home centers); paper; paper toweling; newspaper *(optional)*; masking tape; transparent tape; cotton rags *(optional)*; rubbing alcohol *(optional)*.

General Directions:

1. Cutting a Stencil: Enlarge the stencil design onto paper following the directions on page 215. Cut a piece of Mylar or acetate an inch larger than the stencil design all around. Tape the acetate over the design with masking tape. Trace the design onto the acetate with the black felt-tip pen. Using the cardboard, piece of glass with taped edges, or piece of acrylic as a cutting board, cut out the traced stencil sections with the craft or utility knife. Pull the knife toward you, and cut in a continuous motion. If the design needs to be turned, turn the acetate rather than the knife. Once the knife tip pierces the acetate, do not lift the tip again until you have finished cutting the line or curve. If you make a mistake or the acetate tears, repair the spot with a piece of transparent tape.

2. Stenciling: Mask off the stencil cutouts that will not be used for the first color by taping paper under them. Tape the top of the stencil in place with masking tape. Holding a stencil brush like a pencil, dip it into the first color acrylic paint. Using an up-and-down pouncing motion, pounce the brush on folded paper toweling or newspaper until the brush is almost dry. Pounce the brush on the open stencil cutouts, starting at the cut edges. Continue pouncing in circles until the cutouts are filled in with solid color. Let the paint dry. Mask off the first color cutouts. Remove the paper from the second color cutouts, and pounce in the second color. Continue until all the stencil cutouts are colored. Use a different stencil brush for each color used.

3. Cleaning the Stencil and Brushes: Clean the stencil with paper toweling or cotton rags soaked in soapy water or rubbing alcohol. Pat the stencil dry. Store the stencil flat, or between layers of cardboard. Clean the stencil brushes with soap and water until the rinse water runs clear. Let the brushes dry completely before using them again.

PICNIC BASKET

Materials:

General Materials; picnic basket with hinged lid; yellow, green and red acrylic paints; 3 stencil brushes.

Directions:

1. Enlarge and cut a stencil for the design in FIG. II, 5A *(page 82)* following General Directions, Step 1.
2. Stencil the design on the basket lid following General Directions, Step 2. Clean and store the stencil and brushes following General Directions, Step 3.

NAPKINS

Materials:

General Materials; ½ yard of large check blue gingham; matching thread; sewing needle; yellow and green acrylic paints; 2 stencil brushes; iron.

Directions:

1. Cut two 16 x 21-inch rectangles from the gingham. Turn under each edge ¼ inch, and press. Turn under each edge again ⅜ inch, press, and hand-sew the hem in place.
2. Trace and cut a stencil for the full-size design in FIG. II, 5B *(page 83)* following General Directions, Step 1.
3. Place several layers of paper toweling underneath a corner of one napkin. Stencil the design on the napkin corner following General Directions, Step 2. Repeat on the remaining napkin, using fresh paper towel padding underneath. Clean and store the stencil and brushes following General Directions, Step 3.
4. Let the stenciled napkins dry overnight. Cover one napkin with paper toweling, and set the iron one step above the setting for the gingham. Apply heat with a circular motion for 1 minute. Cool the iron to one step below the setting for the gingham, and iron for about 1 minute. Repeat on the remaining napkin.

*Shall I compare thee
to a summer's day?
Thou art more lovely
and more temperate:
Rough winds do shake the darling
buds of May,
And summer's lease
hath all too short a date.*
—William Shakespeare

FIG. II, 5A   PICNIC BASKET STENCIL   1 SQ. = 1″

R = RED
Y = YELLOW
G = GREEN

FIG. II, 5B NAPKIN STENCIL   FULL SIZE

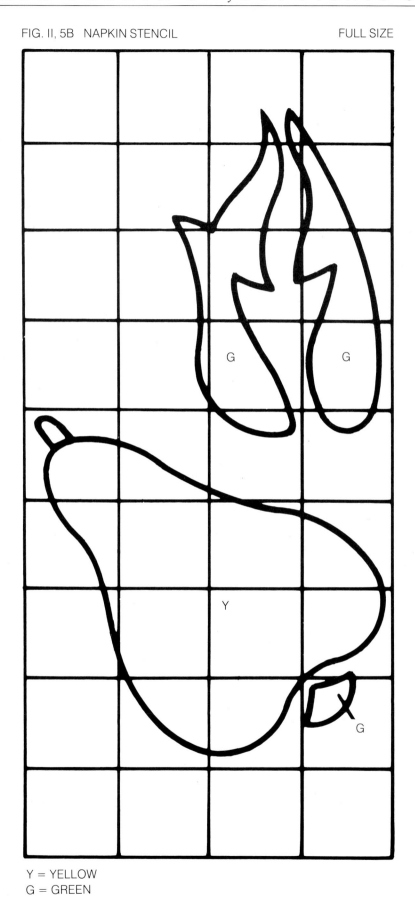

Y = YELLOW
G = GREEN

83

C·O·U·N·T·R·Y
RUGS

Create your own
country floor coverings with traditional rug-making
techniques: punch-hooking, needlepoint or knitting
with fabric scraps.

"WELCOME HOME" HOOKED RUG
(about 21 x 33 inches)

Average: For those with some experience
in rug hooking.

Materials:
1 yard of 45-inch-wide 15-mesh jute canvas or closely
woven rug burlap; rug frame; rug punch needle; Aunt
Lydia's Heavy Rug Yarn (60-yard skeins): 8 skeins of
Hemlock (No. 620), and 1 skein each of Lilac (No. 010),
Red (No. 120), Watermelon (No. 135), Brick (No. 145),
True Blue (No. 317), Tangerine (No. 315), Burnt
Orange (No. 320), Brown (No. 420), Light Yellow
(No. 505), Buttercup (No. 540), Gold (No. 559), Grass
Green (No. 615), Putty (No. 610), Light Avocado
(No. 635), Forest Green (No. 660) and Natural
(No. 905); black fine-point permanent felt-tip pen;
dressmaker's carbon; tracing wheel, or dry ballpoint
pen; 2 quarts of liquid rug latex; 4 x 8 inches of
cardboard; plastic drop cloth; scissors; tracing paper.

Directions:
1. *Pattern:* Enlarge the design in FIG. II, 6 *(page 86)*
onto tracing paper, following the directions on page
215. Using the black felt-tip pen, draw a 21 x 33-inch
rectangle in the center of the canvas or burlap. Using
the dressmaker's carbon and tracing wheel or dry
ballpoint pen, center and trace the design within
the rectangle. Turn the tracing paper design
counterclockwise, match the broken lines and floral
design, and trace to complete the oval design. Go over
the tracings on the canvas with the black felt-tip pen.
The marked side of the canvas will be the wrong side of
the rug; the letters will be backwards.
2. *Rug Frame:* Allowing 2 inches of space between
the edge of the design and the frame, fasten the canvas,
marked side up, to the frame. The canvas must be taut;
if it sags while working, tighten and fasten it again.
3. *Punching:* Roll the yarn skeins into balls. Following
the punch needle manufacturer's directions, and
beginning near the center of the frame, outline the
design shapes with two rows of hooked yarn. Fill in the
shapes by working back and forth in straight rows, or
by following each shape's contour toward its center.
The punch needle's point should slip through the
canvas weave without ripping the fabric. The loops
should be of equal height, and should cover the
backing. Do not make the loops too tight, or the rug
will buckle. To avoid creating ridges, end with ragged,
rather than straight, rows and interlace new stitches
with the old stitches. Avoid targeting small shapes
(working in circles around them) to prevent puckering.
Use the points of the scissors to push yarn ends
through the canvas to the front. When the rug is
finished, clip the yarn ends flush with the loops. When
you have worked the design, outline the rectangle with
two rows of Forest Green, and complete the
background with Hemlock. Work the stitches on the
outside rows very close together so the canvas edges
will be well covered when they are turned under.
4. *Finishing:* Trim the canvas 2½ inches from each
edge of the hooked work. Spread the drop cloth over a
flat surface, and place the rug on top, wrong side up.
Using the cardboard, spread the latex over the rug
back, making sure every yarn loop is saturated. Spread
a thin layer of latex over the empty canvas borders. At
each corner, fold the canvas diagonally to the back so
the canvas point just touches the edge of the hooked
work, and finger press the canvas smooth. Fold the four
canvas borders to the back, miter the corners, and
press the canvas smooth. Spread latex over the raw
canvas edges to keep them from fraying. Place a weight
over each corner, and let the rug dry overnight.

FIG. II, 6 "WELCOME HOME" HOOKED RUG

*A handful of patience
is worth more
than a bushel of brains.*
—Dutch proverb

KNITTED RAG RUG AND PILLOW

Average: For those with some experience in knitting.

RUG
(about 36 x 60 inches)

Materials:
45-inch-wide calico fabric: 3½ yards of yellow, 2½ yards of white and 3¾ yards each of pink, lilac, turquoise and blue; 1 pair size 13 knitting needles, OR ANY SIZE NEEDLES TO OBTAIN GAUGE BELOW; crochet hook; large-eyed tapestry needle; particle mask; liquid rug latex *(optional)*; plastic drop cloth *(optional)*; cardboard *(optional)*.

Gauge: 7 sts = 3 inches; 8 rows = 2 inches.

Directions:
1. Fabrics: Wash the fabrics, and dry them. Wearing the particle mask, tear the fabrics into ¾-inch-wide strips to make 186 yards of yellow, 140 yards of white and 200 yards each of pink, lilac, turquoise and blue. Piece each color into 5-yard lengths, and roll each length into a ball. From the yellow fabric, also tear about 24 yards of ¼-inch-wide strips.

2. Knitting: With ¾-inch yellow strips, cast on 7 stitches. Work in garter stitch (k every row) for 36 inches, tying in new strips on the wrong side. Bind off loosely. Make three more yellow blocks. Make three white blocks the same size as yellow blocks. With turquoise strips, cast on 12 stitches (5 inches). Work in garter stitch for 36 inches, and bind off loosely. Make one more turquoise block. Make two pink, two lilac and two blue blocks the same size as turquoise blocks.

3. Joining: Using the tapestry needle and ¼-inch yellow strips, sew a turquoise block to a yellow block by weaving the strip between the two blocks through every knitted stitch on the long edges; tie the strip's starting end to fasten it. Sew the opposite long edge of the yellow block to a lilac block. Continue joining the blocks as follows: white, blue, yellow, pink, and white (center block). Reverse the order for the other side of the rug, ending with a turquoise block.

4. Fringe: Cut ¾-inch turquoise strips into 10-inch lengths. Fold one length in half crosswise to make a loop. Using the crochet hook, draw the loop between the first two knitted rows at one short end of the rug. Draw the strip's loose ends through the loop, and pull tightly to knot the fringe. Continue tying fringes across the short end of the rug. Repeat on the opposite end.

5. Finishing (optional): Place rug, wrong side up, on top of a plastic drop cloth. Use a piece of cardboard to spread liquid rug latex over back of rug, making sure every stitch is saturated. Let rug dry overnight.

PILLOW
(14 inches square)

Materials:
¾-inch-wide calico fabric strips *(see Rug, Step 1)*: about 150 yards in colors desired; ½ yard of calico fabric for pillow back; matching thread; 14-inch square pillow form; 1 pair size 13 knitting needles, OR ANY SIZE NEEDLES TO OBTAIN GAUGE BELOW; sewing needle; particle mask.

Gauge: 7 sts = 3 inches; 8 rows = 2 inches.

Directions:
1. Pillow Front: With fabric strips, cast on 31 stitches. Work in garter stitch (k every row) for 14 inches, tying in colors on the wrong side in the order desired. Bind off loosely.

2. Assembling: Cut a 15-inch square pillow back. Center and pin the knitted pillow top to the fabric pillow back right sides together. Hand-sew the pillow top to the pillow back around three sides and four corners. Turn the pillow right side out, and stuff it. Turn in the open edge, and slipstitch the opening closed *(see Stitch Guide, page 214)*.

3. Tassels: Cut four 10-inch lengths from the fabric strips. Knot the lengths together at the centers, and sew a tassel at the knot to each corner of the pillow.

NEEDLEPOINT RAG RUGS

What makes it country? Muted colors and primitive farmyard motifs that make the rugs look like antiques.

Easy: Achievable by anyone.

General Materials:
24 x 28 inches of 3.3 mesh rug canvas; contrasting color thread; masking tape; particle mask; tapestry needle; thumbtacks, or push pins; blocking board, or clean muslin; clean cloth; liquid rug latex *(optional)*; plastic drop cloth *(optional)*; cardboard *(optional)*.

General Directions:

1. *Canvas:* Tape the edges of the canvas with masking tape. Baste across the center vertical and horizontal mesh rows; the basted rows will match the arrow-marked center rows in Figs. II, 7A to 7F *(pages 90-95)*.

2. *Fabrics:* Wash the fabrics, and dry them. Wearing the particle mask, tear each fabric into 1-inch-wide strips and roll the strips into a ball; roll a separate ball for each fabric.

3. *Needlepoint:* Using one fabric strip in the needle, work the design of your choice in Figs. II, 7A to 7F in continental stitch, starting at the center of the design *(see Stitch Guide, page 214)*. Each square in Figs. II, 7A to 7F represents one continental stitch in the color indicated. Stitch somewhat loosely so the fabric fills the mesh. Turn the canvas upside down at the end of each row to start the next row.

4. *Edges:* When you have worked to within 4 or 5 squares from each edge of the design, fold the canvas to the back at the last row of the design. Trim the canvas hem to 1 inch, and finish working the needlepoint through both layers, mitering and trimming off the excess canvas at each corner. Overcast the folded canvas edges with the same fabric used on the outside row of stitches.

5. *Blocking:* Using the thumbtacks or push pins, pin the finished rug face down to the blocking board, or to an old table covered with the muslin, with the rug's edges straight and the corners squared. Dampen the clean cloth, and place it over the rug. Iron the rug until the backs of the stitches are moist, pulling the canvas into a true rectangle. Let the rug dry completely before unpinning it.

6. *Finishing (optional):* Place the rug, wrong side up, on top of a plastic drop cloth. Use a piece of cardboard to spread liquid rug latex over the back of the rug, making sure every stitch is saturated. Let the rug dry overnight.

COUNTRY WAYS

• Bed Rugs •

In early America, most folks kept their floors bare. The American textile industry was very new, and its products were too costly to be walked on. Even painted floor cloths and woven mats were too expensive for most families to afford.

Yet we have examples of rugs that were made as long ago as the early 1700's. These rugs primarily were used as bed covers, and probably were part of a colonial woman's dowry. Most of the oldest examples of rug-making were signed and dated by their makers.

Handmade rugs also were draped over furniture, and sometimes hung on walls. It wasn't until about 1830 that rugs were used widely as floor coverings.

COUNTRY WAYS

• Rugs for the Hearth •

When wealthy people began covering their floors with large Oriental carpets, they didn't want their expensive hand-loomed pieces damaged by sparks flying out of the fireplace. To protect the carpets, their owners placed a small "hearth" rug in front of each fireplace.

The hearth rug also brightened up the hearthstone during the months when the fireplace was not in use. Often the hearth rug was accompanied by a painted or embroidered fireplace screen that made the unused fireplace more pleasing to the eye.

We know that Thomas Jefferson had hearth rugs in the White House in 1809 — they are mentioned in his household inventory. In his 1828 dictionary, Noah Webster defined a rug as "a woven cloth used for a bedcover and, in modern times particularly for covering the carpet before the fireplace."

Many hearth rugs featured colorful floral designs. Patriotic motifs were very popular after the War of 1812. Collectors also have found many examples of nautical motifs, and some evidence that sailors may have designed and sewn rugs during their long voyages.

Here Skugg lies snug
As a bug in a rug.
—Benjamin Franklin

RUNNING HORSE
(photo, page 89; about 19 x 24 inches)

Materials:
General Materials; 45-inch-wide cotton or cotton-blend broadcloth weight calico fabrics: 1⅞ yards of cranberry, 1⅛ yards of ecru, ⅔ yard of blue, ⅓ yard of black, and ¼ yard of gray.

Directions:
Tear 85 yards of cranberry strips, 50 yards of ecru strips, 30 yards of blue strips, 15 yards of black strips, and 12 yards of gray strips. Following the General Directions *(page 88)*, work the design in FIG. II, 7A.

FIG. II, 7A RUNNING HORSE

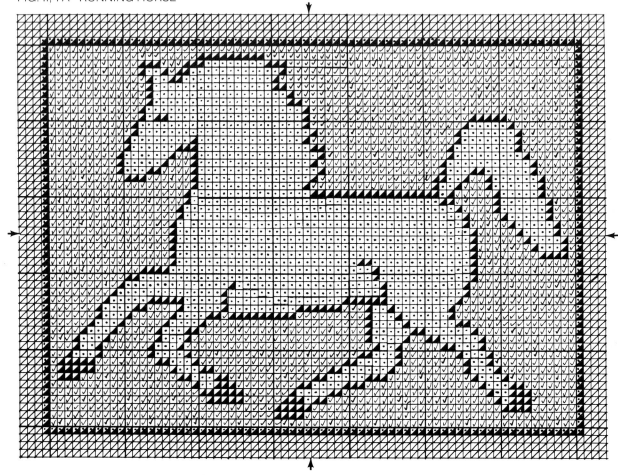

- ◨ BLACK
- ◸ BLUE
- ☑ CRANBERRY
- ⊡ ECRU
- ◪ GRAY

FOLK ART BASKETS
(photo, page 89; about 17¼ x 23¼ inches)

Materials:

General Materials; 45-inch-wide cotton or cotton-blend broadcloth weight calico fabrics: 2 yards of ecru, 1 yard of medium blue, ⅔ yard of light blue, ⅓ yard each of pink and light green, and ⅙ yard of rose.

Directions:

Tear 90 yards of ecru strips, 45 yards of medium blue strips, 30 yards of light blue strips, 15 yards each of pink and light green strips, and 8 yards of rose strips. Following the General Directions *(page 88)*, work the design in FIG. II, 7B.

FIG. II, 7B FOLK ART BASKETS

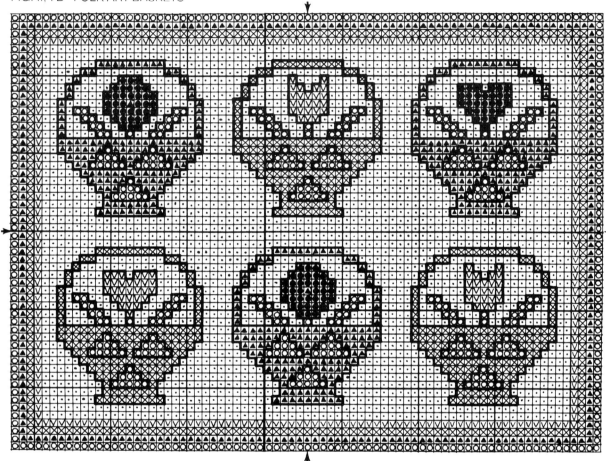

- ▲ MEDIUM BLUE
- ● ROSE
- ◎ LIGHT GREEN
- ⊠ LIGHT BLUE
- ⋁ PINK
- ⊡ ECRU

PEACEABLE LAMB
(photo, page 89; about 17½ x 24 inches)

Materials:

General Materials; 45-inch-wide cotton or cotton-blend broadcloth weight calico fabrics: 1 yard of turquoise, ⅞ yard of white, ⅝ yard of light green, ½ yard of light blue, ⅓ yard of peach, ¼ yard of black, and ⅛ yard of dark rose; 45-inch-wide cotton or cotton-blend broadcloth weight solid color fabric: ⅜ yard of ecru.

Directions:

Tear 45 yards of turquoise strips, 40 yards of white strips, 29 yards of light green strips, 23 yards of light blue strips, 19 yards of ecru strips, 15 yards of peach strips, 12 yards of black strips, and 6 yards of dark rose strips. Following the General Directions *(page 88)*, work the design in FIG. II, 7C.

FIG. II, 7C PEACEABLE LAMB

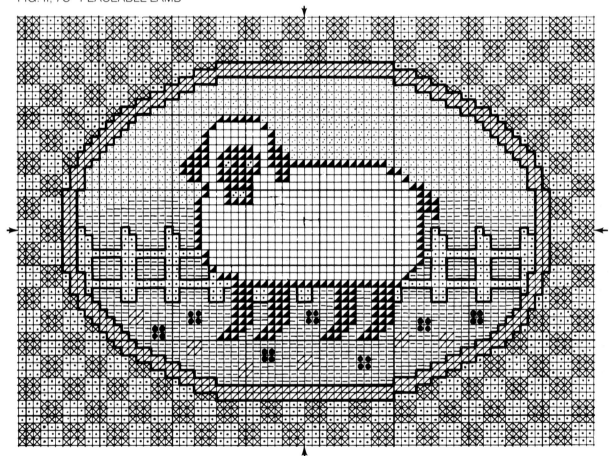

⊠ TURQUOISE
◩ PEACH
◤ BLACK
⊡ WHITE
⊡ LIGHT BLUE
⊟ LIGHT GREEN
⬤ DARK ROSE
☐ ECRU

MR. MALLARD

(photo, page 89; about 17½ x 23 inches)

Materials:

General Materials; 45-inch-wide cotton or cotton-blend broadcloth weight calico fabrics: 1¼ yards of black, 1 yard each of ecru and dark green, ½ yard each of rust, light brown and dark brown, and ¼ yard each of tan and gold.

Directions:

Tear 56 yards of black strips, 45 yards each of ecru and dark green strips, 23 yards each of rust, light brown and dark brown strips, and 12 yards each of tan and gold strips. Following the General Directions *(page 88),* work the design in FIG. II, 7D.

FIG. II, 7D   MR. MALLARD

◤ BLACK
◿ RUST
▱ TAN
▼ DARK GREEN
☐ ECRU
☒ DARK BROWN
▪ LIGHT BROWN
◎ GOLD

LOG CABIN SQUARES
(photo, page 89; about 18 x 23½ inches)

Materials:

General Materials; 45-inch-wide cotton or cotton-blend broadcloth weight solid color fabrics: ½ yard of black, ⅜ yard of dark green, ⅓ yard each of medium blue, dark blue, light green, medium green and dark purple, ¼ yard each of light blue and medium purple, and ⅙ yard of light purple.

Directions:

Tear 23 yards of black, 19 yards of dark green, 15 yards each of medium blue, dark blue, light green, medium green and dark purple, 12 yards each of light blue and medium purple, and 8 yards of light purple. Following the General Directions *(page 88)*, work the design in FIG. II, 7E.

FIG. II, 7E   LOG CABIN SQUARES

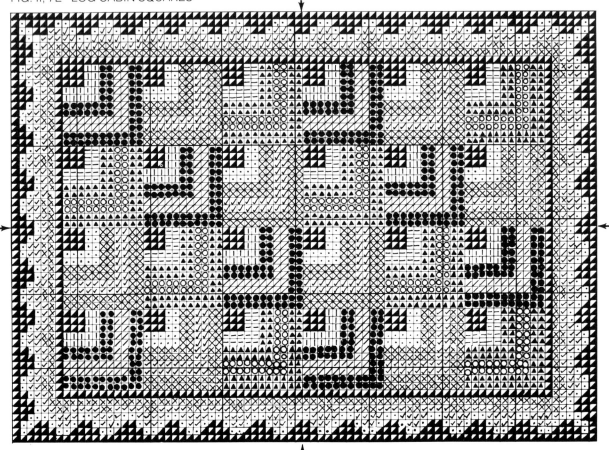

- ◨ BLACK
- ⊡ LIGHT BLUE
- ☑ MEDIUM BLUE
- ⊠ DARK BLUE
- ⊟ LIGHT GREEN
- ◎ MEDIUM GREEN
- ▲ DARK GREEN
- 🅸 LIGHT PURPLE
- ◪ MEDIUM PURPLE
- ● DARK PURPLE

CAT NAPPING
(photo, page 89; about 17½ x 23½ inches)

Materials:
General Materials; 45-inch-wide cotton or cotton-blend broadcloth weight calico fabrics: 2 yards of black, ⅔ yard of aqua, ½ yard each of white, ecru, and light blue, and ⅜ yard of pink.

Directions:
1. *Fabrics:* Tear 30 yards of aqua strips, 23 yards each of white and light blue strips, and 19 yards of pink strips. If you wish to work the cat in continental stitch, also tear the black and ecru fabrics into 1-inch-wide strips (90 yards of black, and 23 yards of ecru). If you

wish to work the cat in turkey stitch *(see photo)*, tear the black and ecru fabrics into ½-inch-wide strips.

2. *Stitches:* Following the General Directions *(page 88)*, work the entire design in Fig. II, 7F in continental stitch, if you wish. Or work the design in the following stitches *(see photo)*: Work the cat fur in turkey stitch, leaving about a ½-inch-long loop between stitches *(see Stitch Guide, page 214)*. When you have finished working the rug, cut the loops to make the fringed fur. Work the outside and interrupted inside borders in continental stitch. Work the rest of the design in long straight stitch to fill in colors for each shape *(see Stitch Guide)*. Break up the white background into horizontal rows of straight stitches about 5 mesh threads long.

FIG. II, 7F CAT NAPPING

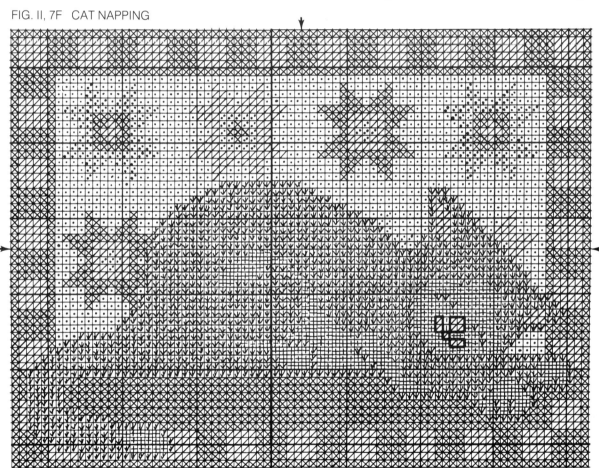

- ☒ AQUA
- ◨ PINK
- ⊡ LIGHT BLUE
- ⊙ WHITE
- ☑ BLACK
- ⊞ ECRU

D · O · L · L · S
AND TEDDIES

A handmade toy or doll always is special. Make one of these sweet playthings for your own "country child," or sit one on a mantel or shelf to add country charm to your home.

BIG AND LITTLE SISTER DOLLS

(big sister doll: about 19 inches tall; little sister doll: about 15 inches tall)

What makes it country? A classic soft doll complete with rosy cheeks, yarn hair, and a ruffled pinafore dress.

Challenging: Requires more experience in sewing and doll making.

Note: *Materials are given for the Big Sister doll. Changes for the Little Sister doll are in parentheses; when parentheses are not shown, the Little Sister doll uses the same amount.*

Materials:

¼ yard of 45-inch-wide muslin; ⅓ yard (¼ yard) of white cotton fabric; ½ yard (⅓ yard) of print fabric for dress; 6 x 9 inches (5 x 7 inches) of print fabric for apron; 2 yards (1⅓ yards) of ⅜-inch-wide matching color grosgrain ribbon; 9 x 12 inches of black felt; worsted weight yarn: 200 yards of Light Brown (100 yards of Yellow); matching sewing threads; 2 yards (1¾ yards) of 1-inch-wide ruffled eyelet lace; ⅔ yard (½ yard) of ⅛-inch-wide elastic; embroidery floss: small amounts of Pink, Red, Tan, Brown and Black; embroidery hoop; embroidery needle; sewing needle; synthetic stuffing; Velcro fastener; 5½ x 12 inches of cardboard; paper for patterns.

Directions (¼-inch seams allowed):

1. Patterns: Enlarge the Big Sister doll and clothing pattern in FIG. II, 8 *(page 99)* onto paper following the directions on page 215, and using a ratio of 1 square = 1 inch. Enlarge the Little Sister doll and clothing pattern onto a separate sheet of paper using a ratio of 1 square = ¾ inch. Label each set, and cut out the pattern pieces.

2. Cutting: For each doll, cut two Heads, two Bodies, two Arms, two Leg/Foot pieces, and two Foot Bottoms from the muslin. Transfer the face to one Head piece, and place the Head piece in the embroidery hoop. Using three strands of floss in the embroidery needle, and the photo as a color guide, vertically satin stitch the center of the pupils and cheeks. Backstitch all the other facial lines and outlines *(see Stitch Guide, page 214)*.

3. Arms: Fold each Arm in half, right side in. Leaving the top (shoulder) edge open, sew the Arm seam; leave a small opening in the seam for stuffing. Clip the inside corner at the thumb. Turn the Arms right side out.

4. Legs: Fold each Leg/Foot piece in half, right side in, and stitch the seam; leave open the top of the Leg, bottom edge of the Foot, and 2 inches in the seam. Clip the curves. Pin a Foot Bottom to the bottom of each Leg/Foot, and stitch. Turn the Legs right side out.

5. Assembling: Sew a Head piece to each Body piece at the neck edges. Pin the Arms and Legs to the front Body piece, tucking the upper edges of the Arms and Legs to fit between the marks on the pattern; make sure the thumbs and toes face front. Baste the Arms and Legs in place. Sew the front and back Body/Head pieces right sides together, with the limbs tucked inside, leaving an opening in one Body side seam for turning. Turn the doll right side out. Stuff all parts, turn in the open edges, and slipstitch the openings closed *(see Stitch Guide)*.

6. Big Sister's Hair: Wrap the Light Brown yarn 75 times around the cardboard's 5½-inch width. Clip the yarn at one edge, open the strands flat, and spread them out evenly to measure 4½ inches wide. Stitch across the strands 2½ inches from one cut edge. Hand-sew the yarn hair at its stitch line to the Head seamline, with 2½-inch-long bangs at the front. Trim the bangs evenly. Smooth the longer yarn hair over the back of the Head. Wrap Light Brown yarn around the cardboard's 5½-inch width 100 times. Clip the yarn at one edge, open the strands flat, spread them 4 inches wide, and stitch across them at the center. Hand-sew the yarn hair at its "part" line from the front of the Head to the back above the neck. Smooth the hair around the Head. At cheek level, backstitch the hair by hand to the back of the Head. Backstitch again ½ inch below the first stitch line. Trim the hair below the stitching at the back neck hairline.

7. *Big Sister's Curls:* Wrap Light Brown yarn 12 times around the cardboard's 12-inch length, and knot the yarn ends together. Using one finger from each hand, place a finger inside along each edge of the cardboard, and pull the yarn off the cardboard; twist the yarn tightly between the same two fingers. Fold the twisted yarn at the center, and bring the two fingers together. Tie a separate length of yarn through the yarn openings at your fingers, and knot the ends of the yarn length together; the twisted yarn will form a curl. Make seven curls. Sew the curls to the Head over the backstitched hairline. At each side of the Head, loop a 12-inch length of grosgrain ribbon through the hair above the side, and tie the ribbon into a bow *(see photo, page 96).*

8. *Little Sister's Hair:* Wrap the Yellow yarn around the cardboard's 5½-inch width 75 times. Clip the yard at one edge, open the strands flat, and spread them out evenly to measure 3 inches wide. Stitch across the strands 1½ inches from one cut edge. Hand-sew the yarn hair at its stitch line to the Head seamline, with 1½-inch-long bangs at the front. Trim the bangs evenly. Smooth the longer yarn hair over the back of the Head. Wrap Yellow yarn around the cardboard's 12-inch length 75 times. Clip the yarn at one edge, open the strands flat, and spread them 4 inches wide. Stitch across the strands at the center to create a "part" in the hair. Pin the "part" to the Head behind the bangs. Braid the hair at the sides, and tie each braid with a grosgrain ribbon bow. At the doll's eye level, tack the braids to the Head *(see photo).*

9. *Pantaloons:* Cut two Pantaloons pieces from the white fabric, and sew them together at the center front seam. Press under the waist edge ⅜ inch. Cut a 9-inch (7½-inch) length of elastic, and sew it to the wrong side of the waist edge, stretching the elastic to fit. Lap ruffled eyelet over the raw bottom edge of each Pantaloon leg, and stitch. Cut two 6-inch (4-inch) lengths of elastic. Sew a length to each Pantaloon leg 1 inch (¾ inch) above the eyelet, stretching the elastic to fit. Sew the center back seam. Sew the inner leg seams.

10. *Bodice:* From the dress fabric, cut two 11½ x 4¾-inch (8½ x 3¼-inch) sleeves, two 20 x 9-inch (10 x 6½-inch) skirt pieces, two Bodice backs, and one Bodice front. Sew the Bodice front to the Bodice backs at the shoulders. Turn the neck edge ⅛ inch to the inside, lap it over ruffled eyelet, and topstitch. Turn up the eyelet, and turn down the neck seam. Stitch along the neck edge. Do not stitch the side seams yet.

11. *Sleeves:* Sew the underarm seam of each sleeve. Turn the sleeves right sides out. Overcast one long edge of each sleeve. Gather this edge to fit a 7½-inch (5-inch) length of ruffled eyelet. Lap the eyelet ⅜ inch over the gathered sleeve edge, and stitch. Gather the opposite edge of each sleeve to fit a Bodice sleeve opening, opened flat, and stitch. Turn under the open center edges of the Bodice backs ¼ inch, and topstitch.

12. *Skirt:* Gather one long edge of each skirt piece to fit a Bodice bottom edge. Pin one skirt piece to the Bodice front. At the back, overlap the Bodice center edges ⅜ inch, and pin the remaining skirt piece to the bottom edge of the Bodice back. Stitch both waistlines. Sew the side seams up to the armholes. Press under the skirt's bottom edge ¼ inch.

13. *Skirt Ruffle:* Cut 2-inch-wide strips from the full width of the dress fabric, and piece them together to make a 76-inch-long (56-inch-long) strip. Sew the short ends of the strip together to make a loop. Fold the loop in half, wrong side in and raw edges even, and press. Gather the raw edge of the loop. Lap the skirt's bottom edge over the ruffle's raw edge, and stitch. Sew the Velcro fastener to the back neck edges of the dress.

14. *Big Sister's Apron:* Cut a 9 x 4¾-inch apron, and topstitch ruffled eyelet over the side and bottom edges. Gather the waist edge to 6 inches. Cut a 32-inch length of grosgrain ribbon. Pin the ribbon over the waist edge, matching centers, and topstitch, leaving the excess ribbon extending beyond the sides for ties.

15. *Little Sister's Pinafore:* Cut a 6½ x 3½-inch apron, and topstitch ruffled eyelet over the side and bottom edges. Gather the waist edge to 5 inches. Cut a 2 x 1¾-inch bib from the apron fabric. Turn under the upper edge ¼ inch, and topstitch. Cut two 5-inch lengths of ruffled eyelet, and topstitch one length to each side of the bib, with the excess eyelet extending at the top. Pin the wrong side of the apron waist edge over the right side of the bib bottom edge. Cut a 24-inch length of grosgrain ribbon. Center the ribbon over the pinafore waist and topstitch, leaving the excess ribbon for ties. Sew the end of each extending bib eyelet strip to the back of the ribbon tie on the same side of the pinafore 1 inch from the apron edge.

16. *Shoes:* Using the Shoe Top portion of the Leg/Foot pattern, and placing the heel on the fold, cut two Shoe Tops from the black felt. Also cut two Shoe Soles. Fold each Shoe Top in half, right side in, and stitch the seam. Stitch a Shoe Sole to the bottom edge of each Shoe Top, and turn the Shoe right side out.

FIG. II, 8 BIG AND LITTLE SISTER DOLLS

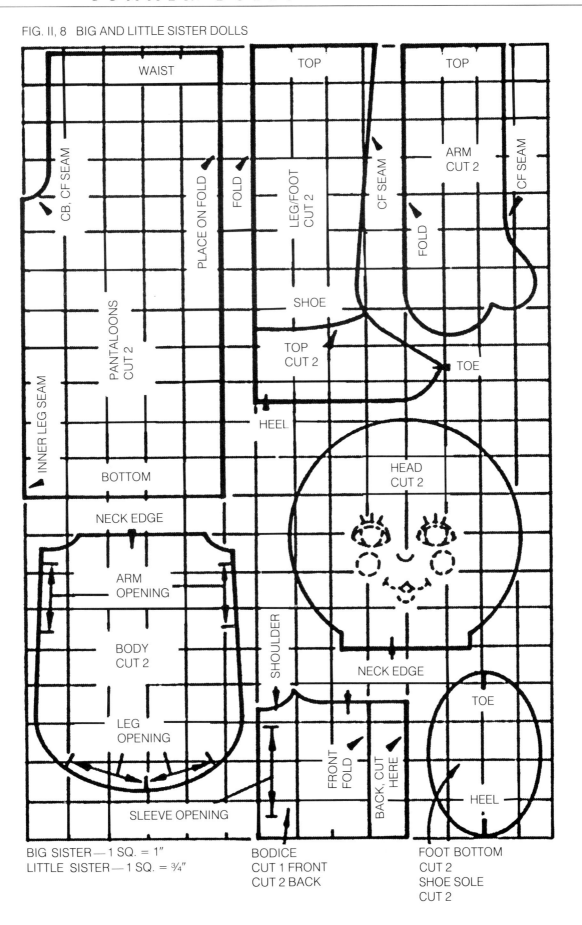

WAIST

TOP

TOP

CB, CF SEAM

PLACE ON FOLD

FOLD

LEG/FOOT
CUT 2

CF SEAM

ARM
CUT 2

CF SEAM

FOLD

PANTALOONS
CUT 2

SHOE

TOP
CUT 2

TOE

INNER LEG SEAM

HEEL

BOTTOM

HEAD
CUT 2

NECK EDGE

ARM
OPENING

SHOULDER

BODY
CUT 2

NECK EDGE

TOE

LEG
OPENING

FRONT
FOLD

BACK, CUT
HERE

HEEL

SLEEVE OPENING

BIG SISTER — 1 SQ. = 1"
LITTLE SISTER — 1 SQ. = ¾"

BODICE
CUT 1 FRONT
CUT 2 BACK

FOOT BOTTOM
CUT 2
SHOE SOLE
CUT 2

AN OLD-FASHIONED GIRL

Average: For those with some experience in sewing and doll making.

Materials:

45-inch-wide fabric: 1 yard of pink or peach percale, 1 yard of white polyester/cotton, and 1¼ yards of small plaid polyester/cotton; 8 yards of coordinating color double-fold bias tape; ⅓ yard of 1½-inch-wide coordinating color grosgrain ribbon; 1½ yards of ⅜-inch-wide coordinating color satin ribbon; scraps of black or dark brown imitation suede fabric; 1 pair of Misses size 6-8½ white nylon knee socks; matching sewing threads; 3 yards of 1-inch-wide white coarse lace; 1½ yards of ¾-inch-wide white fine lace; 1 yard of 1½-inch-wide white fine lace; 6-strand needlepoint yarn (40-yard skeins): 2 skeins of Brown; embroidery floss: small amounts of Rose, Blue, Dark Brown and White; embroidery needle; sewing needle; synthetic stuffing; Velverette® glue tube (available at craft supply stores); snap fasteners; 5¼ x 3 inches of stiff cardboard; miniature silk flowers *(optional)*; dressmaker's pencil; straight pins; rubber bands; paper for pattern.

COUNTRY WAYS

• Dolls: Plain and Fancy •

In Colonial America, children played with very simple dolls made from rags, wood or cornhusks. Seeing these dolls today, one might think their crude faces would be rather frightening to a child. Yet they were loved and coddled as much as any modern baby doll. Some old-fashioned dolls didn't even have faces because certain sects believed it was sinful to recreate the human image; only God could do that.

It was a very fortunate child who owned a fancy-dressed doll imported from Europe. These dolls may have descended from dressmakers' "babies" — dolls dressed in copies of the latest fashions that were sent by clothiers to their customers as early versions of showroom models.

Directions (¼-inch seams allowed):

1. Pattern: Enlarge the pattern in FIG. II, 9 *(page 103)* onto paper, following the directions on page 215.

2. Cutting: From the pink or peach percale, cut one Body Front, two Body Backs, four Arm pieces, four Leg pieces, and two Foot Soles. Using the dressmaker's pencil, transfer the Face to the head of the Body front.

3. Legs: Sew the Leg pieces in pairs, right sides together, leaving the tops and bottoms open. Sew a Foot Sole to the bottom edge of each Leg, and turn the Leg right side out. Stuff the Legs firmly, keeping the seams at the center front and center back. Stitch across the top of each Leg ½ inch below the edge.

4. Arms: Sew the Arm pieces in pairs right sides together, leaving the tops open. Turn the Arms right side out. Stuff each hand lightly, and stitch to indicate fingers. Stuff each Arm firmly up to the stuffing line, and stitch across the Arm on that line; leave the remainder of the Arm unstuffed. Turn in the top seam allowances, and stitch the Arms closed.

5. Assembling: Sew all the darts in the Body Front and Body Backs. Sew the Body Backs right sides together along the center seam, leaving the opening as marked. Sew the Body Back to the Body Front, leaving the bottom edge open. Turn up the seam at the Body bottom edge, and stitch. Insert the tops of the Legs into the bottom of the Body. Sew the bottom of the Body closed to fasten the Legs to the Body. Stuff the Body firmly through the back opening, turn in the open edges, and slipstitch the opening closed *(see Stitch Guide, page 214)*. Slipstitch the Arms to the sides of the Body at the shoulder, using the front shoulder dart and the mark at the back as placement guides. Using the embroidery needle and floss, and the photo as a color guide, embroider the Face in satin stitch and outline stitch *(see Stitch Guide)*.

6. Hair: Wrap the yarn 40 times around the cardboard's 5¼-inch width. Tie the wrapped yarn at the top and bottom edges with separate lengths of yarn. Remove the wrapped yarn from the cardboard to give a double tassel. Sew one tie point to the center of the head where the head front meets the head back. Arrange the yarn to cover the sides of the head, and sew the opposite tie point where it lies. Cut the cardboard's 5¼-inch width to 4½ inches, and wrap yarn 20 times around it. Tie and remove the wrapped yarn as for the first double tassel. Twist the double tassel on itself to make a chignon, and tie the tie points together to fasten the chignon. Glue the chignon to the back of the head, using pins and rubber bands to hold the chignon in place until the glue dries.

7. *Stockings:* Turn the socks inside out, and cut off the foot portions. Slip a sock tube onto one Leg. Pin the tube along the back Leg seam to fit the Leg and foot snugly. Remove the sock tube and cut off the excess sock, leaving a seam allowance. Sew the sock seam, and overcast the raw edge. Turn the sock right side out, and slip the sock onto the Leg. Repeat.

8. *Underpants:* Cut two Underpants pieces from the white fabric, and sew them right sides together along the center front and center back seams. Hem the back opening, and the bottom edges of the legs. Sew coarse lace to the right side of each Underpants leg hem. Sew the Underpants inner leg seams. Turn the Underpants right side out, and place them on the doll. Pleat the waist edge to fit the doll, and pin the pleats. Remove the Underpants from the doll, sew the pleats, and roll a hem at the pleated waist edge. Sew a snap fastener to the back opening.

9. *Petticoat:* From the white fabric, cut a 10¾ x 45-inch petticoat skirt, a 2¾ x 24-inch petticoat waistband, two Petticoat Bodice backs, and one Petticoat Bodice front. Turn up 1 inch along one long edge of the petticoat skirt, and hem it. Sew coarse lace to the hemmed edge on the right side of the fabric, allowing the edge of the lace to extend slightly beyond the edge of the fabric. Sew a second coarse lace border above the first. Gather the opposite long edge of the skirt to fit one long edge of the waistband, and sew the skirt and waistband together. Roll a hem on each short end of the waistband. Sew the Petticoat Bodice front to the Petticoat Bodice backs at the shoulders. Roll a hem on the arm openings, and sew the underarm seams. Turn in and hem the back opening. Gather the top edge of the petticoat waistband to fit the bottom edge of the Petticoat Bodice, and stitch. Sew the short ends of the petticoat skirt together. Sew snap fasteners to the back of the Petticoat Bodice.

10. *Shoes:* From the imitation suede, cut two Shoe Tops and two Shoe Soles. Fold each Shoe Top in half, right side in, and stitch the back seam. Sew a Shoe Sole to the bottom edge of each Shoe Top, stitching from the center back toward the center front and easing A to B on the Shoe Top to fit the Sole. Turn the Shoes right side out.

11. *Dress:* From the plaid fabric, cut two 16¼ x 36-inch dress skirt pieces, two Sleeves, two Dress Bodice backs, and one Dress Bodice front. Cutting crosswise on the plaid fabric, cut two 4 x 9-inch bias strips and two 2½ x 11-inch bias strips. From the white fabric, cut two 3¾ x 2-inch cuffs. Sew the skirt pieces together along a short end to make a 72-inch-long skirt strip. Turn up 1¾ inches along one long edge of the strip, and hem it.

Roll a hem on each short end that measures 5 inches from the top raw long edge. Using a zigzag stitch and contrasting thread, sew two rows of bias tape to the skirt near the hemmed bottom edge. Sew the Dress Bodice front to the Dress Bodice backs at the shoulders. Roll a hem on the Bodice neckline. Sew the Sleeves to the Bodice. Turn the bottom edge of each Sleeve to the right side; do not turn in the edge. Using a zigzag stitch and contrasting thread, sew bias tape over the raw bottom edge of each Sleeve, and a second row of bias tape below the first. Gather one long edge of each 9-inch bias strip, and stitch it invisibly to the inside of a Sleeve under the lower row of bias tape. Stitch the short ends of each 9-inch bias strip together using a narrow seam allowance. Gather the bottom edge of each 9-inch bias strip, and sew it to a long edge of a cuff, allowing ¼ inch of cuff to extend beyond the bias strip. Finish the cuffs. Sew a length of ¾-inch-wide fine lace over the right side of each cuff, sewing the lace's inner edge to the wrong side of the cuff *(see photo, page 101)*. Repeat with another length of ¾-inch-wide fine lace on the neckline. Turn in and sew the Bodice back opening allowances. Sew the underarm seams. Fit the Bodice to the doll, and tighten the waist edge if necessary. Fold each 11-inch bias strip in half lengthwise, wrong side in, and press. Using a zigzag stitch and contrasting thread, sew bias tape over the long raw edge of each strip. Using the photo as a placement guide, pin and stitch the bias strips in place on the Dress Bodice. Trim the bias strip ends even with the Dress Bodice bottom edge. Cut a 10-inch length of grosgrain ribbon. Turn in ¾ inch at each cut end of the ribbon, and hem. Pin one long edge of the ribbon to the bottom edge of the Dress Bodice, using a ¼-inch seam allowance. Adjust the Bodice bottom edge to fit, and stitch. Gather the raw top edge of the dress skirt, and sew it to the bottom edge of the ribbon. Stitch the back skirt seam. Sew snap fasteners to the cuffs and the back of the Dress Bodice.

12. *Headdress:* Cut a 31-inch length of 1½-inch-wide fine lace. Fold it into an arch, non-scalloped edges together and overlapping, and stitch to make double-width lace. Attach the lace to the head around the chignon, and drape the ends of the lace over the doll's shoulders. Cut two 10-inch lengths of satin ribbon, and fold them in half. Cut the remaining satin ribbon to make loops to sew to the folded ends of the ribbon lengths. Pin or sew the ribbon lengths to each side of the head over the double-width lace *(see photo)*.

13. *Nosegay (optional):* Arrange miniature silk flowers into a nosegay tied with ribbon, and tack them to the doll's hand.

FIG. II, 9   AN OLD-FASHIONED GIRL   1 SQ. = 1"

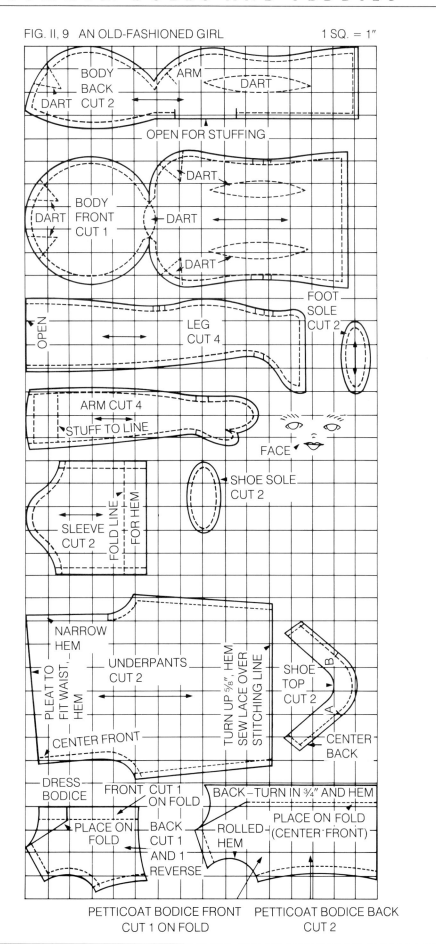

BODY BACK CUT 2
ARM
DART
DART
OPEN FOR STUFFING

BODY FRONT CUT 1
DART
DART
DART
DART

LEG CUT 4
FOOT SOLE CUT 2
OPEN

ARM CUT 4
STUFF TO LINE
FACE

SLEEVE CUT 2
FOLD LINE FOR HEM
SHOE SOLE CUT 2

NARROW HEM
UNDERPANTS CUT 2
PLEAT TO FIT WAIST, HEM
CENTER FRONT
TURN UP ⅝", HEM SEW LACE OVER STITCHING LINE
SHOE TOP CUT 2
B
A
CENTER BACK

DRESS BODICE
FRONT CUT 1 ON FOLD
PLACE ON FOLD
BACK CUT 1 AND 1 REVERSE
BACK – TURN IN ¾" AND HEM
ROLLED HEM
PLACE ON FOLD (CENTER FRONT)

PETTICOAT BODICE FRONT
CUT 1 ON FOLD

PETTICOAT BODICE BACK
CUT 2

*There's the flaxen-haired doll
that is lovely to see
And really expensively dressed,
Left alone, all uncared for,
and strange though it be,
She likes her rag dolly the best.*
—Edgar A. Guest

BABY LOUISE
(about 11 inches tall)

Average: For those with some experience in sewing and doll making.

Materials:
45-inch-wide fabric: ½ yard of solid white, pink or brown for doll, and ½ yard of floral print for clothes; 1 yard of 1-inch-wide white lace with scalloped edge; matching sewing threads; ¼-inch-wide ribbon to complement fabric; embroidery floss: small amounts in colors for eyes and mouth; yarn scraps for hair in color desired; embroidery needle; tapestry needle; synthetic stuffing; dressmaker's pencil; paper for pattern.

Directions (¼-inch seams allowed):
1. Pattern: Enlarge the pattern in FIG. II, 10A onto paper, following the directions on page 215. From the solid fabric, cut two Doll pieces. From the floral print fabric, cut two Dress pieces *(see FIG. II, 10B)*, and a 4½ x 11½-inch bonnet. Using the dressmaker's pencil, transfer the face to one Doll piece.

2. Doll: Sew the Doll pieces together, leaving an opening between the circles. Clip, and turn. Stuff the legs and arms, and stitch on the broken lines. Stuff the head and body, turn in the open edges, and slipstitch the opening closed *(see Stitch Guide, page 214)*. Using embroidery floss and needle, work the eyes in French knots, anchoring the floss at the back of the head to indent the eyes. Work the mouth in backstitch. Using tapestry needle and yarn, work French knots for hair.

3. Dress: With the Dress pieces right sides together, stitch the underarm and side seams. Clip the corners. Roll and stitch a narrow hem at the bottom, neck and sleeve edges. Turn the dress right side out. Cut a piece of lace the length of one sleeve edge, plus ½ inch. Turn under ¼ inch at each short end of the lace. Starting ¼ inch from the raw shoulder edge, stitch a lace casing around the sleeve: Pin the lace to the sleeve, matching the lace's straight edge to the sleeve edge. Stitch ¼ inch from the matched edges. Fold the lace's scalloped edge down over the stitchline; the scalloped edge should extend ½ inch beyond the sleeve's edge. Topstitch as close to the sleeve's edge as possible. Repeat at the other sleeve's edge. Stitch the shoulder seams, and clip the corners. Make the neck lace casing stopping and starting at the center front. Cut a piece of lace the length of the bottom edge of the dress. Topstitch the lace to the dress with the scalloped edge of the lace extending ½ inch beyond the edge of the dress.

4. Bonnet: Fold the bonnet lengthwise, right sides in, and stitch the long edges together; turn right side out. Turn in the short ends, and topstitch ¼ inch from the long seamed edge to make the back casing. Lap the scalloped edge of a piece of lace ½ inch over the folded bonnet edge. Topstitch along the straight lace edge and the bonnet folded edge.

5. Insert ribbon into each casing, and tie into a bow.

FIG. II, 10A BABY LOUISE 1 SQ. = 1"

FIG. II, 10B

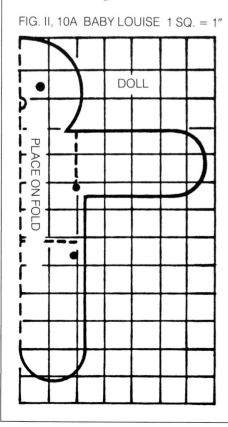

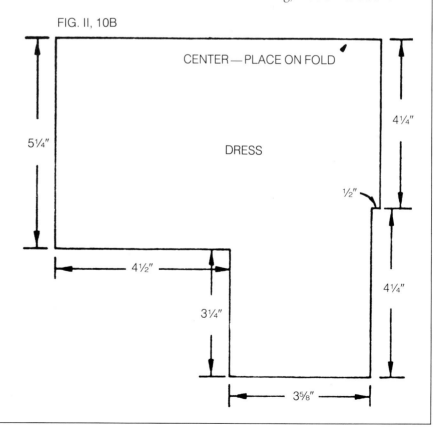

BABETTE THE NEEDLEPOINT BEAR
(about 16 inches tall)

Average: For those with some experience in needlepoint and sewing.

Materials:
½ yard of 36-inch-wide 10-mesh needlepoint canvas; Coats & Clark Red Heart 3-ply Persian needlepoint and crewel yarn (12-yard pull skein): 9 skeins each of White and Tan, 2 skeins each of Light Pink and Dark Coral, and 1 skein each of Rose, Natural, Dark Brown and Black; ¼ yard of 45-inch-wide pink calico cotton fabric; 1 package of white stretch lace seam binding; pink, white and tan sewing threads; 1 small snap fastener; synthetic stuffing; No. 18 tapestry needle; sewing needle; rustproof pins; black fine-point permanent felt-tip pen; masking tape *(optional)*; paper for pattern.

Directions:
1. Pattern: Enlarge the pattern in FIG. II, 11 *(page 108)* onto paper, following the directions on page 215. Leaving a 1½-inch margin all around each piece, cut the number of canvas pieces indicated for each pattern piece in FIG. II, 11. If you wish, cover the edges of the canvas pieces with masking tape to prevent them from raveling. Place each canvas piece over its pattern piece. Using the black felt-tip pen, trace the solid lines of the pattern piece onto the canvas.

2. Needlepoint: Using 18-inch lengths of 3-ply yarn in the tapestry needle, and following FIG. II, 11 for the colors, work each bear piece in continental stitch to one stitch beyond the outline *(see Stitch Guide, page 214)*. Begin and end each length of yarn by running it through stitches on the back of the canvas.

3. Blocking: Using the rustproof pins, pin the finished needlepoint pieces to shape. Dampen the pieces, and let them dry.

4. Assembling: Trim the excess canvas on each needlepoint piece ⅛ inch beyond the outside stitches all around. Using corresponding color yarn and the tapestry needle, whipstitch the Body pieces wrong sides together, leaving an opening for stuffing *(see Stitch Guide)*. Stuff the Body, and whipstitch the opening closed. Repeat with the Head Front and Head Back. Fold each Leg, Ear and Arm, wrong side in, along its fold line. Whipstitch together the edges of each piece, stuffing the piece before completing the whipstitching. Using corresponding color sewing thread, and the photo as a guide, sew the Head, Arms and Legs to the Body. Sew the Ears to the Head.

5. Lace Edgings: Cut two 15-inch lengths of lace. Gather each length to fit the top of a Leg, and sew the lace in place. Repeat with an 8-inch length of lace around each Arm where the White and Tan stitches meet. Gather a 1-yard length of lace, and place it around the neck.

6. Pinafore Apron: Cut two 40 x 4-inch calico rectangles, and sew them together to make an 80 x 4-inch strip for the apron. Gather one long edge of the strip to measure about 12 inches. Cut a 12½ x 1-inch calico strip for the waistband, and fold it in half lengthwise, wrong side in. Fold under the long raw edges ⅛ inch, and press. Open the waistband, and pin one raw edge to the gathered edge of the apron. Stitch the waistband to the apron using the ⅛-inch fold line as a stitch guide. Bring the opposite waistband edge up and over the gathered stitched edge, and slipstitch the waistband in place *(see Stitch Guide)*. Fold under the short back ends ¼ inch, and stitch in place. Sew the snap fastener to the back ends of the waistband. Fold under the apron's lower edge ½ inch twice, and press. Slipstitch the hem in place.

7. Pinafore Bib: Cut a 5 x 3-inch calico rectangle for the bib. Fold the rectangle in half, right sides in, to make a 2½ x 3-inch rectangle. Using a ½-inch seam allowance, sew the long edge and two short ends together, leaving an opening for turning. Turn the bib right side out. Turn in the open edges, and slipstitch the opening closed. Leaving 1½ inches of the bib extending above the waistband, sew the bib in place along the center front of the waistband.

8. Pinafore Straps: Cut two 6 x 1½-inch calico strips for the shoulder straps. Fold each strip in half lengthwise, right side in, and sew its raw long edges together. Turn the straps right side out. Sew one short end of each strap to each side of the bib's top edge. Cross the straps, and sew the other short ends on the back of the apron. Place the pinafore on the bear.

9. Finishing: Draw two strands of Black yarn across the instep of each foot for a shoe strap. Make a small calico bow measuring about 1½ inches across, and tack the bow to the bear's right Ear *(see photo)*.

*I am a Bear of Very Little Brain,
and long words Bother me.*
—A.A. Milne

FIG. II, 11 BABETTE THE NEEDLEPOINT BEAR   1 SQ. = 1"

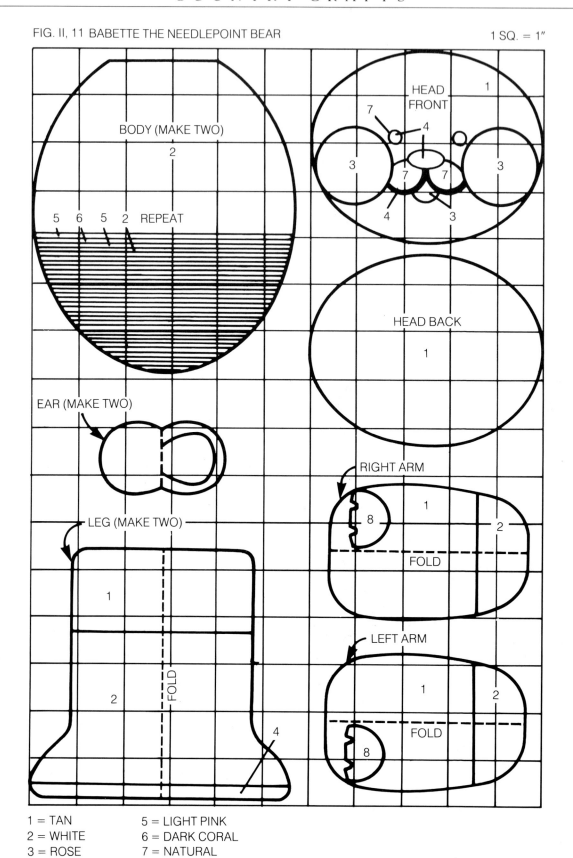

1 = TAN   5 = LIGHT PINK
2 = WHITE   6 = DARK CORAL
3 = ROSE   7 = NATURAL
4 = BLACK   8 = DARK BROWN

TINY TEDDY
(7 inches tall)

Average: For those with some experience in crocheting.

Materials:
Worsted weight yarn: 2 ounces in color desired, and 1 yard of Brown; size F crochet hook, OR ANY SIZE HOOK TO OBTAIN GAUGE BELOW; synthetic stuffing; ½ x 10 inches of wool fabric for scarf; darning needle.

Gauge: 9 sts = 2 inches; 6 rnds = 1 inch.

Directions:
1. Head: Starting at the tip of the nose, ch 2. **Rnd 1:** 6 sc in 2nd ch from hook. **Rnd 2:** (2 sc in next sc, sc in next sc) 3 times—9 sc. **Rnd 3:** Sc in each sc around. **Rnd 4:** (2 sc in next sc, sc in each of next 2 sc) 3 times—12 sc. **Rnd 5:** Sc in each sc around. **Rnd 6:** Sc in each of next 2 sc, 2 sc in each of next 8 sc, sc in each of next 2 sc—20 sc. **Rnd 7:** Sc in each of next 8 sc, 2 sc in each of next 4 sc, sc in each of next 8 sc —24 sc. **Rnds 8 and 9:** Sc in each sc around. **Rnd 10:** (Sc in each of next 5 sc, 2 sc in next sc) 4 times—28 sc. **Rnd 11:** Sc in each sc around. **Rnd 12:** (Sk next sc, sc in each of next 5 sc) 4 times—24 sc. **Rnd 13:** (Sk next sc, sc in each of next 4 sc) 4 times—20 sc. **Rnd 14:** (Sk next sc, sc in each of next 3 sc) 4 times—16 sc. Stuff the Head firmly. **Rnd 15:** (Sk next sc, sc in each of next 2 sc) 4 times—12 sc. **Rnd 16:** (Sk next sc, sc in next sc) 4 times—8 sc. **Rnd 17:** *Draw up a lp in each of next 2 sc, yarn over hook, draw through all 3 lps on hook; rep from * 3 times more. Sl st in next sc. Fasten off.

2. Ear (make 2): Starting at the base of the Ear, ch 5.
Row 1: Sc in 2nd ch from hook, sc in each of next 3 ch—4 sc. Ch 1, turn. **Row 2:** Sc in each sc across. Ch 1, turn. **Row 3:** (Sk 1 sc, sc in next sc) 2 times—2 sc. Ch 1, turn. **Row 4:** Sl st in 2nd sc. Fasten off, leaving an

8-inch-long end for sewing. Sew the base of the Ears, 1 inch apart, to Rnd 10 of the Head.

3. Body: Starting at the neck edge, ch 8. Join with sl st to form ring. **Rnd 1:** 12 sc in ring. **Rnd 2:** (2 sc in next sc, sc in each of next 2 sc) 4 times—16 sc. **Rnd 3:** Sc in each of next 2 sc, (2 sc in next sc, sc in each of next 3 sc) 3 times, 2 sc in next sc, sc in next sc—20 sc. **Rnd 4:** Sc in each sc around. **Rnd 5:** (Sc in each of next 4 sc, 2 sc in next sc) 4 times—24 sc. **Rnds 6 to 9:** Sc in each sc around. **Rnd 10:** Sc in each of next 12 sc, ch 12, sk next 12 sc. **Rnd 11:** Sc in each of next 12 sc, ch 12, sk the same 12 sc. **Rnd 12:** Sc in each of next 12 sc, sc in the 12 skipped sc of Rnd 10 (front edge), sc in first 12 sc of rnd (back edge). Fasten off. Stuff the Body firmly. Push the two ch 12's inside the Body. Sew the front and back edges together.

4. Leg (make 2): Starting at the center of the footpad, ch 2. **Rnd 1:** 6 sc in 2nd ch from hook. **Rnd 2:** 2 sc in each sc—12 sc. **Rnds 3 to 10:** Sc in each sc around. Fasten off, leaving an 8-inch-long end. Stuff the Leg firmly. Pinch the top edge of the Leg; using the darning needle and yarn end, sew the opening flat. From the back of the Body, sew Legs to the Body bottom seam.

5. Arm (make 2): Work same as the Leg for 7 rounds. Stuff and sew the opening flat as for the Leg. Sew the Arms to the sides of the Body, leaving the first 2 rnds of the Body free. Sew the Head firmly to the neck edge.

6. Features: With Brown and the darning needle, embroider the nose in satin stitch over the first two rnds above the starting ring of the face. Work a ½-inch-long straight stitch under the center of the nose; backstitch a curved line below for the mouth. Working over Rnd 5 of the Head, satin stitch the eyes 1 inch apart. Work the eyebrows in straight stitch *(see Stitch Guide, page 214)*.

7. Scarf: Fringe the narrow edges of the wool fabric by pulling the threads. Tie the scarf around the bear's neck.

UMN

There's a crispness to the air, a clarity to the light and the sky is that perfect middle shade of blue. Overnight, the green leaves of summer turn into a mass of gold and red and russet. Autumn has come to the country.

Traditionally the season of the harvest, autumn is a time both of anticipation and fulfillment. The crops are brought in, and Christmas is just around the corner.

Capture autumn's beauty with dried flower crafting. Create Victorian-style pressed flower pieces or preserve late summer roses in an exquisite mini-wreath.

This Halloween put a different kind of face on your jack-o'-lantern, from E.T. to Humpty Dumpty, with our creative carving ideas. When November arrives, make Thanksgiving decorations to add a special touch to your table.

Woodworking and autumn seem to go hand-in-hand, so we offer a dazzling array of wood crafts. From household items to terrific toys, these projects will make any woodworker happy—and they make great Christmas gifts, too!

Autumn in the country means so many wonderful things: the first fire, falling leaves, crisp apples and getting your favorite warm woollies out of storage. Now you can celebrate the season with crafts as well.

P·R·E·S·E·R·V·I·N·G
NATURE

The blossoms of spring
and summer may be long gone, but you still can enjoy
their beauty with these dried and pressed flower
projects. We've given you all you need to know to
craft with Nature's most perfect materials.

WILD GRASSES WREATH

*What makes it country? An arrangement of field
grasses and branches collected on a leisurely autumn
afternoon walk.*

Average: For those with some experience in crafting.

Materials:
Supple branches, such as birch, dogwood or willow;
bunches of dried field grasses, such as king artemisia,
yarrow and lavender (also available at florists or
nurseries); stems of fresh ivy, or fresh flowers such as
carnations or daisies; 18-inch-diameter wire wreath
form; medium-gauge floral wire; floral water vials.

Directions:
1. Bend the supple branches around the wreath form,
wiring the branches as needed, until the form is
covered completely.
2. Tuck bunches of the dried field grasses into the
branches at random, using different hues for contrast.
3. Fill the water vials with warm water, and insert one
ivy stem or fresh flower into each vial. Slip the vials into
the wreath at random.

*Listen! the wind is rising,
and the air is wild with leaves,
We have had our summer evenings,
now for October eves!*
— Humbert Wolfe

C O U N T R Y   W A Y S

• *Wild Grasses* •

Wild grasses are one of the loveliest sights in
the country. While they often take a back seat to
wildflowers, wild grasses tell a beautiful story
in their own right.

Artemisia, the first grass used in the Wild
Grasses Wreath, is named for Artemis, the
Greek goddess of the hunt. The plant genus,
which includes wormwood and sagebrush, was
sacred to the goddess. In medieval times,
wormwood and rosemary were packed away
with clothing as moth repellants.

Yarrow also is an ancient plant. It is said that
Achilles was taught by Chiron the Centaur to
use the lacy, multi-leaved plant in an ointment
that would heal the wounds of his warriors
during the siege of Troy. This story may explain
yarrow's Latin name—*Achillea millefolium*.
With its pleasingly nutty, autumnal fragrance,
yarrow has been used over the centuries as a
love charm, an herbal tea, and a remedy for
everything from hair loss to fever and chills.

Lavender comes to mind immediately when
we think of a classic English garden, but most
European wild lavender is found in the warm,
dry regions of southern Europe, such as France
and Italy. Lavender's pretty purple flowers and
delicate fragrance have made it popular since
ancient times. Its name comes from the Latin
word *lavo*, to wash, probably because in
ancient days the flowers were distilled to
perfume bathing water.

SWEET CITRUS POTPOURRI

What makes it country? A fresh scent, one of the sweetest, most subtle ways to decorate the home.

Easy: Achievable by anyone.

Materials:
4 ounces of dried cut orange peel; 4 ounces of dried marigold flowers; 3 ounces of dried chamomile flowers; 1 ounce of dried cut lemon grass; 3 ounces of lemon verbena leaves; 1 ounce of powdered orrisroot; 20 drops of lemon oil; roomy paper bag; wax paper; clothespin.

Directions:
1. Place the orange peel, marigolds, chamomile, lemon grass, and orrisroot in a glass bowl. Combine the ingredients with a large spoon. Stir in the lemon oil. Mix in the lemon verbena.
2. Line the paper bag with wax paper. Place the potpourri in the lined bag, fold the bag, and seal it with the clothespin. Store the bag in a dry, dark, cool place for 2 weeks, mixing the potpourri every other day.

DRIED ROSE MINI-WREATH

What makes it country? It's a lovely Victorian bit of nature that lasts all year, in any room.

Easy: Achievable by anyone.

Materials:
About 8 dozen dried rosebuds and flower heads *(see Drying Roses, page 116)*; 5-inch-diameter straw wreath form; sphagnum moss (available at nurseries and floral supply stores); white glue; lightweight picture hanger; clear acrylic spray, or hairspray.

Directions:
1. Cover the top and sides of the wreath form with the sphagnum moss, gluing the moss in place.
2. Glue the dried rosebuds and flower heads over the moss to cover the top and sides of the wreath. Let the glue dry completely.
3. Attach the picture hanger to the back of the wreath. To protect the wreath from dust, spray it with two coats of clear acrylic or hairspray, letting the spray dry between coats.

Gather ye rose-buds while ye may:
Old Time is still a-flying.
—Robert Herrick

DRYING ROSES

Roses are best dried in a medium of sand or silica gel. For the Dried Rose Mini-Wreath (page 114), you will need only flower heads and buds; cut off the stems before drying the roses.

Easy: Achievable by anyone.

Materials:
Fresh rosebuds and flower heads; slotted spoon; small paintbrush. **For Silica Gel Method:** Silica gel (available at floral supply stores and some nurseries); covered, airtight, preferably lightproof container.
For Sand Method: Sand; container for cleaning sand; shallow container for drying sand; sturdy container such as shoe box, cake tin, or plastic container.

Directions:
1. Silica Gel: Spread a 2-inch layer of silica gel in the container. Settle the rosebuds and flower heads face up in the gel so they do not touch each other. Pour more gel over the roses until the petals are covered completely. Place the lid on the container. The silica gel, normally blue in color, will turn pink as it absorbs the moisture from the roses.
2. Check the drying roses daily. The roses will dry in 3 to 7 days. Do not let them overdry, or they will disintegrate when they are touched. The roses will feel crisp when they are dry.
3. Remove the dried roses from the gel with the spoon. Use the paintbrush to brush off any gel remaining on the petals. Handle the dried roses gently.
4. To reuse the silica gel, let it dry until it turns completely blue again.
5. Sand: Some people prefer to dry flowers with sand because silica gel can be dangerous to breathe. Sand for flower drying must be clean and dry. Place the sand in the cleaning container, and pour water over it. Stir the sand so the dirt rises to the top. Let the sand settle, and pour off the dirty water. Repeat until the sand is clean. Spread out the sand in the shallow container, and let the sand dry in the sun.
6. Spread a 2-inch layer of clean, dry sand in the sturdy container. Settle the rosebuds and flower heads face up in the sand so they do not touch each other. Pour more sand gently over the roses until the petals are covered. Leave the container open.
7. The roses will dry in 3 to 5 weeks. The sand does not absorb the roses' moisture, but holds the roses' shapes while they dry naturally.
8. When the roses are dry, remove them from the sand with the spoon. Use the paintbrush to brush off any sand remaining on the dried petals.

COUNTRY WAYS

• The Language of Roses •

No flower has ever captured human interest and imagination like the rose. Poets praise it. Gardeners raise it in an infinite number of varieties. Avid horticulturists even work to propagate antique rose varieties that date back as far as the 16th century.

One of the most charming customs of the early 19th century was the use of flowers as a means of communication. In those romantic Victorian days, hundreds of plants and flowers were given symbolic meanings. When a suitor wished to express his love for a young woman, he would send her a bouquet of flowers to "speak" his message.

In general, the rose signified love. With so many varieties existing, however, the rose became the most "eloquent" of flowers. Here are some examples:

Cabbage Rose—Ambassador of love
Carolina Rose—Love is dangerous
Damask Rose—Brilliant complexion; freshness
Deep Red Rose—Bashfulness
White Rose—I am worthy of you
White and Red Roses together—Unity
Yellow Rose—Friendship
Red Rosebuds—Purity and loveliness
White Rosebuds—Girlhood

O, my luve's like a red, red rose,
That's newly sprung in June;
O, my luve's like the melodie
That's sweetly play'd in tune.
— Robert Burns

PRESSING FLOWERS

Easy: Achievable by anyone.

Materials:
Fresh flowers, petals or greenery; cinderblock and heavy book, such as a phone book, or Flower Press *(directions, below).*

Directions:
1. Place the fresh flowers, petals or greenery between the pages of the heavy book, with at least 1 inch of pages between every two flowers. Weight down the book with the cinderblock. Or, if you plan to press many flowers, use the Flower Press.
2. Let the flowers dry completely in the book for about 2 weeks, or in the Press for 2 to 3 days. When all the moisture is gone from the flowers, remove them from the book or Press. Store the pressed flowers in a closed box in a cool place until you are ready to use them.

FLOWER PRESS

Easy: Achievable by anyone.

Materials:
Two 10-inch plywood squares; 10-inch corrugated cardboard squares; 10-inch blotter paper squares; four ¼-inch-diameter lag bolts; 4 washers and wing nuts to fit lag bolts; sandpaper; tack cloth; paint in color desired; paintbrush; drill with ¼-inch bit.

Directions:
1. Sand the plywood squares smooth on both sides, and wipe off all the sawdust with the tack cloth. Paint both sides of the plywood squares.
2. Drill a hole in each corner of one plywood square. Making sure the holes match, repeat on the second plywood square.
3. Cut off the corners of the cardboard and blotter paper squares to allow room for the lag bolts.
4. Slip the lag bolts through the holes in one plywood square, and place the square on a flat surface with the bolts facing up. Place a cardboard square on top of the plywood square, then two blotter paper squares. Continue to stack the layers in this way, ending with a cardboard square.
5. To press flowers, place one flower between two adjacent blotter paper squares in the Press. Repeat for each flower you wish to press. Slide the remaining plywood square over the bolts. Place the washers and wing nuts on the bolts, and tighten the wing nuts to tighten the Press.

PRESSED FLOWER PICTURE

What makes it country? It's an authentic Victorian craft that can be used as a border for framed invitations, announcements, or photographs.

Average: For those with some experience in crafting.

Materials:
Variety of pressed flowers and ferns *(see Pressing Flowers, at left);* 8 x 10-inch shadow box frame with glass; 9 x 11 inches of felt or velvet; clear-drying white or craft glue; tweezers; ribbon.

Directions:
1. Cover the frame's cardboard insert with the felt or velvet, turning the fabric ½ inch to the back on each edge. Clip the corners so the fabric lies flat. Glue the fabric in place on the back of the cardboard, and let the glue dry completely.
2. If you are making a pressed flower border for a card or photograph, center the card or photo on the fabric-lined cardboard, and glue the card in place with a dab of glue in each corner. Arrange the pressed flowers and ferns around the card, using the tweezers to lift and place the flowers gently.
3. When you have a pleasing arrangement, affix each flower in place with a dab of glue. Glue ribbon bows and streamers around the flowers. Let the glue dry for 24 hours before framing the pressed flower picture.

DECOUPAGE FLOWER ACCESSORIES

What makes it country? Real flowers captured forever to beautify household items.

Easy: Achievable by anyone.

Materials:
Variety of pressed flowers and greens *(see Pressing Flowers, page 117)*; ceramic, wood or glass item to be decoupaged; tweezers; paintbrush; decoupage glue.

Directions:
1. Make sure the item to be decoupaged is thoroughly clean and dry.
2. Arrange the pressed flowers and greens on the item, using the tweezers to lift and place the flowers gently.
3. When you have a pleasing arrangement, affix each flower in place with a dab of glue. Let the glue dry.
4. Brush a coat of glue over the entire design area, and let the glue dry completely.

COUNTRY WAYS

• *The Dried Garden* •

The art of pressing flowers was begun by gardeners and horticulturists as a way to preserve different varieties of flowers for study. Such collections of floral specimens were known as "dried gardens" or "winter gardens." The oldest known dried garden was made by John Tradescant the Elder, gardener to King Charles I of England in the mid 17th century; the collection survives to this day.

When horticulturists of that era traveled, they collected samples of interesting or unusual plants and pressed them between the pages of a book. Later, the specimens might be fastened to the book pages with a special type of glue. John Tradescant included in his book flowers collected on a trip to Virginia. Historians believe that the Tradescant dried garden is in such good condition today because of the glue that was used on the flowers.

Autumn is the bite of a harvest apple.
—Christina Petrowsky

H·A·R·V·E·S·T
TIME

Allhallow eve has been celebrated for centuries; Thanksgiving is unique to America, although there are similar holidays in Canada and Australia. However you choose to honor the harvest, from festive jack-o'-lanterns to special table decor, craft it country-style.

CREATIVE CARVING FROM THE PUMPKIN PATCH

All you need is a paring knife and a good imagination! What makes it country? An old tradition, natural materials, and the spirit of invention.

Average: For those with some experience in crafting.

Materials:
Pumpkin; paring knife; pencil; toothpicks; votive candle in holder.

Directions:
1. Take a good look at the pumpkin; its shape may inspire a design. In the photo at left, a lumpy, rather sinister-looking pumpkin became a little demon *(see pumpkin on lower right)*. An egg-shaped pumpkin became Humpty Dumpty *(see photo at left and photo, page 122)*, and a squat, oval pumpkin looked like E.T. Or take inspiration from a favorite storybook character; the pumpkin on the upper right was inspired by the "wild things" created by the artist/author Maurice Sendak. Or use the photo as a guide to create a design.

(Continued on page 123)

From ghoulies and ghosties and long-leggety beasties And things that go bump in the night, Good Lord, deliver us!
— Cornish prayer

• *Jack-O'-Lanterns* •

Credit the Irish with introducing jack-o'-lanterns to America. The legend of the jack-o'-lantern varies with the telling; here is one version.

In Ireland long ago there was a man named Jack who was notorious for drunkenness and being "tight" with his money. One night, while Jack was downing a pint at the local pub, the Devil appeared and sat beside him. Jack realized that Satan had come to claim his soul, but Jack wasn't quite ready to go. He cleverly persuaded the Devil to have one last drink with him before they pushed off for the other world.

To pay for the drink, the Devil turned himself into a sixpence, which Jack immediately tucked into his wallet. To the Devil's surprise, the wallet had a catch shaped like a cross; once inside, he could not escape!

Jack agreed to let the Devil go on the condition that he not return for another year. One year later, the Devil came back and Jack played another practical joke on him. The Devil was not amused.

Years passed, and Jack's body wore out. He was too much of a sinner to go to Heaven, and the Devil would not let him into Hell. Poor Jack was doomed to eternal wandering!

He begged the Devil for a light, and the Devil obliged him with a live coal. Jack put the coal into a turnip he was chewing, and from that day, Jack has used the makeshift lantern to light his way as he walks the earth waiting for Judgment Day.

In Ireland, as well as Scotland where the legend also was known, people carved oversized turnips and rutabagas into jack-o'-lanterns. It wasn't until the Irish came to America and discovered pumpkins — which lend themselves so well to carving — that jack-o'-lanterns began to be made from pumpkins.

2. Draw the design lightly on the pumpkin in pencil. Using the paring knife, cut out a circular hole in the bottom of the pumpkin; this creates a flat base for the jack-o'-lantern to stand on. It also eliminates the difficulty of reaching into the top of the pumpkin to light the candle.

3. Scoop out the pumpkin seeds and stringy pulp; save the pumpkin seeds for toasting.

4. Cut out and remove most of the facial features from the pumpkin. To give the pumpkin face texture and depth, use the paring knife to scratch the design details into the pumpkin's surface *(see photo, page 120)*. When the pumpkin is placed over the lighted candle, the light will shine brightly through the cut outs, and glow softly through the scratches. If you wish, make the entire pumpkin face using the scratching technique *(see photo, page 122)*.

5. To make stand-up ears or horns, leave part of each cut out attached to the pumpkin, and bend the cut out forward until you achieve the desired effect. If necessary, hold the cut out in place with a toothpick.

6. Light the votive candle, and carefully place the pumpkin over it.

COUNTRY WAYS

• *Halloween in History* •

Halloween has been celebrated for centuries, dating back to the Celts who inhabited Western Europe before the birth of Christ. In ancient days, Allhallow eve was a time for good people to feast and ghosts to walk abroad. Folks dressed in animal skins, and lit candles to ward off evil spirits. Eventually the masqueraders began visiting their neighbors and asking for "treats." Those who were generous were assured of a good year to come; the stingy were tormented by "evil spirits."

When the Romans conquered England and France, they added their own harvest traditions: bobbing for apples, and the giving of nuts as treats. As the celebration of Halloween spread through Western Europe, other traditions emerged. In Italy, folks gave bread and water, and left lamps burning through the night to ward off evil. The wandering spirits in other countries were left doughnuts and milk. There even was a custom of making a circle of empty chairs, allowing one chair for each family member and one extra for a visiting ghost.

Irish immigrants are credited with introducing Halloween to America during the 19th century.

The one red leaf, the last of its clan,
That dances as often as dance it can,
Hanging so light, and hanging so high,
On the topmost twig that looks up
at the sky.
— Samuel Taylor Coleridge

CORNHUSK PILGRIM AND INDIANS

Challenging: Requires more experience in crafting.

Materials:

About 120 dyed and natural-color cornhusks, or natural-color cornhusks and fabric dyes *(see photo for colors)*; Feel-O-Fleece®: 16 inches of brown, and 25 inches of black; three 1-inch-diameter Styrofoam® balls; ½-inch-diameter wooden bead; ¹⁄₁₆ x 1 x 3-inch wooden board; miniature pumpkin and corn; small twigs; 8 cotton balls; string; 16 inches of jute twine; drinking straw, or pencil; No. 20 and No. 26 wire; wire cutters; scissors; glue gun; plastic bags.

Note: *Cornhusks are ribbed on one side, and smooth on the other. Use the ribbed side as the right side, and work with the grain. The cutting directions first give the width of the husks, across the ribs, and then the length.*

Directions:

1. *Preparing the Cornhusks:* If you are dyeing cornhusks, prepare the fabric dyes following the package directions. Drop the husks one at a time into the dyes. Remove the husks when they have turned the desired colors, rinse them in cold water, and drain them. Soak the undyed and, if using them, purchased dyed husks in warm water for 20 minutes. Separate the husks, and drain them until they are slightly moist. Place all the moist husks in plastic bags to keep them from drying out, or they will crack easily. If necessary, moisten the husks again before working with them.

2. *Head:* Place a Styrofoam ball in the center of a 2 x 8-inch husk. Cover the ball by bringing the husk ends together and tucking in the sides neatly. Gather the husk at the base of the head, and wrap the gather with No. 26 wire. Cut a 6-inch length of No. 20 wire, and insert one end into the base of the head for the neck and backbone. Glue a small husk strip tightly around the neck.

3. *Hands:* Make a ½-inch loop at each end of a 10-inch length of No. 20 wire. Wrap each loop with a 1 x 8-inch husk, and secure the husk with glue.

4. *Sleeves:* Gather one 6-inch edge of a 6 x 5½-inch husk, smooth side out, around the wrist of one hand, with the other 6-inch husk edge extending beyond the end of the hand *(see* FIG. III, 1A*)*. Wrap the gather with No. 26 wire. Repeat on the other hand. Turn the sleeves right side out by pulling the ungathered ends of the husks carefully to the center of the arm wire *(see* FIG. III, 1B*)*. Gather these ends, and secure them to the center of the arm wire with No. 26 wire. Wrap a 12-inch length of No. 26 wire around the center of the arm wire

several times, leaving two wire tails *(see* FIG. III, 1C*)*. Attach the neck to the center of the arm wire by wrapping the neck with the wire tails in a crisscross pattern *(see* FIG. III, 1D*)*.

FIG. III, 1A SLEEVE

FIG. III, 1B SLEEVE

FIG. III, 1C SLEEVES

FIG. III, 1D SLEEVES

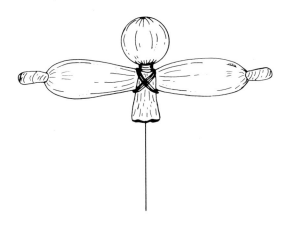

(Continued on page 126)

COUNTRY WAYS

• *The Pilgrims' Thanks* •

The story of the Pilgrims' journey to the New World to find religious freedom is well known. The first year was disastrous for the colonists, who would have perished but for the help given by the Native Americans living nearby. After the Pilgrims' successful harvest in 1620, they celebrated with a feast of Thanksgiving, and invited their Native American friends to share in the bounty.

The date of the actual celebration still is being debated. Some scholars believe the first Thanksgiving may have been held in February. Also, there is no evidence that the Pilgrims and their guests dined on turkey, cranberry sauce or pumpkin pie.

Abraham Lincoln proclaimed the last Thursday in November as the official date to observe Thanksgiving, but Congress did not make it a national holiday until 1941.

**A joy that's shared
is a joy made double.**
— English proverb

5. Bodice: Place two cotton balls side by side in the center of the smooth side of a 6 x 8-inch husk *(see* FIG. III, 1E*).* Turn the long side edges 1 inch over the cotton balls, and bring the short ends together. Place the bodice piece against the center of the arm wire, with the fold at shoulder level and the raw edges at the bottom. Gather the raw edges to form a waist. Secure the waist to the backbone wire with No. 26 wire. Using a 2 x 5-inch husk, cover the bodice piece from the right front waist diagonally over the left shoulder to the left back waist. Using another 2 x 5-inch husk, cover the other half of the bodice from the left front waist diagonally over the right shoulder to the right back waist. Gather the husk ends at the waist, and secure them with No. 26 wire.

FIG. III, 1E BODICE

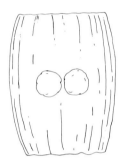

6. Underskirt: Attach twenty 1½ x 6-inch husks around the waist with No. 20 wire, gathering the husk ends as you go, and covering the bodice, neck and head *(see* FIG. III, 1F*).* Pull down the free ends of the husks gently to a skirt position.

FIG. III, 1F UNDERSKIRT

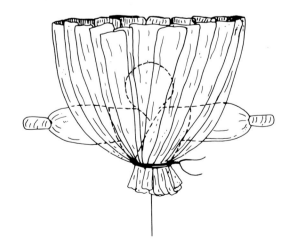

7. Overskirt: Place four 7 x 5½-inch husks around the waist over the underskirt. Gather the husk ends at the waist, and secure them with No. 20 wire. Glue together the sides of the overskirt pieces. Position the doll's arms while they are still moist *(see photo, page 125).*

8. Pilgrim Apron: Center a 6 x 4½-inch husk on top of an 8 x 5-inch husk. Gather them together at the top edges, and attach them to the front of the Pilgrim doll's waist with No. 20 wire. Curl the apron's corners by rolling them around the straw or pencil *(see photo).* Glue a narrow husk strip over the wired waist for the apron waistband. Cut two ¾ x 6-inch husk strips for the apron ribbons. Taper the width of each ribbon at one end to ¼ inch. Curl the ribbons around the straw. Trim the ¾-inch ribbon ends into fishtails. Glue the ¼-inch ribbon ends to the center back of the apron waistband. Glue the fishtail ends to the back of the skirt. Cut a ½ x 2½-inch husk, and overlap the short ends to form a ring. Compress the ring, and glue a ¼ x 1-inch husk around the middle to form a bow *(see* FIG. III, 1G*).* Glue the bow to the center back of the apron waistband over the ribbons.

FIG. III, 1G PILGRIM APRON BOW

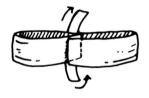

9. Pilgrim Collar: Cut a 3-inch-diameter husk circle. Fold the circle in half twice, and cut off the corner to form a small neck hole *(see* FIG. III, 1H*).* Unfold the circle, and cut a wedge out of it *(see* FIG. III, 1H*).* Glue the collar to the Pilgrim doll's shoulders, with the cut out wedge at the front. Make a small bow with streamers from a ⅛ x 5-inch husk strip. Curl the streamers around the straw, and glue the bow to the center front of the collar.

FIG. III, 1H PILGRIM COLLAR

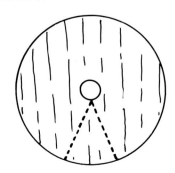

10. *Pilgrim Hair:* Place a line of glue along the top front of the head from temple to temple. Place two 8-inch lengths of brown Feel-O-Fleece side by side on the line of glue, with 1 inch of the fleece to the rear, and the rest hanging down over the face *(see* FIG. III, 1I)*.* Let the glue set for 5 minutes. Flip back the front hair, and tie the ends together at the base of the head with a small piece of string. Roll under the hair ends, and glue them to the nape of the neck.

FIG. III, 1I PILGRIM HAIR

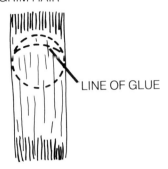

LINE OF GLUE

11. *Pilgrim Hat:* Cut a 3-inch husk square. Cutting with the grain, cut two 1-inch slits at the bottom edge of the square to form the back panel; cut the first slit 1 inch from the left edge, and the second slit 1 inch from the right edge. Cut off the lower corner on each side of the back panel *(see* FIG. III, 1J)*.* Bring point A to point B underneath the back panel, and glue the section to the inside of the back panel. Repeat with point C to point D. Fold back the hat brim carefully *(see photo, page 125)*. Glue the inside of the hat to the top of the Pilgrim doll's head.

FIG. III, 1J PILGRIM HAT

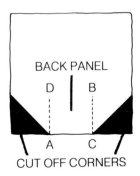

BACK PANEL

D | B

A | C

CUT OFF CORNERS

12. *Indian Apron:* Cut a 5-inch husk square. Cut one edge into a V by folding the square in half to form a rectangle, and cutting off the corner at one short end. Unfold the husk. Cut 1-inch slits ¼ inch apart along the V edges to give a fringed look *(see photo)*. Gather the apron's upper edge, and attach it to the Indian doll's waist with No. 20 wire. Glue a narrow husk strip around the wired waist for the apron waistband.

13. *Indian Shawl:* Cut a 5 x 8-inch husk. Cut the top and bottom edges into V's, and fringe them, following the directions in Step 12. Fold the husk in half twice, and cut off the corner to form a neck hole. Cut a slit from the point of the bottom V to the neck hole *(see* FIG. III, 1K)*.* Glue the shawl to the Indian doll's shoulders, with the slit at the front. Make a small husk bow with curled streamers following Step 9, and glue the bow to the front of the shawl at the neck.

FIG. III, 1K
INDIAN SHAWL

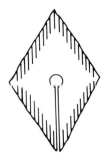

14. *Indian Braided Hair:* Place a line of glue down the middle of the head from the forehead to the nape of the neck. Center a 12-inch length of black Feel-O-Fleece on the glue line, with half the length to the left and half the length to the right. Let the glue set for 5 minutes. Separate each half of the fleece into three strands, and braid the strands up to the glue line. Tie a small piece of string around the ends of each braid.

15. *Indian Headband:* Glue a narrow husk strip around the top of the head.

16. *Papoose:* Make the papoose head following the directions in Step 2, using the wooden bead in place of the Styrofoam ball, and a 2 x 4-inch husk; omit the neck and backbone wire. Glue a 1-inch piece of black Feel-O-Fleece to the top of the head for hair. Wrap and glue a ¾ x 3-inch husk over the top and sides of the head for a hood. Glue the back of the head to the top of the wooden board. Glue two cotton balls, one above the other, to the board below the head for the body. Wrap a 3 x 3½-inch husk around the body and board, placing the top edge of the husk at the papoose's neck, and gluing the side and bottom edges to the back of the board. Tie the jute twine around the papoose in a crisscross pattern. Glue the papoose to the back of one of the Indian dolls; hold the papoose in place until the glue sets.

17. *Finishing:* Glue the miniature pumpkin to the Pilgrim doll's hands, holding the pumpkin in place until the glue sets. Peel and whittle the small twigs to look like firewood, and glue them to the arms and hands of one of the Indian dolls *(see photo)*. Glue the miniature corn to the arms and hands of the other Indian doll; if you wish, glue miniature husks to the sides of the corn first *(see photo)*.

ELEGANT CROCHETED TABLECLOTH
(about 44 x 68 inches)

What makes it country? Painstaking crafting to produce a tablecloth good enough to be "best."

Average: For those with some experience in crocheting.

Materials:
J. & P. Coats Knit-Cro-Sheen Mercerized Cotton (175-yard ball): 29 balls of Pale Yellow; size 7 steel crochet hook, OR ANY SIZE HOOK TO OBTAIN GAUGE BELOW.
Gauge: Each motif = 4 inches in diameter.

Directions:
1. First Motif: Starting at the center, ch 5. Join with sl st to form a ring. **Rnd 1:** Ch 4, (dc in ring, ch 1) 7 times. Join to 3rd ch of ch-4. **Rnd 2:** Sl st in next sp, ch 4, make 4 tr in same sp, (ch 3, 5 tr in next sp) 7 times; ch 3. Join to top of ch-4. **Rnd 3:** Ch 3; holding back on hook last lp of each dc, dc in next 4 tr, thread over and draw through all lps on hook—**starting cluster (cl) made;** ch 8; * holding back on hook last lp of each dc, dc in next 5 tr, thread over and draw through all lps on hook—**5-dc cl made;** ch 8; rep from * around. Join to tip of first cl. **Rnd 4:** Ch 1, * in next lp make 4 sc, ch 3 and 4 sc; rep from * around. Join to first sc. **Rnd 5:** Sl st in next 3 sc and in next ch-3 lp; ch 4, holding back on hook last lp of each tr, make 2 tr in same lp, thread over and draw through all lps on hook—**starting tr cl made;** ch 8; holding back on hook last lp of each tr, make 3 tr in same lp, thread over and draw through all lps on hook—**(3-tr cl made)** twice; * in next ch-3 lp make 3-tr cl and (ch 8 and 3-tr cl) twice; rep from * around. Join to tip of first cl. **Rnd 6:** Ch 1, * in next lp make 4 sc, ch 3 and 4 sc, in tip of next tr cl make sc, ch 3 and sc; in next lp make 4 sc, ch 3 and 4 sc; rep from * around. Join to first sc. Fasten off.

2. Second Motif: Work as for the First Motif through Rnd 5. **Rnd 6:** Ch 1, (in next lp make 4 sc, ch 3 and 4 sc, sc in tip of next cl, ch 1, sl st in corresponding ch-3 lp on First Motif, ch 1, sc in tip of same cl on Second Motif; in next lp on Second Motif make 4 sc, ch 3 and 4 sc) twice; sc in tip of next cl on Second Motif, ch 1, sl st in corresponding ch-3 lp on First Motif, ch 1, sc in tip of same cl on Second Motif; working on the Second Motif only, complete the rnd as for the First Motif. Make 11 rows of 17 motifs, joining 2 corresponding lps to adjacent motifs, and leaving 2 lps free between joinings.
3. Fill-In Motif: Starting at the center, ch 7. Join with sl st to form a ring. **Rnd 1:** Ch 4, (hdc in ring, ch 2) 7 times. Join to 2nd ch of ch-4—8 sps. **Rnd 2:** Sl st in next sp, ch 4, make 2 tr in same sp; now join the Fill-In Motifs to the free ch-3 lp between 4 motifs as follows: * Ch 2, sl st in center of ch-3 lp on Motif, ch 2, sl st in top of last tr made on Fill-In Motif, ch 1, make 3 tr in next lp on Fill-In Motif; rep from * around, end last rep with ch 1, sl st in top of ch-4. Fasten off. Make a Fill-In Motif in each space between 4 motifs.
4. Blocking: Pin the tablecloth to the correct measurements on a padded, flat surface. Steam the tablecloth lightly by holding a steam iron just above it; do not place the iron directly on the tablecloth. Let the tablecloth dry completely before unpinning it.

Our fathers were Englishmen which came over this great ocean, and were ready to perish in this wilderness.
—William Bradford

COUNTRY WAYS

• Ancient Thanksgivings •

The concept of a thanksgiving feast is thousands of years old. It dates back to ancient civilizations such as the Mayans and Aztecs, who feasted and offered sacrifices to their gods to thank them for bountiful harvests.

Strangely enough, these ancients had another thanksgiving tradition that we share. It seems the Mayan thanksgiving celebration included playing a game very similar to our football. People traveled for miles to the holy city of Chichen-Itza to watch the game. There is evidence the festivities included a band to play music during the game.

W · O · O · D
CRAFTS

W ooden accessories
and furnishings belong in every country home. These
wonderful wooden projects can be painted or left
plain; either way, they're country treasures.

WOODEN BEAR ROCKER

Average: For those with some experience
in woodworking and decorative painting.

Materials:

8½ feet of 1 x 12 clear pine lumber; ¼- or ⅜-inch-
diameter wooden dowels; 6d finishing nails; graphite
paper; stylus or dry ballpoint pen; wood glue; wood
putty; sandpaper; tack cloth; red, blue, white, black,
beige and dark brown acrylic paints; antiquing glaze;
clear varnish; artist's paintbrushes; paintbrushes; jigsaw;
drill; hammer; nail set; cheesecloth; tracing paper.

Directions:

1. Cut two 11 x 25-inch pieces, and two 5½ x 12-inch
pieces from the clear pine for the chair sides. Using
glue and dowels, and following FIG. III, 2 *(page 132)*
for the dowels' placement, join one large to one small
wood piece to make a wood piece large enough for the
chair side. Repeat for the other chair side.
2. Enlarge the pattern in FIG. III, 2 onto tracing paper,
following the directions on page 215. Using the
graphite paper and stylus or dry ballpoint pen, transfer
the bear shape to both chair side pieces. Cut out the
bear shapes with the jigsaw. Also cut two arm rests, two
rockers, an 11-inch square for the chair seat, and an
11 x 20-inch rectangle for the chair back.
3. Transfer the chair back top design and heart to the
chair back. Cut out the top and heart with the jigsaw.
4. Sand the edges of the pieces smooth, and wipe off all
the sawdust with the tack cloth. Nail the chair back to
the chair seat *(see* FIG. III, 2*).* Countersink the nails.
5. Using glue and dowels, attach the rockers to the
chair sides *(see* FIG. III, 2*).* Nailing from the outside, nail
one chair side to the back/seat assembly; countersink
the nails. Repeat to attach the other chair side. Fill the
nail holes with wood putty, let the putty dry, and sand it
smooth. Wipe off the sawdust with the tack cloth.

6. Paint the entire chair with two coats of beige paint,
letting the paint dry between coats. Transfer the bear
features to the chair sides. Using the artist's
paintbrushes, and following the chart in FIG. III, 2, paint
the bear features on each chair side. To create the effect
of the fur, use a circular, sweeping motion with a dry
brush. Mix white or black paint with the other colors to
achieve shading. Work quickly to achieve shading
because acrylic paints dry very quickly. Mix black paint
with red paint to make dark red paint, and paint the
two commas on either side of the heart cutout. Using
the photo as a guide, paint "honey" freehand on the jar.
7. Apply a coat of antiquing glaze to the entire chair.
Using the cheesecloth, rub away some of the glaze to
give texture and add highlights *(see photo).* Let the
glaze dry. Finish the chair with three to four coats of
varnish, letting the varnish dry and sanding lightly
between coats.

C O U N T R Y W A Y S

• *Knocking on Wood* •

Knocking on wood to avoid "jinxing" good
fortune is common, but few people know why.
   Folks used to believe that if evil spirits heard
you bragging about your good fortune, the
spirits would become jealous and try to take
your good fortune away. Knocking on wood
prevented spirits from hearing what you said.
   The Druids believed that good spirits lived
in trees, which is why wood and branches often
were part of Druid rituals. The Druids would
touch the bark of a tree and ask a favor of the
wood spirits. When the favor was granted, they
knocked on the tree to say thank you.

FIG. III, 2   WOODEN BEAR ROCKER   1 SQ. = 2"

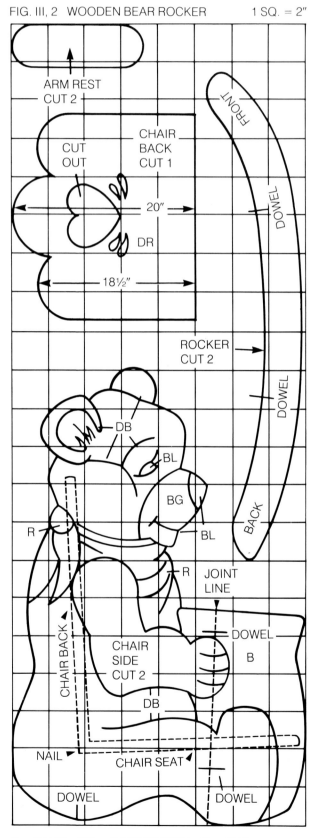

ARM REST
CUT 2

CHAIR
BACK
CUT 1

CUT
OUT

20"

DR

18½"

ROCKER
CUT 2

FRONT

DOWEL

DB

BL

BG

DOWEL

BACK

R

BL

R

JOINT
LINE

DOWEL

CHAIR BACK

CHAIR
SIDE
CUT 2

B

DB

NAIL

CHAIR SEAT

DOWEL

DOWEL

B = BLUE   DB = DARK BROWN   R = RED
BL = BLACK   BG = BEIGE   DR = DARK RED

TABBY BOOKENDS

What makes it country? A familiar face painted in quirky colors for a whimsical touch.

Average: For those with some experience in woodworking.

Materials:

3½ feet of 1 x 6 pine lumber; eight 2-inch drywall screws, or 6d finishing nails; graphite paper; stylus or dry ballpoint pen; wood glue; sandpaper; tack cloth; red, turquoise, purple and white acrylic paints; paintbrushes; handsaw or power saw; sabre saw; jigsaw *(optional)*; drill with assorted bits; screwdriver or hammer; paper for pattern.

CUTTING DIRECTIONS

CODE	PIECES	SIZE
A	2	¾" x 5½" x 7½" Cat
B	2	¾" x 5½" x 6" Bottoms
C	2	¾" x 5½" x 6½" Uprights

Directions:

1. Cut the bookend bottom and upright parts to size. Enlarge the cat pattern in Fig. III, 3 onto paper, following the directions on page 215; cut the pattern in half at the cut line. Using the graphite paper and stylus or dry ballpoint pen, transfer half a cat shape to each of the A cat wood pieces, and cut out the cat shapes with the sabre saw or jigsaw. Drill a ¼-inch-diameter hole for the tail cutout, and cut the taper with the sabre saw.

2. Round off the corners on one short end of each B bottom piece and one tall end of each C upright piece *(see photo)*. Sand all the wood pieces smooth, and wipe off all the sawdust with the tack cloth.

3. Using glue, and screws or nails, attach the square-cut end of a B bottom piece to the square-cut end of a C upright piece to make one bookend *(see photo)*. Repeat to make the other bookend.

4. Paint the bookends turquoise. Transfer the cat features to the A cat pieces. Following the chart in Fig. III, 3, paint the cat features. Mix red with white paint to make pink paint. Mix turquoise with white paint to make light green paint. Let the paint dry. Glue each A cat piece to a bookend.

Nothing should be bought
that can be made
or done without.
—New England saying

FIG. III, 3 TABBY BOOKENDS   1 SQ. = 1"

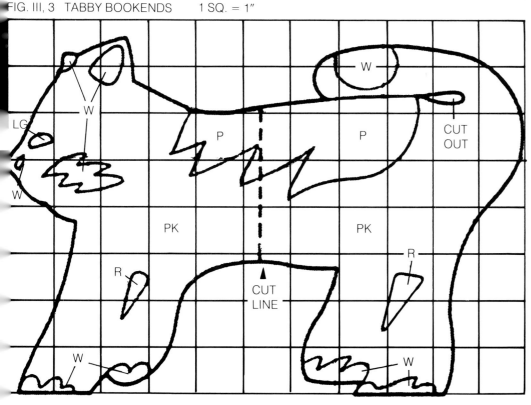

R = RED
LG = LIGHT GREEN
PK = PINK
W = WHITE
P = PURPLE

STRAP-HINGED BOX

What makes it country? A shape like an old desk box, with colonial-style black strap hinges.

Average: For those with some experience in woodworking.

Materials:

8 feet of ½ x 10-inch pine lumber; 2 feet of ½ x 5-inch pine lumber; 2 black strap hinges; black metal drawer pull; 1¼-inch finishing nails; wood glue; sandpaper; tack cloth; wood stain; paintbrush; saw; hammer.

CUTTING DIRECTIONS

CODE	PIECES	SIZE	
A	2	½″ x 9¼″ x 9¼″	Sides
B	1	½″ x 5″ x 16½″	Front
C	1	½″ x 9¼″ x 17½″	Bottom
D	1	½″ x 9¼″ x 16½″	Back
E	1	½″ x 2¾″ x 17½″	Top
F	1	½″ x 7¾″ x 17½″	Lid

Directions:

1. Cut the box parts to size. Measure in 2¾ inches on the top of each A side piece. Measure up 5 inches on the front of each A side piece. Connect the two points with a 7¾-inch-long line, and cut along the line.
2. Glue and nail the box parts together *(see* FIG. III, 4*)*. Sand the box smooth. Round off all the sharp corners and edges. Wipe off all the sawdust with the tack cloth. Stain the inside and outside of the box. When the stain has dried, attach the strap hinges and drawer pull *(see* FIG. III, 4*)*.

FIG. III, 4   STRAP-HINGED BOX

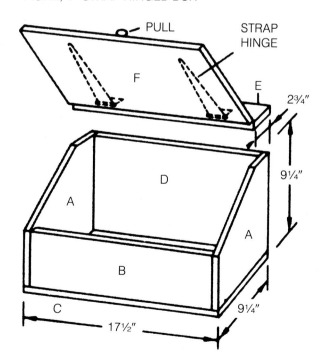

ONE-DRAWER BOOK RACK
(11 x 16 x 13 inches)

Average: For those with some experience
in woodworking.

Materials:

5 feet of ½ x 12-inch, or two 5-foot lengths of ½ x 6-inch
pine lumber; 12 x 10 inches of ⅛-inch-thick plywood;
2 feet of ¼ x 4-inch, 3 feet of ½ x ½-inch, and 2 feet of
½ x 4-inch lattice; two 1-inch-diameter porcelain knobs;
¾- and 1-inch wire brads; graphite paper; stylus or dry
ballpoint pen; wood glue; sandpaper; tack cloth; maple
wood stain; paintbrush; sabre saw, jigsaw or coping
saw; drill; hammer; paper for pattern.

Directions:

1. If ½ x 12-inch pine is not available, or is too
expensive, edge-glue together two 5-foot lengths of
½ x 6-inch pine to get the necessary width.
2. Enlarge the pattern in Fɪɢ. III, 5A *(page 136)* onto
paper, following the directions on page 215. Using the
graphite paper and stylus or dry ballpoint pen, transfer
the pattern pieces to the pine. Lay out the A sides head
to head, to leave a scrap for the A1 brace. Cut the rack

(Continued on page 137)

CUTTING DIRECTIONS

CODE	PIECES	SIZE
A (PINE)	2	½″ x 11″ x 16″ Sides
A1 (PINE)	1	½″ x 2½″ x 12″ Brace
B (PINE)	2	½″ x 11″ x 12″ Top/bottom
B1 (LAT)	2	½″ x ½″ x 2″ Stops
C (LAT)	1	½″ x 3½″ x 12″ Drawer front
C1 (LAT)	1	½″ x 3½″ x 11½″ Drawer back
C2 (LAT)	2	½″ x ½″ x 11½″ Drawer supports
D (LAT)	2	¼″ x 3½″ x 10½″ Drawer sides
D1 (PLY)	1	⅛″ x 11⅜″ x 9¼″ Drawer bottom

FIG. III, 5A ONE-DRAWER BOOK RACK SIDE AND BRACE PATTERNS   1 SQ. = 1"

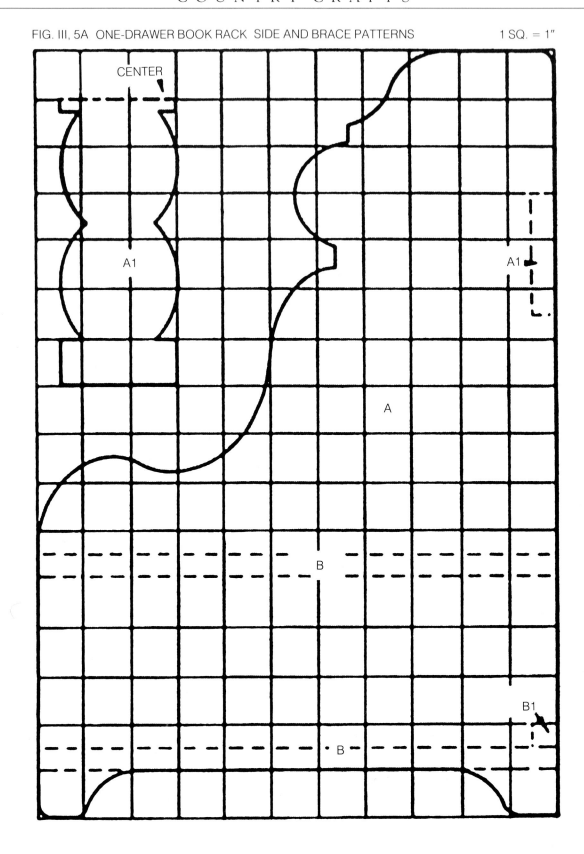

FIG. III, 5B   ASSEMBLY DIAGRAM

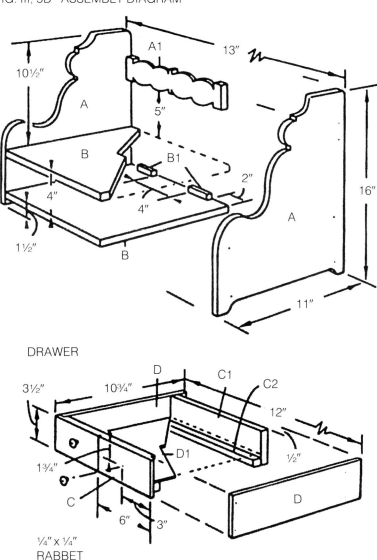

DRAWER

¼" x ¼"
RABBET

and drawer parts to size; the B top/bottom pieces are straight cuts.

3. Using 1-inch brads, glue and nail the A sides to the B top/bottom pieces. Glue and nail the A1 brace between the A sides 5 inches above the B top. Glue and nail the B1 stops in place *(see* FIGS. III, 5A *and* 5B*)*.

4. Cut a ¼-inch square rabbet in both ends of the C drawer front. Make a ¹⁄₁₆-inch-deep saw cut in the outside center of the C drawer front to give the appearance of two drawers. Drill two holes in the C drawer front for the porcelain knobs *(see* FIG. III, 5B*)*.

5. Using ¾-inch brads, glue and nail the D drawer sides to the C drawer front and C1 drawer back. Set in the C1 drawer back ½ inch from the back ends of the D drawer sides. Glue and nail a C2 drawer support to the inside bottom of the C drawer front and C1 drawer

back. Glue the D1 drawer bottom to the C2 drawer supports *(see* FIG. III, 5B*)*.

6. Sand the rack and drawer smooth, and wipe off all the sawdust with the tack cloth. Stain the rack and drawer. When the stain has dried, attach the knobs to the drawer front.

Do what you can,
with what you have,
where you are.
— Theodore Roosevelt

In early America, a home was not complete without wooden boxes. The styles and sizes varied, but boxes were important household items, used to hold clothing, personal belongings, household linens, and even books.

In the 17th century, a family's best clothes and household linens were not stored in closets. They were folded carefully and kept in deep rectangular boxes, with hinged lids, to be used when needed. These boxes sometimes were called Bible boxes, but they were used for more than storing books. Some examples of early wooden boxes are marked with inscriptions that commemorate marriages.

Early wooden boxes usually were made from oak with pine lids. Later, pine alone became popular. After that, a variety of woods were used, including maple, birch and ash. Boxes and their contents were very personal possessions, so they often were part of a woman's dowry, or were presented by the bridegroom to the bride.

Boxes made in the 17th century usually featured carved designs. In the 18th century, elaborate painted motifs became popular. In the 19th century, graining, stenciling and freehand painting were used to decorate boxes.

Anyone can do any amount of work provided it isn't the work he is supposed to be doing at the moment.
— Robert Benchley

SIX-DRAWER SPICE CHEST
(photo, page 135)

Average: For those with some experience in woodworking.

Materials:
5 feet of ½ x 6-inch, and 8 feet of ½ x 4-inch pine lumber; 5 feet of ¼ x 4-inch lattice; six 1-inch-diameter porcelain knobs; ¾- and 1-inch wire brads; wood glue; sandpaper; tack cloth; maple wood stain; paintbrush; saw; drill with ³⁄₁₆-inch bit; hammer.

Directions:
1. Cut the chest and drawer parts to size. The notches in the B sides measure 2 x 3½ inches. Cut ¼-inch square rabbets on the D1 drawer fronts. Drill a ³⁄₁₆-inch-diameter hole in the center of each D1 drawer front for a porcelain knob *(see* Fig. III, 6*)*.
2. Using 1-inch brads, glue and nail the B sides to the A bottom/center pieces; the A center piece should be flush with the top edges of the notches in the B sides *(see* Fig. III, 6*)*.
3. Using 1-inch brads, glue and nail the A1 top to the B sides flush with the sides' upper front and back edges; A1 should overlap B sides equally at each end. Glue the B1 and B2 dividers in place *(see* Fig. III, 6*)*.
4. Using ¾-inch brads, glue and nail the top and bottom drawers together *(see* Fig. III, 6*)*.
5. Sand the chest and drawers smooth, and wipe off all the sawdust with the tack cloth. Stain the chest and drawers; let dry. Attach a knob to each drawer front.

CUTTING DIRECTIONS

CODE	PIECES	SIZE
A (PINE)	2	½″ x 5½″ x 13″ Bottom/center
A1 (PINE)	1	½″ x 3½″ x 14½″ Top
B (PINE)	2	½″ x 5½″ x 8″ Sides
B1 (PINE)	2	½″ x 3½″ x 3½″ Dividers
B2 (PINE)	2	½″ x 5½″ x 3½″ Dividers
C (LAT)	6	¼″ x 3½″ x 5¼″ Bottom drawer sides
C1 (LAT)	6	¼″ x 3½″ x 3¼″ Top drawer sides
D (PINE)	6	½″ x 3½″ x 3½″ Drawer backs
D1 (PINE)	6	½″ x 3½″ x 4″ Drawer fronts
E (PINE)	3	½″ x 3½″ x 4½″ Bottom drawer bottoms
E1 (PINE)	3	½″ x 3½″ x 2½″ Top drawer bottoms

FIG. III, 6 SIX-DRAWER SPICE CHEST

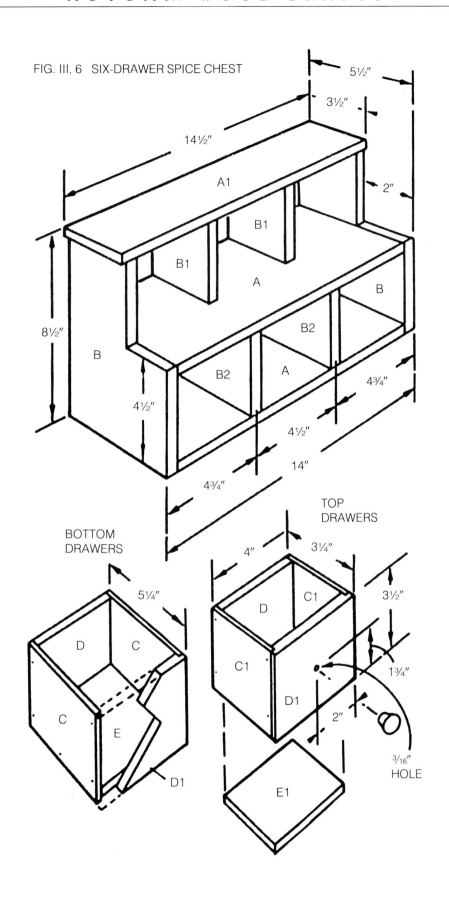

BOTTOM
DRAWERS

TOP
DRAWERS

$^{3}/_{16}$"
HOLE

*The fellow that owns his own home
is always just coming out
of a hardware store.*
— Kin Hubbard

FANCY GRAINED TRUNK

Average: For those with some experience
in woodworking.

Materials:

1¼ panels of ¾-inch-thick 4 x 8-foot AB Interior grade
plywood; 8 feet of ¾-inch cove molding; wallpaper
(optional); 2 decorative brass handles; brass keyhole;
two 3-inch brass hinges; 2-inch finishing nails; graphite
paper; stylus or dry ballpoint pen; wood glue; tack
cloth; sandpaper; 1 quart of acrylic gesso (available at
art supply stores); 1 pint of yellow oxide acrylic paint;
1 pint of acrylic matte medium (available at art supply
stores); 1 large tube of chrome oxide green oil paint;
1 quart of matte varnish; paintbrushes; turpentine;
chamois cloth; cotton cloth; cardboard strip; power
saw; miter box; back saw; hammer; screwdriver; paper.

CUTTING DIRECTIONS

CODE	PIECES	SIZE
A	2	¾" x 19¼" x 24" Sides
B	1	¾" x 24" x 48" Front
C	1	¾" x 24" x 46½" Back
D	1	¾" x 18½" x 46½" Bottom
E	1	¾" x 20" x 48" Lid

Directions:

1. Cut the trunk parts to size. Enlarge the leg cutout pattern in Fig. III, 7B onto paper, following the directions on page 215. Using the graphite paper and stylus or dry ballpoint pen, transfer the leg pattern to the B front and C back, and cut out the front and back legs. Cut the side legs following the dimensions in Fig. III, 7A, rounding the corners. Glue and nail the trunk parts together. Square- or miter-cut the molding, and attach it to the E lid. Attach the E lid to the trunk assembly with the brass hinges *(see Fig. III, 7A)*. Sand the trunk smooth, and wipe off all the sawdust with the tack cloth.

2. Mix all the gesso with all the acrylic matte medium. Paint the trunk with the gesso mixture, and let the mixture dry. Sand and wipe the trunk.

3. Add all the yellow oxide paint to the remaining gesso mixture, and paint the trunk with the yellow mixture. When the yellow coat is dry, sand the trunk lightly, and wipe off all the dust.

4. Mix the green paint with the matte varnish, using enough varnish to give the glaze mixture a creamy texture; too much varnish is better than too little. Paint the trunk lid with the glaze mixture. Wet a 4-inch chamois square, and wring it out. Roll the chamois into a tube, and press it into the glazed lid. Lift up the tube slightly, move it, and repeat to make a wavy design in the glaze. Each time the chamois is pressed into the glaze and lifted, it clears away part of the glaze, revealing the yellow coat underneath. To correct an error, remove the glaze from the area with turpentine and the cotton cloth. Reapply glaze, and repeat.

5. To make the corner shell pattern, hold one end of the cardboard strip in place at a corner, press the cardboard onto the trunk lid, and move the cardboard a little across the trunk lid. Still holding the corner end in place, lift up the cardboard slightly, and repeat to create a rayed effect. When the lid is grained in the desired pattern, let the glaze dry completely before graining another trunk surface. Repeat the glazing and graining on the two sides, front and back. When all the outer surfaces have dried, attach a brass handle to each side, and the brass keyhole to the front.

6. If you wish, paint, glaze and grain the inside of the trunk. Or line the trunk with wallpaper.

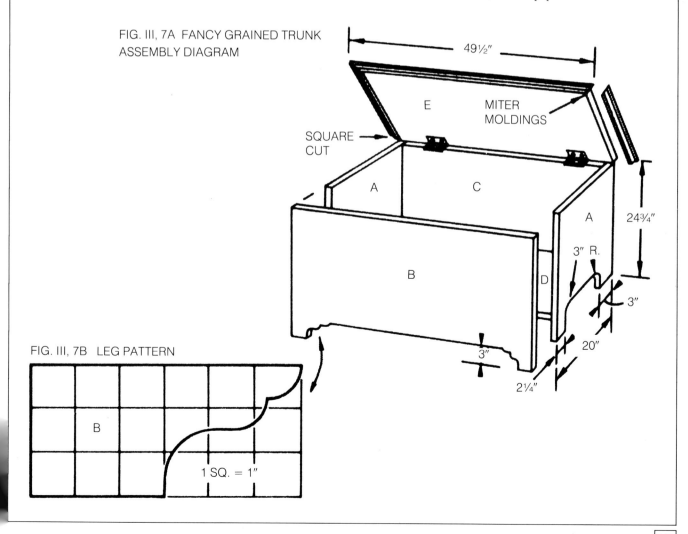

FIG. III, 7A FANCY GRAINED TRUNK ASSEMBLY DIAGRAM

FIG. III, 7B LEG PATTERN

1 SQ. = 1"

FOLK ART CRADLE

Make the cradle for an infant, or for a child to use with dolls at playtime. What makes it country? It's an old-fashioned way to rock baby to sleep, ornamented with classic folk heart decorations.

Average: For those with some experience in woodworking.

Materials:
4 x 4 feet of sanded or overlaid ⅜-inch-thick APA-trademarked plywood; finishing nails; graphite paper; stylus or dry ballpoint pen; wood glue; wood putty; sandpaper; tack cloth; primer; pink, blue and white semigloss latex paints; paintbrushes; sabre saw; drill; hammer; nail set; large compass, or string; tracing paper for pattern.

(Continued on page 144)

CUTTING DIRECTIONS

CODE	PIECES	SIZE
A	2	⅜" x 8¾" x 30" Sides
B	1	⅜" x 12" x 29½" Bottom
C	1	⅜" x 18" x 15¾" Head
C1	2	⅜" x 4¾" x 15½" Head tops
D	1	⅜" x 18" x 15" Foot
D1	2	⅜" x 4" x 15½" Foot tops
E	4	⅜" x 1½" x 18" Rockers

***The hand that rocks the cradle
Is the hand that rules the world.***
—W.R. Wallace

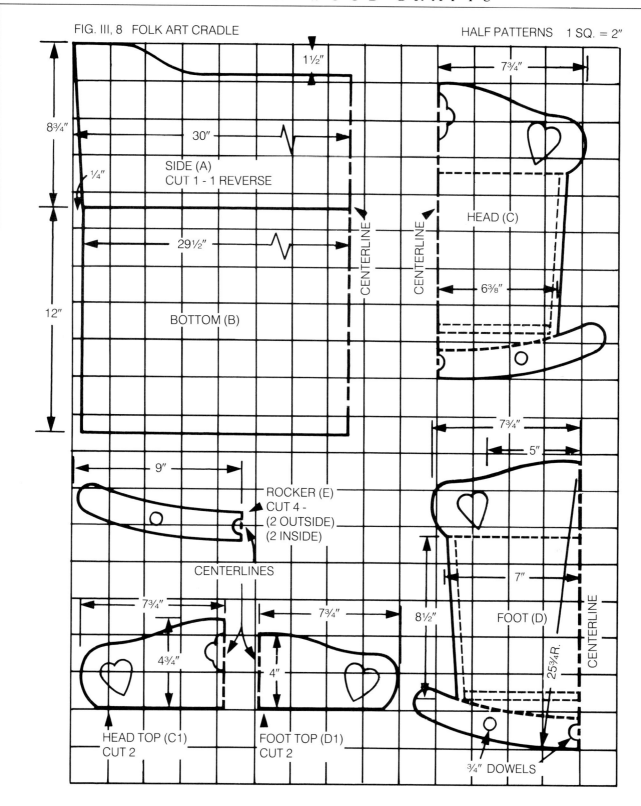

FIG. III, 8 FOLK ART CRADLE

HALF PATTERNS 1 SQ. = 2"

1½"

8¾"

30"

SIDE (A)
CUT 1 - 1 REVERSE

¼"

29½"

BOTTOM (B)

12"

CENTERLINE

CENTERLINE

7¾"

HEAD (C)

6⅜"

CENTERLINE

7¾"

5"

9"

ROCKER (E)
CUT 4 -
(2 OUTSIDE)
(2 INSIDE)

CENTERLINES

7"

8½"

FOOT (D)

25¾ R.

7¾"

7¾"

4¾"

4"

HEAD TOP (C1)
CUT 2

FOOT TOP (D1)
CUT 2

¾" DOWELS

143

Directions:

1. Enlarge the half-patterns in FIG. III, 8 *(page 143)* onto separate sheets of folded tracing paper, following the directions on page 215. Use the large compass or piece of string to draw even curves on the E rocker and on the rocker feet of the C head and D foot. Trace each half-pattern to the other side of the tracing paper, and open the papers for the full patterns.

2. Using the graphite paper and stylus or dry ballpoint pen, transfer the cradle parts to the plywood; use the compass or string to transfer the rocker curves. Cut out the cradle parts with the sabre saw.

3. Glue and nail one E rocker to the bottom front of the C head. Glue and nail a second E rocker to the bottom back of the C head to create a triple thickness rocker foot at the bottom of the C head. Repeat with the remaining E rockers on the D foot. Countersink the nails. Sand to even the triple-thick edges of each rocker foot.

4. Glue and nail one C1 head top piece to the top front of the C head. Glue and nail the other C1 head top piece to the top back of the C head to create a triple thickness head top. Repeat with the D1 foot top pieces on the D foot. Countersink the nails. Sand to even the triple-thick edges of each top.

5. Drill equal-size holes where indicated on the C head for the cloverleaf cutout and tops of the hearts *(see* FIG. III, 8*)*. Repeat for the tops of the hearts on the D foot. Cut out the bottoms of the hearts with the sabre saw. Sand the edges of the cutouts smooth.

6. Rest the B bottom on the top inside edges of the rocker feet on the C head and D foot *(see* FIG. III, 8*)*. Glue and nail the B bottom to the C head and D foot. Countersink the nails.

7. In the same way, glue and nail the A sides to the B/C/D cradle assembly *(see photo, page 142)*.

8. Fill the nail holes with wood putty, let the putty dry, and sand the putty smooth. Sand all the edges of the cradle smooth. Wipe off the sawdust with the tack cloth.

9. Apply a coat of primer to the cradle, and let the primer dry. Using the photo as a guide, paint the cradle.

> ***A hobby is hard work***
> ***you wouldn't do for a living.***
> —Anonymous

COLONIAL WALL RACK

Average: For those with some experience in woodworking.

Materials:

9 feet of ½ x 5½-inch, and 2 feet of ½ x 7½-inch pine lumber; ⅛ x 19 x 31 inches of perforated hardboard; 6 feet of ½ x 1-inch, and 5 feet of ½ x 3¼-inch lattice; 4 feet of 9/16 x 1⅝-inch crown molding; 3 feet of ½ x ¾-inch shoe molding; ⅜-inch-diameter wooden dowel; 3d finishing nails; ½- and 1-inch wire brads; perforated board hooks; graphite paper; stylus or dry ballpoint pen; white glue; sandpaper; tack cloth; rust red paint; honey pine wood stain; paintbrushes; jigsaw or sabre saw; drill with ⅜-inch bit; hammer; paper for pattern.

CUTTING DIRECTIONS

CODE	PIECES	SIZE	
A (PINE)	2	½″ x 5½″ x 32″	Sides
B (PINE)	1	½″ x 5½″ x 19″	Top
C (PINE)	1	½″ x 5½″ x 19″	Bottom
D (LAT)	2	½″ x 1″ x 32″	Back strips
E (HARD)	1	⅛″ x 19″ x 31″	Back
F (PINE)	1	½″ x 7½″ x 23¼″	Outer top
G (LAT)	1	½″ x 3″ x 19″	Front
H (MOLD)	2	9/16″ x 1⅝″ x 7″	Top side molding
J (MOLD)	1	9/16″ x 1⅝″ x 22¼″	Top front molding
K (MOLD)	2	½″ x ¾″ x 6¾″	Bottom side molding
L (MOLD)	1	½″ x ¾″ x 21½″	Bottom front molding
M (DOW)	1	⅜″ dia. x 21″	Dowel
N (DOW)	8	⅜″ dia. x 1″	Pegs
O (LAT)	2	½″ x 3¼″ x 19″	Shelves

Directions:

1. Enlarge the side pattern in FIG. III, 9B *(page 146)* onto paper, following the directions on page 215. Using the graphite paper and stylus or dry ballpoint pen, transfer the side pattern to the A sides. Make the G front pattern by drawing a large single bracket using the dimensions given in the cutting directions; transfer the G front pattern to the 3¼-inch lattice.

(Continued on page 146)

2. Cut the rack parts to size. Drill the holes where indicated in each A side for the M dowel and N pegs *(see* FIG. III, 9B*).* Sand all the rack parts smooth except the hardboard E back. Wipe off all the sawdust with the tack cloth. Paint the E back rust red. Stain all the remaining rack parts honey pine.

3. Using 3d nails, glue and nail the A sides to the B top and C bottom. Using 1-inch brads, glue and nail a D back strip to the back edge of each A side *(see* FIG. III, 9A*).* Turn over the A/B/C/D rack assembly.

4. Using ½-inch brads, nail the E back to the D back strips flush with the A sides, B top and C bottom.

5. Using 3d nails, glue and nail the F outer top to the

B top. The F outer top should be flush with the B top at the back, and centered side to side.

6. Using 1-inch brads, glue and nail the G front to the B top and A sides *(see* FIG. III, 9A*).*

7. Using 3d nails, glue and nail the H top side and J top front molding pieces in place. Repeat with the K bottom side and L bottom front molding pieces. Glue the N pegs in position *(see* FIG. III, 9A*).* Insert and glue the M dowel in the holes in the A sides, centering the dowel between the sides *(see photo, page 145).* Place the O shelves over the N pegs, but do not glue the shelves in place; the shelves are removable. Attach the perforated board hooks to the E back.

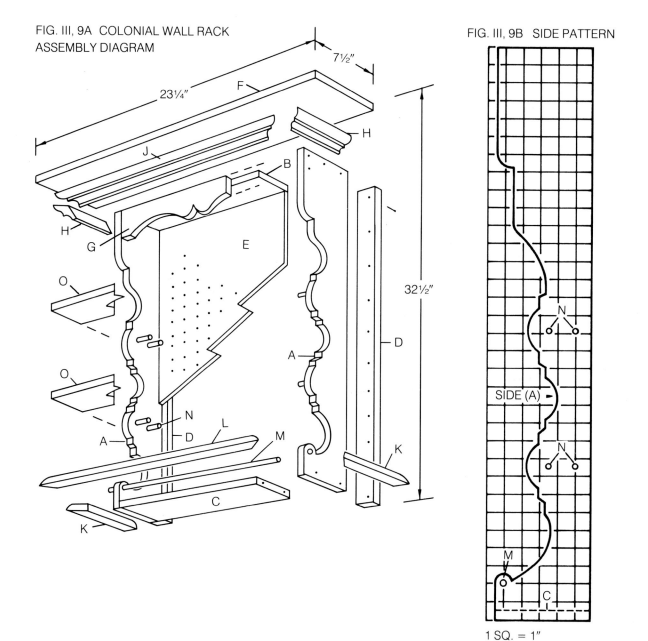

FIG. III, 9A COLONIAL WALL RACK ASSEMBLY DIAGRAM

7½″

23¼″

32½″

FIG. III, 9B SIDE PATTERN

SIDE (A)

1 SQ. = 1″

WOODEN PROP PLANE

Challenging: Requires more experience in woodworking.

Materials:

1 foot of 1⅛ x 1⅛-inch pine lumber; ¼-inch-thick pine scraps; ⅛- and ¼-inch-diameter wooden dowels; two 1½-inch-diameter, and one 1-inch-diameter wooden wheels; three 1-inch-long ¼-inch-diameter wooden axles; wood glue; medium-grade sandpaper; tack cloth; golden yellow, red and navy blue acrylic paints; No. 3 artist's paintbrush; ½-inch paintbrush; saw; drill with assorted bits; rasp; plane; chisel.

Directions:

1. Cut the plane parts to size. Shape the A fuselage with the rasp and plane. Drill two ½-inch-deep ⅞-inch-diameter holes for the pilot seats. Drill two ⅝-inch-diameter holes in the back of the A fuselage, and chisel straight to make a slot for the G tail wheel. Drill a hole on each side of the fuselage at the back for the G1 tail wheel axle *(see Fig. III, 10)*.

2. Glue the C and D tail pieces, and G1 tail wheel axle in place, with the G tail wheel turning freely on the axle. Using sandpaper and glue together, shape the H propellers. Drill a ¼-inch-diameter hole through the center of the H propellers into the center of the A fuselage nose.

3. Drill the holes in the B wings for the E struts *(see Fig. III, 10)*. Glue the A fuselage to the top of the lower B wing. Glue the E struts to the upper and lower B wings. Turn over the plane, and glue the F gear legs and F1 axles in place, with the F2 wheels turning freely on the axles. Attach the H propellers to the A fuselage with the remaining F1 axle.

4. Sand the plane smooth; wipe off the sawdust with the tack cloth. Using the photo as a guide, paint the prop plane.

Cutting Directions

Code	Pieces	Size
A (PINE)	1	1⅛″ x 1⅛″ x 12″ Fuselage
B (PINE)	2	¼″ x 1⅝″ x 10″ Wings
C (PINE)	2	¼″ x 1⅝″ x 2¼″ Tail pieces
D (PINE)	1	¼″ x 1⅝″ x 1½″ Tail piece
E (DOW)	8	⅛″ dia. x 2″ Struts
F (DOW)	2	⅛″ dia. x 1¼″ Gear legs
F1	3	¼″ dia. x 1″ Axles
F2	2	1½″ dia. Wheels
G	1	1″ dia. Tail wheel
G1 (DOW)	1	¼″ dia. x 1″ Tail wheel axle
H (PINE)	2	¼″ x ½″ x 3″ Propellers

FIG. III, 10   WOODEN PROP PLANE

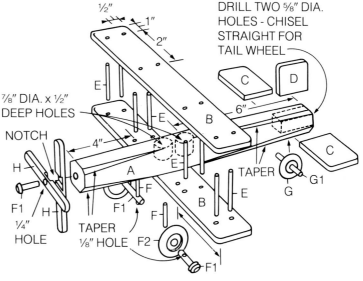

SIT-ON BI-PLANE

Challenging: Requires more experience
in woodworking.

Materials:

⁵⁄₄ x 10 x 30 inches of No. 1 pine lumber; 5½ feet of 1 x 8
No. 2 pine lumber; ⅜-, ¾-, 1-, and 1¼-inch-diameter
wooden dowels; one 3-inch-diameter caster; two 6-
inch-diameter lawn mower wheels; ½-inch No. 6
roundhead screw with 2 washers; 1¼-inch, 1¾-inch,
and 2½-inch No. 6 flathead wood screws; two 3½-inch
lag bolts; 4 washers to fit lag bolts; graphite paper;
stylus or dry ballpoint pen; wood glue; sandpaper; tack
cloth; red, white, blue, silver and olive acrylic paints;
clear polyurethane; paintbrushes; router *(optional)*;
saw; drill with assorted bits; screwdriver; mallet; paper.

Directions:

1. Enlarge the pattern in FIG. III, 11A *(page 150)* onto
paper, following the directions on page 215. Using the
graphite paper and stylus or dry ballpoint pen, transfer
the pattern pieces to the pine, and cut them out. Round
off all the edges; a router with a ¼-inch round over bit
will make the job easier. Cut the other parts to size.
2. Referring to FIG. III, 11A, drill the holes for the
O1 prop dowels, N elevator dowel, L caster tail wheel,
R handle, and F1 center strut. Referring to FIG. III, 11B
(page 151), drill the holes for the J axle, F struts, F1
center strut in the E top wing, O hub dowel in the A
fuselage nose and through the length of the P hub, and
O1 prop dowels on the sides of the P hub. Drill all
holes for a snug fit.
3. Sand the A fuselage smooth, and wipe off all the
sawdust with the tack cloth. Following FIG. III, 11A and
using the photo as a color guide, paint the A fuselage;
do not paint where the seat and wings will be attached.
4. Using glue and 1¼-inch wood screws, attach the B
seat and C seat back to the A fuselage *(see FIG. III, 11B)*.
Glue the F struts to the E top wing and D bottom wing.
5. Put the A fuselage through the D/E/F wing assembly.
Place the D bottom wing in the notch in the A fuselage.
Using glue and 1¾-inch wood screws, attach the D
bottom wing to the A fuselage *(see FIG. III, 11B)*. Place
glue in the holes for the F1 center strut. Using the
mallet, drive the F1 center strut through the E top wing
into the A fuselage until the center strut is flush with
the top of the wing.
6. Using glue and 1¾-inch wood screws, attach the G
gear legs to the H gear block *(see FIG. III, 11B)*. Glue the
J axle in place.
7. Using 1¼- and 2½-inch wood screws, and glue,
attach the G/H/J gear assembly to the underside of the

D bottom wing, centered and 1 inch back from the
wing's front edge.
8. Insert the O hub dowel into the nose of the A
fuselage. Glue the O1 prop dowels to the P hub and Q
prop blades *(see FIG. III, 11B)*.
9. Sand the unpainted plane parts smooth, and wipe off
all the sawdust with the tack cloth. Apply a coat of
polyurethane to the unpainted plane parts.
10. Push the N elevator dowel through the hole in the
A fuselage tail, and press the M elevators onto the
dowel; do not glue the elevators so they can move up
and down.
11. Press the L caster tail wheel into the angled hole in
the A fuselage tail. Drill undersized holes in the J axle
for the lag bolts. Attach the K mower wheels to the J
axle with the lag bolts, and with a washer on each side
of each wheel. Do not over tighten the wheels; they
should be able to spin.
12. Install the R handle. Using the roundhead screw,
attach the O1/P/Q prop assembly to the O hub dowel
on the A fuselage with a washer on each side of the
P hub *(see FIG. III, 11B)*.

CUTTING DIRECTIONS

CODE	PIECES	SIZE
A (PINE)	1	⁵⁄₄″ x 10″ x 29″ Fuselage
B (PINE)	1	¾″ x 5⅝″ x 6″ Seat
C (PINE)	1	¾″ x 3″ x 6″ Seat back
D (PINE)	1	¾″ x 6″ x 22″ Bottom wing
E (PINE)	1	¾″ x 6″ x 24″ Top wing
F (DOW)	4	¾″ dia. x 9″ Struts
F1 (DOW)	1	¾″ dia. x 3″ Center strut
G (PINE)	2	¾″ x 3″ x 5″ Gear legs
H (PINE)	1	⁵⁄₄″ x 3″ x 9″ Gear block
J (DOW)	1	1″ dia. x 10½″ Axle
K	2	6″ dia. Mower wheels
L	1	3″ dia. Caster tail wheel
M (PINE)	2	¾″ x 4″ x 6″ Elevators
N (DOW)	1	⅜″ dia. x 5″ Elevator dowel
O (DOW)	1	⅜″ dia. x 2″ Hub dowel
O1 (DOW)	2	⅜″ dia. x 1⅜″ Prop dowels
P (DOW)	1	1¼″ dia. x 1″ Hub
Q (PINE)	2	¾″ x 1½″ x 6″ Prop blades
R (DOW)	1	¾″ dia. x 5¾″ Handle

When I am grown to man's estate
I shall be very proud and great,
And tell the other girls and boys
Not to meddle with my toys.
— Robert Louis Stevenson

FIG. III, 11A SIT-ON BI-PLANE PATTERN   1 SQ. = 2"

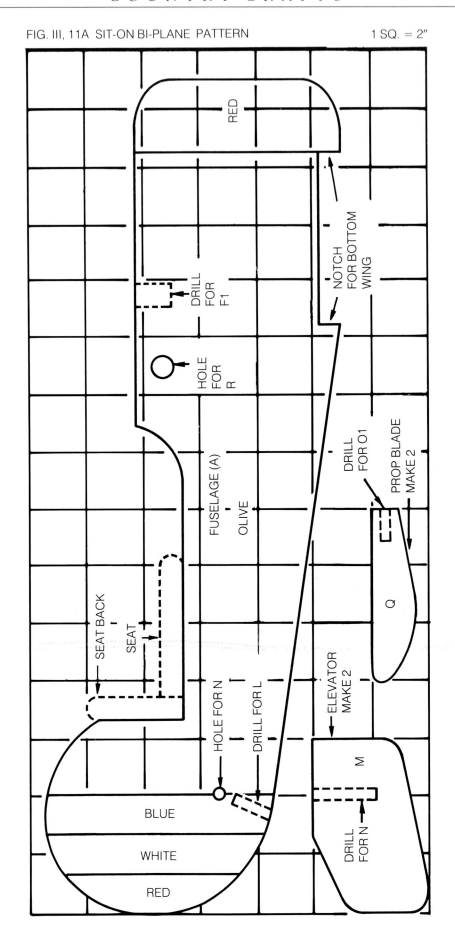

FIG. III, 11B ASSEMBLY DIAGRAM

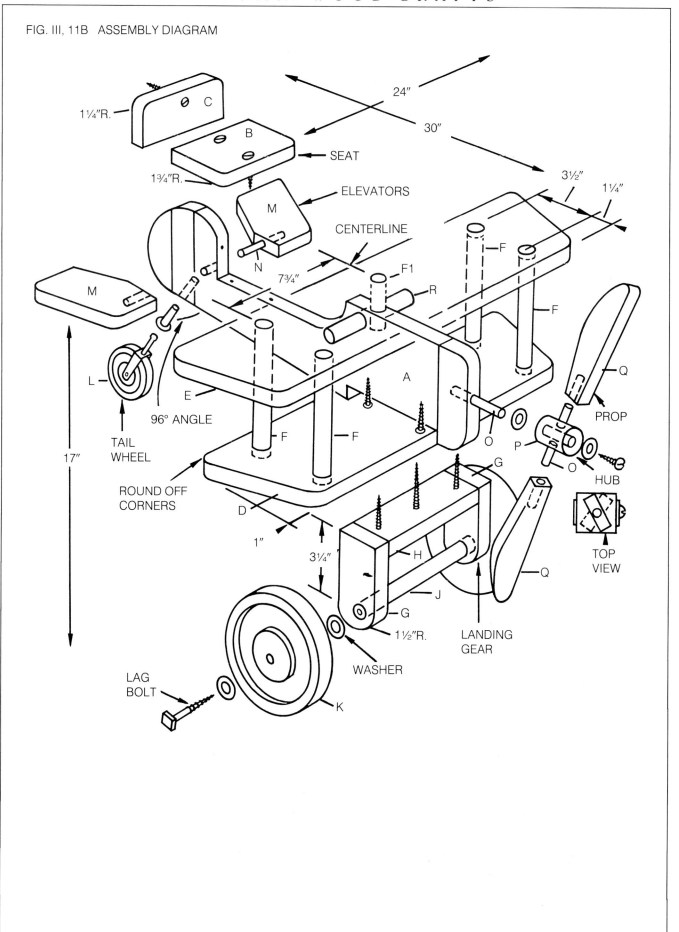

1¼"R.

C

24"

30"

B

SEAT

1¾"R.

ELEVATORS

M

3½"

1¼"

CENTERLINE

N

F

7¾"

F1

R

F

M

F

L

A

Q

E

PROP

96° ANGLE

F

F

O

P

TAIL
WHEEL

O

HUB

17"

G

ROUND OFF
CORNERS

D

1"

H

TOP
VIEW

3¼"

J

Q

G

LANDING
GEAR

1½"R.

WASHER

LAG
BOLT

K

SIT-ON LUMBER TRUCK

What makes it country? A design that recalls an old-fashioned milk truck.

Challenging: Requires more experience in woodworking.

Materials:

Birch plywood: ¼ x 6 x 8 inches, ½ x 12 x 14 inches, and ¾ x 20 x 24 inches; pine scraps: 1 x 3 x 54 inches, 1 x 2 x 18 inches, 1 x 8 x 10 inches, and ½ x ¾ x 12 inches; ⅜- and ⅝-inch-diameter wooden dowels; 4d finishing nails; 1-inch wire brads; 1¾-inch No. 8 flathead wood screws; ⅝-inch and 1-inch No. 8 roundhead wood screws; four ⅜-inch iron washers; white glue; sandpaper; tack cloth; blue, green and black glossy paints; clear and colored polyurethanes; paintbrushes; saw; drill with assorted bits; hammer; screwdriver.

Directions:

1. Cut the truck parts to size. Use the photo and FIG. III, 12 *(page 154)* as guides in shaping the A radiator,
B engine sides, C hood, and D base. Curve the bottom edges of the E axle braces, the side edges of the G bumpers, and the narrow top front edges of the F chassis pieces. Cut out the window in the J divider, rounding the corners slightly. Round the edges of the M side panels, and the front edges of the H seat. Drill blind holes in the D base and K roof for the L roof dowels. Drill a hole in the D base for Q steering post.

2. Sand the truck parts smooth, and wipe off all the sawdust with the tack cloth. Using the photo as a color guide, paint the C hood, H seat, K roof, M side panels, and O wheels. Apply a coat of clear or colored polyurethane to the remaining truck parts.

3. Using 4d nails, glue and nail the C hood to the B engine sides, with the sides recessed ¼ inch from the C hood's side edges. Using glue and 1¾-inch wood screws, attach A radiator, centered, to the B/C assembly flush at the bottom edges of B *(see* FIG. III, 12*)*.

4. Glue the A/B/C engine assembly to the D base centered side to side, and ¼ inch in from the front of D. Then nail through the D base into the B engine sides and A radiator.

5. Glue and nail the H seat to the J divider centered side to side, with the seat's top edge 2½ inches from the divider's bottom edge. Glue the J divider to the K roof centered side to side, and 3¾ inches from the roof's front edge. Then nail through the K roof into the J divider (*see* FIG. III, 12).

6. Turn the H/J/K assembly upside down. Glue the L roof dowels to the K roof. Place glue on the L dowels' open ends, and along the J divider's bottom edge. Place the D base on top of the J/K/L roof assembly, fitting the L roof dowels into the holes in the D base. Nail through the D base into the J divider and each L roof dowel. Turn over the upper truck assembly, and nail through the K roof into each L roof dowel (*see* FIG. III, 12).

7. Drill four holes for 1-inch wood screws in each M side panel (*see* FIG. III, 12). Center each M side panel between a pair of L roof dowels, with the M panel's top edge 3½ inches above the D base. Mark the L dowels for the location of the screw holes, and drill the holes in the dowels. Using 1-inch wood screws, attach the M side panels to the L roof dowels.

8. Glue the R steering wheel to the Q steering post. Glue the Q/R steering assembly to the D base in the hole provided.

9. Using four ⅝-inch wood screws per cover, fasten the N wheel covers to the O wheels (*see* FIG. III, 12).

10. Set the P axles in place on the F chassis pieces (*see* FIG. III, 12). Insert a washer on each end of the axles. Place a dot of glue on each end of the axles, and press the N/O wheel assemblies in place. Glue and nail the E axle braces to the F chassis pieces. Using glue and 1¾-inch wood screws, attach the G bumpers to the front and back edges of the F chassis pieces. Using glue and 1¾-inch wood screws, attach the upper truck assembly to the lower truck assembly by fastening through the D base into the F chassis pieces (*see* FIG. III, 12).

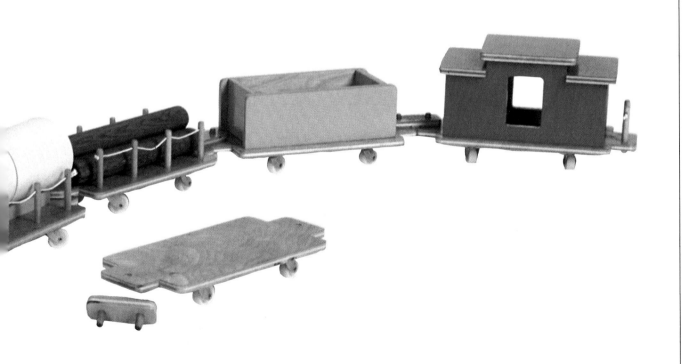

CUTTING DIRECTIONS

CODE	PIECES	SIZE
A	1	½″ x 4″ x 5½″ Radiator
B	2	½″ x 2½″ x 6″ Engine sides
C	1	½″ x 5″ x 7½″ Hood
D	1	¾″ x 24″ x 10″ Base
E	4	½″ x ¾″ x 3″ Axle braces
F	2	¾″ x 2½″ x 22½″ Chassis
G	2	¾″ x 1½″ x 8″ Bumpers
H	1	¾″ x 2″ x 5¾″ Seat

CODE	PIECES	SIZE
J	1	¾″ x 7½″ x 10″ Divider
K	1	¾″ x 10″ x 18″ Roof
L	4	⅝″ dia. x 10¾″ Roof dowels
M	2	½″ x 2½″ x 12″ Side panels
N	4	¼″ x 2½″ dia. Wheel covers
O	4	¾″ x 4″ dia. Wheels
P	2	⅜″ dia. x 8¾″ Axles
Q	1	⅜″ dia. x 4¼″ Steering post
R	1	¼″ x 2½″ dia. Steering wheel

FIG. III, 12   SIT-ON LUMBER TRUCK

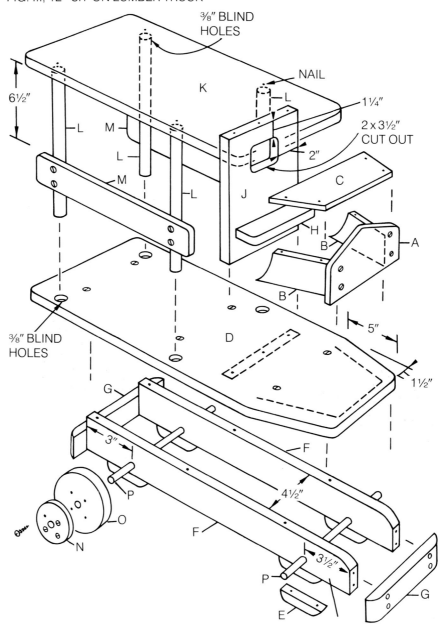

FREIGHT TRAIN
(photo, pages 152-153)

Average: For those with some experience in woodworking.

Materials:

½-inch-thick birch plywood; scrap of 1 x 2 pine; ⅜- and 1¾-inch-diameter wooden dowels; wooden drawer knob; empty wooden spool; one 2-pound, and two 1-pound coffee cans; 6 sets of four 1¼-inch casters; 1¼-inch wire brads; ½-inch roundhead wood screws; ³⁄₁₆ x 1-inch, and ³⁄₁₆ x 1¾-inch bolts with washers and nuts; thin nylon cord; graphite paper; stylus or dry ballpoint pen; white glue; sandpaper; tack cloth; blue and white acrylic paints; clear and colored polyurethanes; paintbrushes; jigsaw or sabre saw; drill with assorted bits; hammer; screwdriver; paper.

Directions:

1. Enlarge the pattern in FIG. III, 13 onto paper, following the directions on page 215. Using the graphite paper and stylus or dry ballpoint pen, transfer one engine base, four standard car bases, one caboose base, two engine cab sides, two coal carrier sides, two caboose sides, and five couplers to the plywood. Cut out the parts, and drill the holes. Also drill four evenly

FIG. III, 13 FREIGHT TRAIN

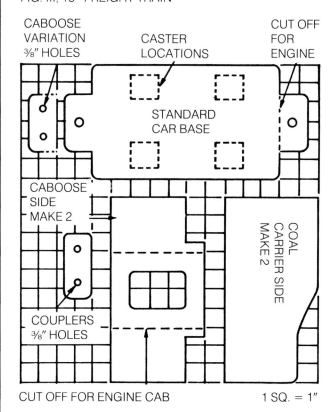

spaced ⅜-inch-diameter holes for dowel rails along each long side of two standard car bases *(see photo, page 152-153)*. Cut the 1 x 2 pine strip to the same length as a car base. Glue and nail the pine strip, centered side to side, to one of the car bases with dowel rail holes to make the tank car base.

2. Using the photo and the cut out plywood parts as guides, also cut out from the plywood one engine cab roof, one coal carrier front end and back end, one caboose long roof piece, two caboose short roof pieces, and two 2-inch-high gondola sides and ends.

3. Sand the wooden train parts smooth, and wipe off all the sawdust with the tack cloth. Using the photo as a guide, apply a coat of clear or colored polyurethane to the wooden train parts. Paint the 2-pound coffee can blue, and the 1-pound coffee cans white.

4. Using the photo as a guide, cut eighteen car rails from the ⅜-inch-diameter dowels. Drill a hole through each rail, near its top, wide enough for the nylon cord to pass through. Sand the dowel rails smooth, and wipe off all the sawdust with the tack cloth. Apply a coat of clear polyurethane to the dowel rails. When the polyurethane is dry, glue the dowel rails in the holes in the two car bases and at the back of the caboose. Thread a length of nylon cord through the rails on each car side to make a railing, and knot the ends of the cord. Repeat on the rails at the back of the caboose.

5. For the tank car, use 1¾-inch bolts to attach 1-pound coffee cans, ends butted, to the pine strip *(see photo)*.

6. For the log hauler, cut the 1¾-inch-diameter dowels to length for logs. Apply a coat of colored polyurethane to the dowel logs, and let the polyurethane dry.

7. For the engine, glue and nail the cab roof to the cab sides. Glue and nail the cab sides to the engine base at the rear. Attach the drawer knob and spool to the 2-pound coffee can *(see photo)*. Using 1-inch bolts, attach the coffee can to the engine base at the front.

8. For the gondola, recess the ends ½ inch along the sides *(see photo)*; glue and nail the ends in place. Glue and nail the sides and ends to a standard car base. Repeat for the coal tender.

9. For the caboose, glue and nail the long roof piece to the sides' top center edges *(see photo)*. Glue and nail the short roof pieces to the sides' top front and back edges. Glue and nail the sides to the base.

10. Using four roundhead screws per caster, fasten a set of casters under each engine, car or caboose base at the locations indicated on the pattern *(see FIG. III, 13)*.

11. Cut ten 1½-inch-long pegs from the ⅜-inch-diameter dowels. Sand the peg ends smooth; wipe off all the sawdust with the tack cloth. Using the pegs and couplers, join together the engine, cars and caboose.

WIN

TER

Spicy-scented pine trees, draped in their winter mantel of soft, white snow. Short days and long nights warmed by the cheerful flickering of a fire. The happy sounds of rosy-cheeked children playing in the tingling, crisp air. Winter, as seen through country eyes, is lovely indeed.

And winter begins with the joy and magic of the Yuletide season. Stitch an array of quilted ornaments to hang on your tree or to decorate a wreath. Capture the tender mystery of Christmas with a hand-crafted balsa wood crèche.

Quilts and afghans go hand-in-hand with winter weather. Stitch heirloom-quality quilts in one of three classic designs, or knit or crochet a chill-chasing afghan. And, as a tip of the hat to St. Patrick's Day, there's a special section devoted to Aran Isle afgans and pillows.

As the winter draws to a close, the promise of Spring fills the air and we celebrate the season of romance. Create one of our "heartfelt" projects and show the one you love just how special they are.

Winter is a time to gather together and celebrate the ending of one year, the beginning of the next—and what better way to enjoy these cozy days, than by crafting something special!

C·H·R·I·S·T·M·A·S
IN THE COUNTRY

E ven if you won't be going "over the river and through the woods" at Christmas time, you can enjoy the old-fashioned warmth and merriment of a country Christmas.

QUILTED ORNAMENTS

What makes it country? A crafting style that's been handed down through the generations from our colonial ancestors.

Easy, Average and Challenging: The directions for the ornaments are arranged in sequence from easy—achievable by anyone, to challenging—requiring more experience in sewing and quilting.

Materials:

42-inch-wide cotton print fabrics: ¼ yard each of 4 greens, 3 reds, 1 cream, and 1 white; muslin; solid white and solid black cotton fabric scraps; synthetic stuffing; cotton/polyester batting; red and green sewing threads; red or green quilting thread; gold metallic thread; DMC embroidery floss: 1 skein of No. 8 Gold; between needle; embroidery needle; ⅓ yard of ½-inch-wide black ribbon; ⅔ yard of narrow gold braid; 6 small white pompons; 6-inch see-through plastic ruler; 12-inch ruler; clear plastic template material (available at craft, quilting and some sewing supply stores), or index cards.

General Directions:

1. Wash and dry all the fabrics to shrink them. Iron the fabrics. The directions for the ornaments that use the largest amounts of fabric are given first. The remaining fabrics can be used as patches in the ornaments that require more piecing.
2. All the patterns *(pages 160-163)* are full size. Trace the pattern for an ornament onto the plastic template material or an index card. If the ornament has more than one pattern piece, trace the pattern pieces separately onto the template material or index cards. When the ornament directions call for adding a seam allowance to the pattern piece templates, add ⅛ inch around the sides of each piece. Cut out the templates.

3. Make the fabric ornament top. Place the top right side up on the batting, and cut the batting using the top as the pattern. Quilt the top to the batting following the ornament directions. Trim the excess batting.

4. Place the quilted ornament top right side down on the right side of one of the print fabrics used to make the top, and cut out the ornament back. Using a ⅛-inch seam allowance, stitch around the outside raw edges, leaving a 1-inch opening along one side. Turn the ornament right side out, and press. Turn in the open edges, and slipstitch the opening closed *(see Stitch Guide, page 214)*. Cut a 7-inch length of gold metallic thread, sew it through a corner of the ornament, and knot the thread ends to make a loop for a hanger.

QUILTED ORNAMENTS

FIG. IV, 1A HEART

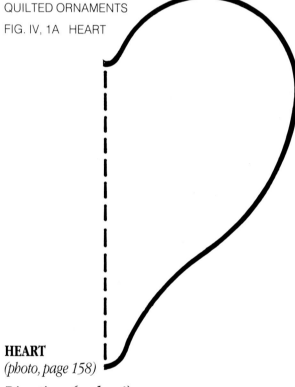

HEART
(photo, page 158)

Directions (makes 4):
1. Cut off the selvages on the red, green, and cream or white print fabrics. Cut two 1 x 9-inch strips from each of the print fabrics, cutting the strips lengthwise on each ¼ yard of fabric. Also cut one 9 x 13-inch rectangle each from the muslin, batting, and one of the print fabrics for the backing.

2. Place the batting on top of the muslin. Place two print strips, right sides together, on top of the batting along the short right-hand edge of the rectangle. Sew a ⅛-inch seam through all layers along the long left-hand edge of the strips. Press the top strip open.

3. Place a third print strip on top of the left-hand strip, right sides together. Sew a ⅛-inch seam along the long left-hand edge of the strips, and press the top strip

open. Repeat until the rectangle is covered with strips.

4. Make a full pattern from the heart half-pattern in FIG. IV, 1A. Make a template of the full heart pattern following General Directions, Step 2 *(page 159)*; do not add a seam allowance. Trace four hearts on the wrong side of the backing rectangle, leaving ½ inch between the hearts. Place the strip-quilted rectangle right side up on a flat surface. Place the backing rectangle, wrong side up, on the strip-quilted rectangle, and pin all the layers together in the centers of the traced hearts.

5. Stitch along each traced heart outline, leaving a 1-inch opening along one side. Cut out the hearts, leaving a ¼-inch seam. Turn the hearts right side out, and press. Turn in the open edges, and slipstitch the openings closed. Attach a hanger at the top of each heart following General Directions, Step 4.

TREE
(photos, pages 158 and 165)

Directions (makes 6):
1. Cut a 9 x 12-inch rectangle from the batting, and from a red or green print fabric. Also cut a 9 x 13-inch rectangle from contrasting fabric for the backing.

2. Make a template of the tree pattern in FIG. IV, 1B following General Directions, Step 2 *(page 159)*; do not add seam allowance. Trace 6 trees on the wrong side of the small fabric rectangle; leave ½ inch between trees.

FIG. IV, 1B TREE

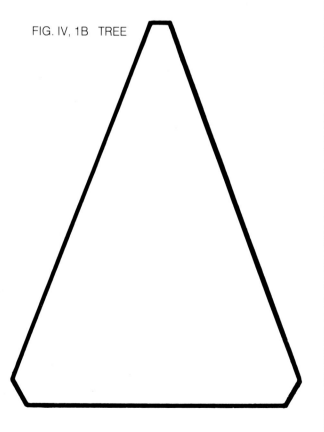

3. Place the backing rectangle, right side up, on top of the batting. Place the rectangle with the traced trees, wrong side up, on the backing. Pin all the layers together in the centers of the traced trees.

4. Stitch around each traced tree, leaving a 1½-inch opening at the bottom edge. Cut out the trees, leaving a ¼-inch seam. Turn the trees right side out, and press.

5. Cut six 2-inch lengths of black ribbon. Turn in the open edges of one tree. Fold one ribbon length in half, and place its raw edges in the tree's seam opening. Slipstitch the opening closed, catching in the ribbon for a tree trunk as you sew. Repeat with the remaining ribbon lengths and trees. Sew a 7-inch length of gold metallic thread through the center of a pompon. Sew the pompon to the top of one tree, and knot the ends of the metallic thread to make a loop for a hanger. Repeat with the remaining pompons and trees.

FIG. IV, 1C
CANDY CANE

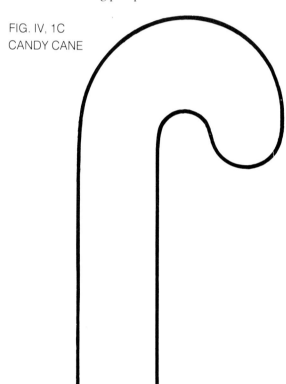

CANDY CANE
(photos, pages 158 and 165)

Directions:

1. Make a template of the candy cane pattern in Fɪɢ. IV, 1C following General Directions, Step 2 *(page 159)*; do not add a seam allowance.

2. Cut a 7-inch square of print fabric. Fold the fabric right sides together, and trace the cane on one wrong side. Stitch around the traced cane, leaving the bottom edge open. Cut out the cane, leaving a ¼-inch seam. Clip the curves, turn the cane right side out, and stuff it.

Turn in the open edges; slipstitch the opening closed.

3. Cut a 7-inch length of gold braid; tie it into a bow around the neck of the cane. Sew a 7-inch length of gold metallic thread through the back seam of the cane under the braid. Pull up the ends of the thread until they are even, and knot the thread at the base to anchor the bow. Knot the thread ends to make a hanger loop.

FIG. IV, 1D   CHECKERBOARD

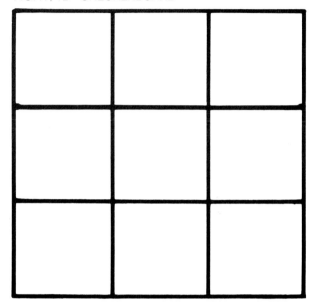

CHECKERBOARD
(photos, pages 158 and 165)

Directions:

1. Using the plastic ruler, draw a 1-inch square on the plastic template material or index card, and add a ⅛-inch seam allowance on all sides. Cut out the square.

2. *Red and Cream Checkerboard:* Cut four red print squares and five cream print squares. Alternating colors, sew squares together to make three rows of three squares each; start one row with a red print square. Placing the row that starts with the red square in the middle, sew rows together, seams matching, to make the ornament top *(see* Fɪɢ. IV, 1D*)*. Cut the batting following General Directions, Step 3 *(page 160)*. Machine-quilt diagonally across the red squares. Finish the ornament following General Directions, Step 4.

3. *Red and Green Checkerboard:* Cut four green print squares and five red print squares. Make the ornament top following the directions in Step 2 above; start one horizontal row with a green print square, and place that row in the middle of the checkerboard. Cut the batting following General Directions, Step 3. Machine-quilt in the ditch of the seams along the sides of the green squares. Finish the ornament following General Directions, Step 4.

APPLIQUÉD HEART IN CENTER SQUARE
(photos, pages 158 and 165)

Directions:

1. Make templates of pattern pieces A through E in Fig. IV, 1E following General Directions, Step 2 *(page 159)*, and adding the seam allowance.

2. Cut four green print A pieces, two red print B pieces, two red print C pieces, one white print D piece, and one red print E piece. Sew the long edge of an A piece to each edge of the D piece, and press the seams toward A. Sew the B pieces to the top and bottom edges of A/D, and press the seams out. Sew the C pieces to the side edges of A/B/D, and press the seams out *(see Fig. IV, 1E)*. Appliqué the E heart in the center of D.

FIG. IV, 1E   APPLIQUÉD HEART IN CENTER SQUARE

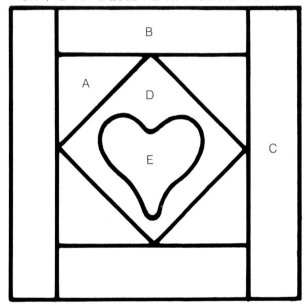

3. Cut the batting following General Directions, Step 3 *(page 160)*. Using the between needle and quilting thread, quilt by hand around the heart *(see Stitch Guide, page 214)*. Quilt by hand or machine in the ditch of the seams. Finish the ornament following General Directions, Step 4.

PINWHEEL
(photo, page 158)

Directions:

1. Make templates of pattern pieces A through C in Fig. IV, 1F following General Directions, Step 2 *(page 159)*, and adding the seam allowance.

2. Cut four green print A pieces, four red print B pieces, and four white print C pieces. Following the diagram in Fig. IV, 1F, sew each B piece to a C piece, and press the seam toward B. Sew each B/C to an A

FIG. IV, 1F PINWHEEL

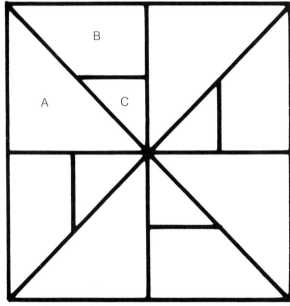

piece along the long edge to make a square, and press the seam toward A. Sew the squares together, with the C pieces in the center, to make the ornament top.

3. Cut the batting following General Directions, Step 3 *(page 160)*. Quilt by hand or machine on the B/C pieces in the ditch of the diagonal A seams. Finish the ornament following General Directions, Step 4.

PIECED HEART
(photo, page 158)

Directions:

1. Make templates of pattern pieces A through D in Fig. IV, 1G following General Directions, Step 2 *(page 159)*, and adding the seam allowance.

2. Cut eight white print A pieces, eight red print A pieces, one red print B piece, one red print C piece,

FIG. IV, 1G PIECED HEART

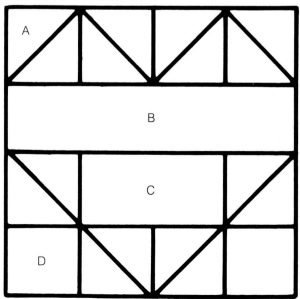

and two white print D pieces. Sew a red A piece and a white A piece together along their long edges to make a square. Repeat with the remaining A pieces. Press four of the squares' seams toward the white pieces, and four toward the red pieces. Following the diagram in Fig. IV, 1G, sew the squares and the C and D pieces together to make three rows. Sew the rows and B piece together from top to bottom to make the ornament top. Press the row seams in one direction.

3. Cut the batting following General Directions, Step 3 *(page 160)*. Quilt by hand or machine in the ditch around the outside seams of the heart. Finish the ornament following General Directions, Step 4.

FOUR-PATCH CENTER *(photo, page 158)*

Directions:

1. Make templates of pattern pieces A through E in Fig. IV, 1H following General Directions, Step 2 *(page 159)*, and adding the seam allowance.

2. Cut two red print A pieces, two green print A pieces, two solid black B pieces, two solid black C pieces, four white print D pieces, two red print E pieces, and two green print E pieces. Alternating colors, sew the red and green E pieces together to form a checkerboard square, and press the seams. Sew the long edge of a D piece to each edge of the checkerboard, and press the seams toward D. Sew the C pieces to opposite side edges of D/E, and press the seams out. Sew the B pieces to opposite side edges of C/D/E, and press the seams out. Sew the long edge of an A piece to each edge of B/C/D/E, and press the seams toward A *(see Fig. IV, 1H)*.

3. Cut the batting following General Directions, Step 3 *(page 160)*. Quilt by hand or machine in the ditch of the seams. Finish the ornament following General Directions, Step 4.

FIG. IV, 1H FOUR-PATCH CENTER

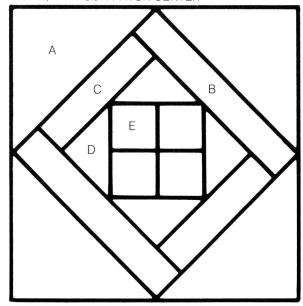

FIG. IV, 1I EMBROIDERED HEART CENTER

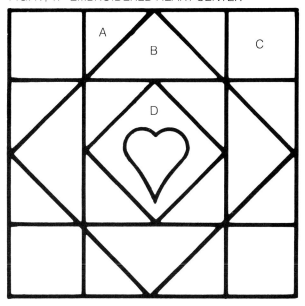

EMBROIDERED HEART CENTER
(photos, pages 158 and 165)

Directions:

1. Make templates of pattern pieces A through D in Fig. IV, 1I following General Directions, Step 2 *(page 159)*, and adding the seam allowance.

2. Cut twelve green print A pieces, four red print B pieces, four red print C pieces, and one solid white D piece. Lightly trace the heart shape in Fig. IV, 1I onto the center of the D piece. Sew the long edge of an A piece to each edge of the D piece, and press the seams toward A. Sew the long edge of an A piece to each short edge of the B pieces, and press the seams out. Sew two A/B rectangles, along their long B edges, to the side edges of the A/D square. Sew a C piece to each short end of the remaining A/B rectangles. Sew these rectangles to the top and bottom edges of A/B/D *(see Fig. IV, 1I)*. Press the seams out.

3. Cut the batting following General Directions, Step 3 *(page 160)*. Quilt by hand or machine in the ditch of the seams.

4. Using the embroidery needle and Gold floss, embroider the heart in the center of the D piece in chain stitch, embroidering through the batting *(see Stitch Guide, page 214)*. Start at the center top of the heart. Embroider the right side, slip the needle back to the top of the heart, and embroider the left side. Finish the ornament following General Directions, Step 4 *(page 160)*.

WOOD-CARVED ORNAMENTS
(photo, page 158)

Average: For those with some experience in crafting.

Materials for One Ornament:
6-inch square of ½-inch-thick clear pine lumber; sharp craft or pocket carving knife; graphite paper; stylus or dry ballpoint pen; medium- and fine-grade sandpaper; No. 0000 steel wool; tack cloth; small can of lacquer or plastic spray; enamel paints for plastic models in colors desired; paintbrushes; scroll saw, coping saw, band saw or jigsaw; drill with ¼-inch bit; ruler; protractor; compass; ribbon or yarn; white glue; paper for pattern.

Directions:
1. Using the ruler and protractor, find the center of the pine square. Using the compass, draw a 4½-inch-diameter circle on the pine. Then draw a 5-inch-diameter circle around the first circle.

2. Enlarge the design of your choice in FIG. IV, 2 onto paper, following the directions on page 215. Using the graphite paper and stylus or dry ballpoint pen, transfer the design within the 4½-inch-diameter pine circle.

3. Drill a ¼-inch-diameter hole in the center of each area of the design you wish to cut away. Saw around the areas carefully, and remove them; a simple design requires less saw work.

4. Use carving to give depth to the design. Using the craft or pocket carving knife, cut a line along the design to mark where you wish to start carving. Carve out small amounts at a time in the direction of the cut line to avoid carving into another part of the pattern. Cut and carve until you achieve the desired results.

5. Using the medium-grade sandpaper, sand the entire ornament to round the edges, and remove saw and knife marks. Using the fine-grade sandpaper and steel wool, sand the ornament as smooth as possible. Wipe off all the sawdust with the tack cloth. Apply a light coat of lacquer or plastic spray to the ornament, and let the ornament dry completely.

6. Paint the ornament from the center outward; paint the border last. If you wish, mark the ornament with the year, or the name of a family member. When the paint is dry, cut a length of ribbon or yarn, fold it into a loop, and glue the loop to the top back of the ornament for a hanger.

FIG. IV, 2   WOOD-CARVED ORNAMENTS

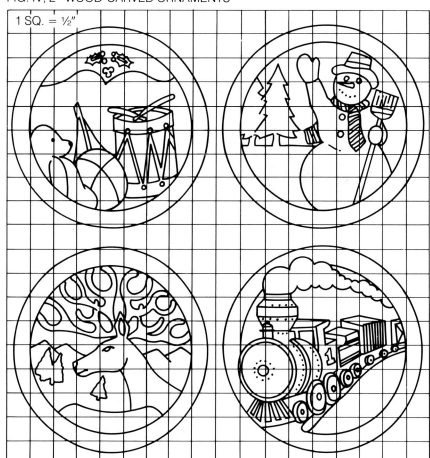

1 SQ. = ½"

CALICO WREATH
WITH QUILTED ORNAMENTS

What makes it country? Christmas-color calicos combined in a cheerful, homey wreath.

Average: For those with some experience in sewing.

Materials:

Quilted Ornaments *(directions, pages 159-163)*; 3 yards of dark green calico fabric; synthetic stuffing; 19-inch square of sturdy cardboard; 7-inch-diameter plate or other circular object; large compass, or ruler, pencil and 9-inch length of string; sewing needle and thread *(optional)*; pinking shears; pins; white glue.

Directions:

1. Using the large compass, trace a 9-inch-radius circle on the cardboard. Or use the ruler to find the center of the cardboard, and pin one end of the string to the center. Stretch the string taut, hold the pencil alongside it, and trace a circle on the cardboard. Cut out the cardboard circle.

2. Place the plate or other circular object in the center of the cardboard circle, and trace around the plate. Cut out the traced smaller circle.

3. Pad both sides of the cardboard wreath form with synthetic stuffing, using glue to hold the stuffing in place. Make the back of the wreath flatter than the front.

4. Using the pinking shears, cut the calico into 2-inch-wide strips. Wrap the calico strips around the wreath form, holding the strips in place with pins where necessary. Or lightly glue the strips in place.

5. Pin the Quilted Ornaments in a pleasing arrangement on the wreath; we used Tree, Candy Cane, Checkerboard, Appliquéd Heart in Center Square, and Embroidered Heart Center ornaments. Or, if you wish, tack the ornaments to the wreath.

BALSA WOOD CRÈCHE

Average: For those with some experience in woodworking and crafting.

Materials:

3 x 36-inch balsa wood planks: 1 each 1/32 inch thick, 1/16 inch thick, 3/32 inch thick, and 1/8 inch thick; graphite paper; stylus or dry ballpoint pen; utility knife with No. 11 blade; natural, colonial pine, and special walnut wood stains; varnish *(optional)*; 3 small paintbrushes; white glue; 4 boxes; tracing paper for pattern.

Directions:

1. Trace the full-size patterns in Figs. IV, 3A and 3B *(pages 168-169)* onto tracing paper. Using the graphite paper and stylus or dry ballpoint pen, transfer the pattern pieces to the balsa wood planks according to the thicknesses indicated for the pieces in Figs. IV, 3A and 3B.
2. Cut out the wood pieces with the utility knife. As you cut the pieces, place them in separate boxes by category: shepherds in one box, wise men in another box, and so on.
3. Stain all the wood pieces designated No. 1 in Figs. IV, 3A and 3B with natural stain, let them dry completely, and return them to their boxes. Repeat with the remaining wood pieces and stains. Cut all the bases from the 1/8-inch-thick balsa, and stain the bases special walnut. Let the stained wood dry for 24 hours before completing the figures.
4. Using Figs. IV, 3A and 3B as placement guides, assemble and glue together each figure. If you wish, finish the figures with a coat of varnish.

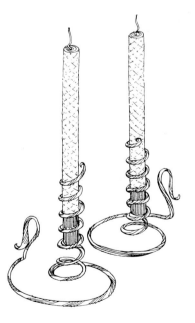

***Glory to God in the highest,
and on earth peace,
good will toward men.***
—The Bible, Luke, 2:14

FIG. IV, 3A   BALSA WOOD CRÈCHE   FULL SIZE PATTERN

STAINS: 1 = NATURAL   2 = COLONIAL PINE   3 = SPECIAL WALNUT

FIG. IV, 3B   BALSA WOOD CRÉCHE   FULL SIZE PATTERN

BALSA WOOD THICKNESS: A = $\frac{3}{32}$"   B = $\frac{1}{16}$"   C = $\frac{1}{32}$"   D (BASES ONLY) = $\frac{1}{8}$"

Q · U · I · L · T · S
FOR A
WINTER'S NIGHT

Τ he cold nights
of winter make warm bedclothes a necessity. These
classic quilts provide protection against the chill,
and add beauty to any room in your home.

SQUARE-IN-THE-MIDDLE QUILT
(about 85 x 97 inches)

What makes it country? A simple, classic design carried out in old-fashioned calico.

Average: For those with some experience in quilting.

Materials:
45-inch-wide fabric: 6 yards of solid brown for quilt back and binding, 3 yards of brown/orange calico (A), 4½ yards light shade calico (B), and 3¼ yards of brown/white calico (C); matching sewing threads; brown crochet thread; synthetic batting; clear plastic template material (available at craft, quilting and some sewing supply stores), or crisp cardboard; sharp white and hard lead pencils; safety pins, or quilter's pins and darner or milliner's needle; curved needle *(optional)*; masking tape.

Directions (¼-inch seams allowed):
1. Pattern: Draw a 3-inch square, a 4-inch square, and a 5⅞-inch square on the plastic template material or cardboard, making sure the squares' corners are 90°. Label the squares small, medium, and large. Also trace the triangle in FIG. IV, 4A *(page 172).* Cut out the templates carefully; they include the ¼-inch seam allowance. Using the white and hard lead pencils, trace around the templates on the wrong side of the fabrics.
2. Cutting: From fabric A, cut two 4 x 83-inch borders, two 4 x 68-inch borders, and 50 large squares.
From fabric B, cut two 4 x 90-inch borders, two 4 x 75-inch borders, 12 medium squares, 196 small squares, and 200 triangles. **From fabric C,** cut two 4 x 97-inch borders, two 4 x 82-inch borders, and 245 small squares.

(Continued on page 172)

COUNTRY WAYS

• *Quilts North and South* •

In colonial America, pieced or patchwork quilts were the most common type of quilt among frugal Northerners. Women pieced together their quilts from scraps of worn-out clothing, and neighbors often traded patches to make their quilts more interesting and beautiful.

Appliqué quilts, on the other hand, were symbols of affluence. Northern women would have considered it wasteful to use new fabric just for appliqués, but Southern women — the wives and daughters of plantation owners — practiced their appliqué needlework on fine fabrics such as silks and satins. Most fine appliqué quilts that date back to colonial times came from the South. The less elaborate, everyday Southern bed coverings usually were made by plantation slaves.

It is possible to guess an antique quilt's origin, and perhaps its age, by examining the number of cotton seeds left in the batting. Quilts made in the North before the invention of the cotton gin in 1793 usually have far more seeds than those made in the South during the same period, when slaves picked the seeds from the cotton by hand.

*Let us love winter,
for it is the spring of genius.*
—Pietro Aretino

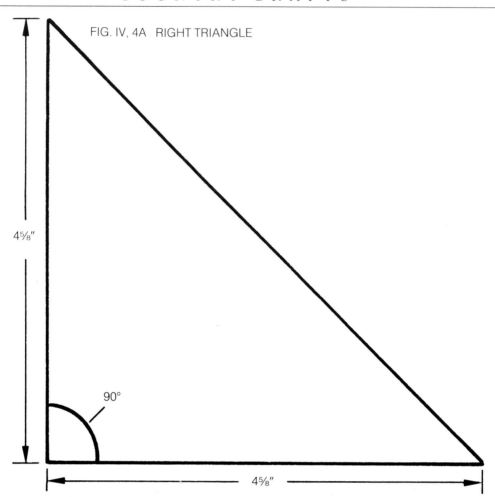

FIG. IV, 4A   RIGHT TRIANGLE

4⅝"

90°

4⅝"

3. *Diamond Block:* Sew the long edge of a B triangle to each edge of a large A square *(see* Fig. IV, 4B*)*. Make 50 Diamond blocks.

4. *Nine-Patch Block:* Following the diagram in Fig. IV, 4C, sew small B and C squares side by side to make three horizontal rows of three squares each. Sew the rows together from top to bottom, seams matching, to make the block. Make 49 Nine-Patch blocks.

FIG. IV, 4B   DIAMOND BLOCK

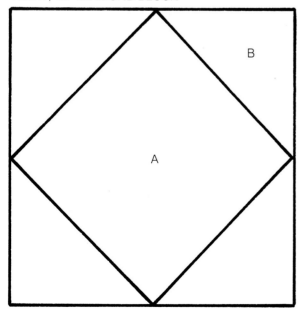

B

A

FIG. IV, 4C   NINE-PATCH BLOCK

C	B	C
B	C	B
C	B	C

FIG. IV, 4D   SQUARE-IN-THE-MIDDLE QUILT

B						C						B
	B					B					B	
		B				A				B		
			D	9	D	9	D	9	D	9	D	
			9	D	9	D	9	D	9	D	9	
			D	9	D	9	D	9	D	9	D	
			9									
			D									
C	B	A	9							A	B	C
			D									
			9									
			D									
			9									
			D									
		B				A				B		
	B					B					B	
B						C						B

5. Assembling: Following the diagram in FIG. IV, 4D, and alternating Diamond and Nine-Patch blocks, sew eleven horizontal rows of nine blocks each. Start six rows with a Diamond block, and five rows with a Nine-Patch block. Alternating starting blocks, sew the rows together from top to bottom, seams matching.

6. Borders: Sew an 83-inch A border to each side edge of the patchwork. Sew a medium B square to each end of the 68-inch A borders. Sew these borders to the top and bottom edges of the patchwork. Repeat to attach the remaining borders, side edges first *(see* FIG. IV, 4D*)*.

7. Quilt Back: Cut across the quilt back fabric to make two 3-yard-long 45-inch-wide pieces. Sew the pieces together side by side along a selvage.

8. Basting: Spread the quilt back, wrong side up, on a clean, flat surface, and tape down the corners. Cut a piece of batting to fit the quilt back. Spread the batting and then the quilt top, right side up and centered, on top of the quilt back. Using safety pins, pin-baste the quilt layers together from the center straight out to each edge, and diagonally out to each corner. Add more rows of pins about 6 inches apart. Or pin with quilter's pins, and then use a darner or milliner's needle, single lengths of light-colored sewing thread and long stitches to baste through the quilt layers in the same way you pinned.

9. Binding: Trim the batting flush with the quilt top. Trim the quilt back to extend 1¼ inches beyond the quilt top on all sides. Fold the raw edges of the quilt back over the quilt top to be the binding, and pin the binding in place. Turn under the binding's raw edges, and slipstitch the binding to the quilt top, mitering the corners *(see Stitch Guide, page 214)*.

10. Tying: Use a curved needle or a darner needle; a curved needle will make the stitching easier. Thread the needle with a length of crochet thread; do not knot the thread. Starting at the center of the quilt, and working from the top, take a short stitch through all three layers, leaving a 2-inch tail of thread. Take another stitch on top of the first. Cut the thread about 2 inches away from the stitches. Tie the thread tails into a square knot, and trim the ends to ½ inch. Space more ties evenly across the quilt about 4 to 6 inches apart, making sure to tie in the same places within each kind of quilt block. Remove the basting.

• Pin Magic •

Pins have been associated with magical things since ancient times. Historians tell us the earliest pins were made from thorns and sanded animal bones, and were used to make clothing and tents.

Metal always has been associated with magic. When pins first were fashioned from metal, it was believed witches would use the pins to cast spells. This probably is the origin of the children's rhyme, "see a pin and pick it up, and all the day you'll have good luck;" if good folks picked up stray pins, witches couldn't use the pins to hex them.

Like many old saws, rhymes about pins sometimes contradict each other. Here are a few examples:

Pick up a pin, pick up a sorrow.
See a pin, let it lie, and all the day
    you'll have to cry.
Pass up a pin, pass up a friend.
Lend a pin, spoil a friendship.

COURTHOUSE STEPS QUILT
(about 83 x 99 inches)

What makes it country? Courthouse Steps is a variation on the Log Cabin motif, one of the oldest American quilt patterns.

Average: For those with some experience in quilting.

Materials:
45-inch-wide fabric: 6 yards of solid off-white for quilt back and binding, about 5½ yards of different dark shade calicos, about 4 yards of different light shade calicos, and ⅛ yard of medium shade calico; matching sewing threads; coordinating color crochet thread; 7¼ yards of muslin or similar fabric; synthetic batting; safety pins, or quilter's pins and darner or milliner's needle; curved needle *(optional)*; masking tape.

Directions:
1. *Cutting: From the muslin,* cut thirty 17-inch squares. ***From the medium shade fabric,*** cut thirty 2-inch center squares. Make sure the squares' corners are 90°. Cut or tear **the light and dark fabrics** carefully into 2-inch-wide strips.

2. *Courthouse Steps Block:* Fold a muslin square in half along both diagonals, and press to find the square's center. Repeat with a medium-shade center square. Pin the center square over the muslin square, matching centers *(see* Fig. IV, 5A, *page 176)*. Baste along the edges of the center square *(see* Fig. IV, 5B*)*. With right sides together, pin a light strip to the top edge of the center square, with the left and top edges flush *(see* Fig. IV, 5C*)*. Stitch ¼ inch from the top edge. Trim the right edge flush with the center square. Press the seam up. Repeat at the bottom edge, and press the seam down. Stitch a dark strip to the right edge of the patches the same way *(see* Fig. IV, 5D*)*. Press the seam out. Repeat on the left edge *(see* Fig. IV, 5E*)*. Continue to add strips in the same order, light strips at the top and bottom, dark strips at the sides *(see* Fig. IV, 5F*)*, until the muslin is covered with five rows of strips around the center square. The strips around the outside edges will look ¼ inch wider to allow for the seams in assembling the quilt top. Baste around the edges of the quilt block. Make 30 quilt blocks.

3. *Assembling:* With dark edges matching, sew six horizontal rows of five quilt blocks each. Sew the rows together vertically, seams matching, to complete the quilt top *(see photo)*.

4. *Finishing:* Finish the quilt following the directions in Square-in-the-Middle Quilt, Steps 7 to 10 *(page 173)*. When tying the quilt, tie within a center quilt block, then repeat within the other quilt blocks.

COURTHOUSE STEPS QUILT

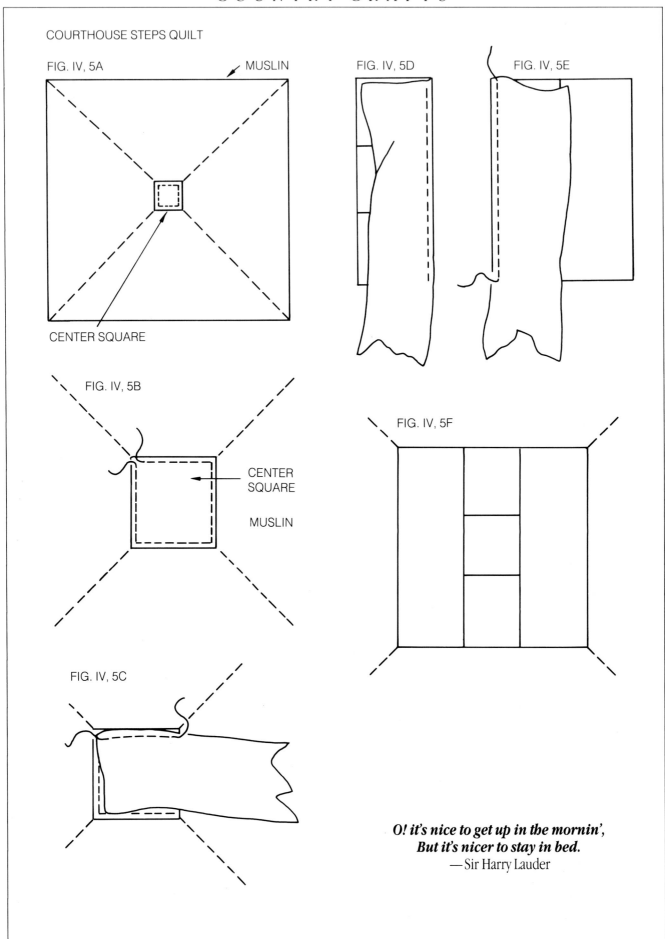

FIG. IV, 5A

MUSLIN

CENTER SQUARE

FIG. IV, 5B

CENTER
SQUARE

MUSLIN

FIG. IV, 5C

FIG. IV, 5D

FIG. IV, 5E

FIG. IV, 5F

O! it's nice to get up in the mornin',
But it's nicer to stay in bed.
— Sir Harry Lauder

COUNTRY WAYS

• *Quilting Bees* •

In pioneer towns and rural areas, the quilting bee often provided the only opportunity a woman had to enjoy the companionship of other women. Although men traveled and worked together, women spent most of their days tending a family and house or farm. The quilting bee was a good way for women to work together and visit. Quilting bees were so important to women's lives that Susan B. Anthony began her crusade for women's suffrage by speaking at quilting bees.

A woman usually pieced a quilt top herself. When the top was finished, she invited friends and neighbors to help her quilt it. After a full day's stitching, the women would be joined by their men for supper and, perhaps, dancing.

The quilting bee was a place for women to exchange the latest news. Often young women held quilting bees to announce their engagements officially and to make bridal quilts. Sometimes a prospective bride would piece the bridal quilt herself, but in some communities it was considered bad luck for the bride-to-be to work on the quilt at all. Her friends would work together to make the quilt as a gift for the bride. Usually each friend made a quilt block, which she signed as a remembrance of their friendship.

Friendship, or remembrance, quilts were made not only for brides, but for friends, clergymen, and town elders. In some communities, teenage girls gathered together for friendship quilt parties. Each girl brought scraps of her old dresses from which to make her quilt block, which she embroidered with her name and the date. The finished blocks were stitched together into a quilt top, which was presented to one of the group. The recipient then hosted a quilting bee to finish the quilt, thus providing the chance for two get-togethers.

COUNTRY WAYS

• *Caring for Quilts* •

Whether you own an antique quilt handed down through the generations, or have created your own heirloom-quality quilt, these tips will help you care for your quilts so you can enjoy them for years to come.

Airing Quilts: The safest method for airing a quilt 50 or more years old is to place it outdoors in the shade on a nice, breezy day. Never hang a quilt on a clothesline; this weakens the stitches. To air a quilt indoors, drape the quilt over a chair for half a day.

Cleaning Quilts: Lay the quilt flat on a bed or other clean surface. On top of the quilt, place a 24-inch square of fiberglass screening with all its edges taped. Slowly and gently vacuum over the screen using a low-power, hand-held vacuum with a clean brush attachment. When the first section is clean, carefully move the screen to another part of the quilt, and repeat the vacuuming. When the top of the quilt is done, turn back half the quilt and vacuum the bed or surface under it. Repeat with the other half of the quilt. Turn over the quilt, and repeat the screen vacuuming on the back. This method should not be used more than once a year. Never vacuum a quilt with beading on it.

Dry or wet cleaning of a quilt should be done only by an expert who specializes in quilt cleaning. There is no guarantee that either method will work, or that the cleaning process will not damage the quilt.

Storing Quilts: Wrap each quilt in acid-free tissue paper, washed muslin, washed cotton, or cotton/polyester-blend sheets. If the quilt has a metal part attached to it, remove the metal, if possible, before wrapping the quilt for storage. Place the wrapped quilt in an acid-free box, and store the box in a cool area that is clean, dry, dark, and well-ventilated. Relative humidity should be about 50%. Do not store quilts in the attic or basement, which tend to be damp. Do not store quilts in Styrofoam®, plastic, or any product made from wood, such as cardboard or regular (not acid-free) paper.

PIECED STAR QUILT
(about 86 x 96 inches)

What makes it country? The pattern is a variation on the classic star patchwork motif.

Average: For those with some experience in quilting.

Materials:

45-inch-wide fabric: 6 yards of solid off-white for quilt back and binding, 3 yards of first dark shade calico (A), 1 yard of medium shade calico (B), 1¼ yards of second dark shade calico (C), and 6¼ yards of light shade calico (D); matching sewing threads; off-white crochet thread; synthetic batting; clear plastic template material (available at craft, quilting and sewing supply stores), or crisp cardboard; sharp white and hard lead pencils; safety pins, or quilter's pins and darner or milliner's needle; curved needle *(optional)*; masking tape.

Directions (¼-inch seams allowed):

1. Patterns: Draw a 4⅞-inch right triangle, and a 6½-inch right triangle, on the plastic template material or cardboard. Label the triangles small and large. Also draw a 2½-inch square, and a 2½ x 16½-inch rectangle, making sure their corners are 90°. Cut out the templates carefully; they include the ¼-inch seam allowance. Using the white and hard lead pencils, trace around the templates on the wrong side of the fabrics.

2. Cutting: From fabric A, cut two 4½ x 98-inch borders, two 4½ x 88-inch borders, and 160 small triangles. **From fabric B,** cut 80 small triangles. **From fabric C,** cut 80 small triangles, and 12 squares. **From fabric D,** cut two 4½ x 90-inch borders, two 4½ x 80-inch borders, 31 rectangles, 80 large triangles, and 160 small triangles.

3. Pieced Star Block: Sew a small C triangle and a small D triangle together along their long edges to make a square. Repeat to make four C/D squares. Make four squares with small A and D triangles the same way. Following the diagram in FIG. IV, 6, sew the A/D squares together to make a large square. Sew the long edges of a small A triangle and a small B triangle to the short edges of a large D triangle, with the A triangle on the left, to make a rectangle. Repeat to make four A/B/D rectangles. Following FIG. IV, 6, sew two A/B/D rectangles to the side edges of the large square to make Row 2. Sew a C/D square to each short end of the remaining A/B/D rectangles, with the C triangle outward, to make Rows 1 and 3. Sew the rows together from top to bottom, seams matching, to make the quilt block. Make 20 quilt blocks.

4. Assembling: Using the photo as a placement guide, and alternating quilt blocks and D rectangles, sew five wide horizontal rows of four blocks and three rectangles. Alternating D rectangles and C squares, sew four narrow horizontal rows of four rectangles and three squares. Alternating wide and narrow rows, sew the rows together from top to bottom, seams matching.

5. Borders: Sew a 90-inch D border to each side edge of the patchwork, and trim the borders' ends flush with the patchwork. Sew the 80-inch D borders to the top and bottom edges of the patchwork, and trim the ends flush with the side borders. Attach the A borders the same way to complete the quilt top.

6. Finishing: Finish the quilt following the directions in Square-in-the-Middle Quilt, Steps 7 to 10 *(page 173)*. When tying the quilt, tie within a center quilt block, then repeat the tying in the same places within the other quilt blocks.

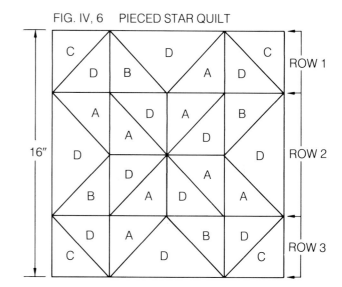

FIG. IV, 6   PIECED STAR QUILT

*Love is meat and drink,
and a blanket to boot.*
—New England saying

CHILL-CHASING
A·F·G·H·A·N·S

These snuggly warm coverlets practically invite you to curl up on the sofa. There are afghans both to knit and crochet, and each would make a lovely addition to any home.

FLUFFY AFGHAN
(about 37 x 43 inches, plus fringe)

Average: For those with some experience in crocheting.

Materials:
Mohair-type yarn (50-gram, 130-yard ball): 7 balls of Lavender (A), and 3 balls each of Aqua (B) and Winter White (C); size M crochet hook, OR ANY SIZE HOOK TO OBTAIN GAUGE BELOW; 11½-inch-long piece of cardboard.

Gauge: In Pattern Stitch, 17 sts (1 pattern repeat) = 5¼ inches; 5 rows = 3 inches.

Notes: *When working Rows 2 to 13 of the Pattern Stitch, work only in the back loop of each stitch.*

When changing colors, draw the new color through the last 2 loops of the stitch you are working on.

When working over a strand of yarn, keep the strand at an even tension, neither too loose nor too tight. At the end of each color section, pull the strand that is carried so it is at an even tension.

Directions:
1. Afghan: Starting at the bottom edge with A, ch 122. Now beg Pattern Stitch as follows. **Row 1:** Sc in 2d ch from hook, * sk next ch, sc in each of next 7 ch, 3 sc in next ch, sc in each of next 7 ch, sk next ch; rep from * across, ending with sc in last ch — 121 sc. **Row 2 (right side):** Ch 1, turn, working in back loops only, sc in first sc, [* sk next sc, sc in each of next 8 sc, insert hook back into the last st worked and with A draw up a loop so there are two loops on hook *; drop A strand in front of work but do not cut and draw B through the 2 loops on hook to complete sc; working over A strand and using B, sc in same st as last sc (3 sc in one st made); sc in each of next 6 sc; insert hook into next st and with B draw up a loop; drop B in front of work, pick up A and draw through the 2 loops on hook; working over B strand and using A, sk next st]; rep from

[to] until 18 sts rem, then rep from * to * once; drop A strand in back of work and draw B through the 2 loops on hook, sc in same st as last sc (3 sc in one st made); sc in each of next 7 sc, sk next sc, sc in last sc. **Row 3:** With B, ch 1, turn, sc in first sc, [* sk next sc, sc in each of next 8 sc; insert hook back into last st worked and with B draw up a loop *; drop B strand in front of work and draw A through 2 loops on hook; working over B strand and using A, sc in same st as last sc (3 sc in one st made); sc in each of next 6 sc; insert hook into next st and with A draw up a loop; drop A in front of work, pick up B and draw through 2 loops on hook; working over A strand and using B, sk next st]; rep from [to] until 18 sts rem, then rep from * to * once; drop B strand in back of work and draw A through 2 loops on hook, sc in same st as last sc (3 sc in one st made); sc in each of next 7 sc, sk next sc, sc in last sc. **Rows 4 and 6:** Rep Row 2. **Rows 5 and 7:** Rep Row 3. At the end of Row 7, draw C through the last 2 loops of the last sc. Fasten off B. **Row 8:** With C, ch 1, turn, sc in first sc, [* sk next sc, sc in each of next 8 sc; insert hook back into last stitch worked and with C draw up a loop *; drop C strand in front of work and draw A through 2 loops on hook; working over C strand and using A, sc in same st as last sc (3 sc in one st made); sc in each of next 6 sc; insert hook into next st and with A draw up a loop; drop A strand in front of work, pick up C and draw through the 2 loops on hook; working over A strand and using C, sk next st]; rep from [to] until 18 sts rem, then rep from * to * once; drop C strand in back of work and draw A through 2 loops on hook, sc in same st as last sc (3 sc in one st made); sc in each of next 7 sc, sk next sc, sc in last sc. **Row 9:** With A, ch 1, turn, sc in first sc, [* sk next sc, sc in each of next 8 sc; insert hook back into last st worked and with A draw up a loop *; drop A strand in front of work and draw C through 2 loops on hook; working over A strand and

using C, sc in same st as last sc (3 sc in one st made); sc in each of next 6 sc; insert hook into next st and with C draw up a loop; drop C strand in front of work, pick up A and draw through 2 loops on hook; working over C strand and using A, sk next st]; rep from [to] until 18 sts rem, then rep from * to * once; drop A strand in back of work and draw C through 2 loops on hook, sc in same st as last sc (3 sc in one st made); sc in each of next 7 sc, sk next sc, sc in last sc. **Rows 10 and 12:** Rep Row 8. **Rows 11 and 13:** Rep Row 9. Rep Rows 2 to 13 for Pattern Stitch until Afghan measures 43 inches from beg, ending with Row 13. Fasten off C; do not cut A.

2. Edging, Row 1: Working across the top edge of the Afghan, with A, ch 1, turn, sc in each st across. **Row 2:** Do not turn, ch 1, working from left to right, sc in each st across for reverse sc. Fasten off. Work on the bottom edge as follows: With the right side facing you, join A in last st of foundation ch, ch 1. Continue to work the edging the same way as the other edge. Fasten off.

3. Fringe: Wind A 9 times around the 11½-inch length of the cardboard. Clip the yarn at one edge to make 23-inch-long strands. Holding the strands together, fold them in half to make a loop. Insert the crochet hook from the back to the front in the first st on the bottom edge of the Afghan, and draw the loop through. Draw the strands' loose ends through the loop, and pull tightly to knot the fringe. Repeat in every 3rd st along the bottom edge of the Afghan, ending with the last st. Repeat along the top edge. Trim the fringe ends evenly.

Extreme cold when it first arrives
seems to generate
cheerfulness and sociability.
For a few hours
all life's dubious problems
are dropped in favor
of the clear and congenial task
of keeping warm.
— E.B. White

VIOLET AFGHAN
(about 49 x 71 inches)

Average: For those with some experience in crocheting and cross stitch.

Materials:
Brunswick Windrush yarn (3½-ounce skein): 9 skeins of Ecru (A), 2 skeins of Light Denim (B), and 1 skein each of Purple (C), Earth Green (D), Meadow Green (E), and Maize (F); size 10 or J afghan hook, OR ANY SIZE HOOK TO OBTAIN GAUGE BELOW; size J crochet hook *(optional)*; tapestry needle.

Gauge: Each rectangle = 12 x 14 inches.

Note: *The cross stitch design is embroidered on the rectangles after they are crocheted, but before they are joined together.*

Afghan Stitch: With the afghan hook, crochet chain indicated. **Row 1:** Draw up a lp in 2nd ch from hook and each ch across, leaving all lps on hook. Work off lps as follows: Yo, draw through 1 lp, * yo, draw through 2 lps; rep from * across, leaving 1 lp on hook. **Row 2:** Skip first upright bar, draw up a lp in next upright bar and each upright bar across, leaving all lps on hook; work off lps as for Row 1. Repeat Row 2 to end.

Directions:
1. Rectangle (make 20): With A, ch 29. Work in afghan st for 33 rows. If you wish, work the last row and the rectangle edging with a size J crochet hook instead of the afghan hook. **Last Row:** Sl st in each st across; do not fasten off.

2. Rectangle Edging, Rnd 1: Ch 1, 2 sc in same corner sp, sc in end of each row to next corner, 3 sc in

(Continued on page 184)

FIG. IV, 7   VIOLET AFGHAN

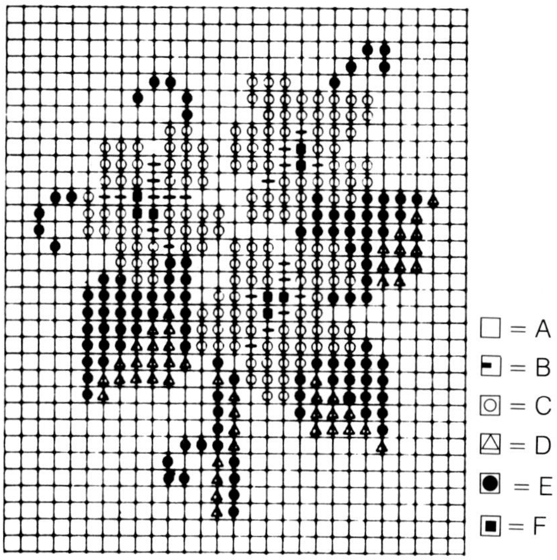

□ = A
▣ = B
◎ = C
△ = D
● = E
▪ = F

corner, sc in other side of each ch to next corner, 3 sc in corner, sc in end of each row to next corner, 3 sc in corner, sc in each sl st to corner, 1 more sc in first corner; drop A, with B, join with sl st to first sc.

Rnd 2: With B, ch 3, 1 dc in same corner st, dc in each sc around, working 3 dc in each corner, end with 1 more dc in first corner, fasten off B; with A, join with sl st to 3rd ch of starting ch. **Rnd 3:** With A, ch 3, 3 dc in same corner st, dc in each dc around, working 5 dc in each corner, end with 1 more dc in first corner, join with sl st to 3rd ch of starting ch. Fasten off A.

3. Blocking: Pin each rectangle to the finished measurements on a padded, flat surface. Cover the rectangles with a damp cloth, and let them dry; do not press the rectangles.

4. Embroidering: Using the tapestry needle, cross stitch the violet design in Fig. IV, 7 *(page 182)* centered on each rectangle *(see Stitch Guide, page 214).* Each symbol in Fig. IV, 7 represents one cross stitch in the color indicated.

5. Joining: With A, working through the back lp of each dc, sew the rectangles together from the center of a corner to the center of the next corner, matching sts. Sew the rectangles in 5 rows of 4 rectangles each.

6. Afghan Edging: Join A in any corner, ch 3, dc in same sp, dc in each dc to next afghan corner, 3 dc in corner; continue in this way, end with 1 more dc in the first corner, join with sl st to 3rd ch of starting ch. Fasten off.

COUNTRY WAYS

• Crochet •

The name crochet comes from the French word meaning "hook." The origin of the craft is not clear, but the technique has been known for hundreds of years.

Crochet came to America with the first European settlers, but did not become widely popular in Europe or America until the early 19th century. The Irish, immigrating to the United States in large numbers, popularized crocheted trims and garments in this country.

Today we work crochet in wool and heavy yarns as well as cotton thread, but the earliest crocheted work was done with the finest threads of cotton and silk — much like early lace-making.

PINEAPPLE STRIP AFGHAN
(about 53 x 69 inches, including border)

Average: For those with some experience in crocheting.

Materials:
Red Heart Super Sport 3-ply yarn (3-ounce ball): 11 balls of Pale Green; size G aluminum crochet hook, OR ANY SIZE HOOK TO OBTAIN GAUGE BELOW; tapestry needle.

Gauge: Pineapple Strip = 4¾ inches wide, including border; Popcorn Strip = 3 inches wide, including border; for both Strips, 7 rows = 3 inches.

Note: *Afghan is worked in strips, then sewn together.*

Directions:

1. Pineapple Strip (make 7): Starting at a narrow end, ch 19. **Row 1:** Dc in 4th ch from hook, ch 5, sk next 6 ch, in next ch work dc, ch 3, dc; ch 5, sk next 6 ch, dc in each of next 2 ch. **Row 2 (right side):** Ch 2 loosely (counts as first dc), turn, dc in next dc, ch 3, sk next 5 ch, 7 dc in ch-3 sp between next 2 dcs, ch 3, sk next 5 ch, dc in next dc, dc in top of turning ch. ***Hereafter ch 2 at beg of row counts as first dc unless otherwise stated. Row 3:*** Ch 2, turn, dc in next dc, ch 1, sk next 3 ch, dc in next dc, (ch 1, dc in next dc) 6 times; ch 1, sk next 3 ch, dc in next dc, dc in 2nd ch of turning ch. **Row 4:** Ch 2, turn, dc in next dc, ch 1, sk next ch-1 sp, *yo, insert hook in ch-1 sp between next 2 dc, yo and draw up a lp, yo and through first 2 lps on hook, yo, insert hook in same sp, yo and draw up a lp, yo and through first lp on hook, yo and through all 4 lps on hook —* **cluster (cl) made;** (ch 1, cl in next ch-1 sp) 5 times; ch 1, sk next ch-1 sp, dc in next dc, dc in 2nd ch of turning ch. **Row 5:** Ch 2, turn, dc in next dc, ch 2, cl in sp bet first 2 cl, (ch 1, cl in sp bet next 2 cl) 4 times; ch 2, sk next ch, dc in next dc, dc in 2nd ch of turning ch. **Row 6:** Ch 2, turn, dc in next dc, ch 3, cl in sp bet first 2 cl, (ch 1, cl in sp bet next 2 cl) 3 times; ch 3, sk next 2 ch, dc in next dc, dc in 2nd ch of turning ch. **Row 7:** Ch 2, turn, dc in next dc, ch 5, cl in sp bet first 2 cl, (ch 1, cl in sp bet next 2 cl) twice; ch 5, sk next 3 ch, dc in next dc, dc in 2nd ch of turning ch. **Row 8:** Ch 2, turn, dc in next dc, ch 6, cl in sp bet first 2 cl, ch 1, cl in sp bet next 2 cl, ch 6, sk next 5 ch, dc in next dc, dc in 2nd ch. **Row 9:** Ch 2, turn, dc in next dc, ch 5, work dc-ch 3-dc in sp bet next 2 cl, ch 5, sk next 6 ch, dc in next dc, dc in 2nd ch —pineapple pattern completed. Rep Rows 2 to 9 for a total of 18 pineapples. Rep Rows 2 to 8 once. **Last Row:** Ch 2, turn, dc in next dc, ch 5, work dc-ch 1-dc in sp bet next

(Continued on page 186)

*We shall never be content
until each man makes his own
weather and keeps it to himself.*
—Jerome K. Jerome

2 cl, ch 5, sk next 6 ch, dc in next dc, dc in 2nd ch—153 rows. Mark the top edge. Fasten off.

2. Pineapple Strip Border: Work around each strip. **First Long Edge:** From the right side, attach yarn with sl st to 2nd ch at upper left corner, ch 6, dc in same ch, * ch 1, dc in top of next row; rep from * across, end with ch 1, dc in foundation ch of beg ch-3, ch 3, dc in same ch. **Bottom Edge:** Work along the base chain. Ch 1, sk next dc, dc in next ch, (ch 1, sk next ch, dc in next ch) 6 times; ch 1, sk next ch, work dc-ch 3-dc in end ch. **Second Long Edge:** * Ch 1, dc in top of next row; rep from * across, end with dc in top of end dc, ch 3, dc in same dc. **Top Edge:** * Ch 1, sk next dc, dc in next ch, (ch 1, sk next ch, dc in next ch) twice *, ch 1, sk next dc, dc in next sp; rep from * to * once, ch 1, sk next dc, join with sl st to 3rd ch at beg. Fasten off.

3. Popcorn Strip (make 6): Starting at a narrow end, ch 11. **Row 1:** Dc in 4th ch from hook, ch 2, sk next 2 ch, sl st in next ch, *ch 1 (yo, insert hook in same st, yo and draw up a lp, yo and through first 2 lps on hook) twice, yo, insert hook in same st, yo and draw up a lp, yo and through first lp on hook, yo and through all 5 lps on hook, sl st in same st—popcorn stitch (pcn st) made on reverse side;* ch 2, sk next 2 ch, dc in each of next 2 ch. **Row 2 (right side):** Ch 2 (counts as first dc), turn, dc in next dc, ch 2, tilt work toward you, work dc through the 2 lps at back of pcn st, ch 2, dc in next dc, dc in top of turning ch. **Row 3 (pcn st row):** Ch 2, turn, dc in next dc, ch 2, sl st in next dc, pcn st in same dc, ch 2, dc in next dc, dc in top of turning ch. Rep Rows 2 and 3 for a total of 77 pcn sts—153 rows. End with pcn st row. Mark the top edge. Fasten off.

4. Popcorn Strip Border: Work around each strip. **First Long Edge:** Work the same as the border for the Pineapple Strip. **Bottom Edge:** Work along the base chain. Ch 1, sk next dc, dc in next ch, (ch 1, sk next ch, dc in next ch) twice, ch 1, sk next ch, work dc-ch 3-dc in end ch. **Second Long Edge:** Work the same as the border for the Pineapple Strip. **Top Edge:** Ch 1, sk next dc, dc in next ch, ch 1, sk next ch, dc in back 2 lps of pcn st, ch 1, sk next ch, dc in next ch, ch 1, join with sl st to 3rd ch at beg. Fasten off.

5. Blocking: Pin each Pineapple Strip right side down on a padded, flat surface to measure 4¾ x 67½ inches. Holding a steam iron over the strip, steam the strip lightly; do not place the iron directly on the strip. Let the strip dry thoroughly before removing the pins. Pin each Popcorn Strip right side up on a padded, flat surface to measure 3 x 67½ inches. Steam the Popcorn Strips the same way as the Pineapple Strips.

6. Assembling: Starting at the lower right corner of the afghan, from the right side, pin the strips together in alternating order starting and ending with a Pineapple Strip. With yarn and the tapestry needle, sew the strips together from the right side with an overcast st, working through the back lp only of each st and keeping the seams as elastic as the strips. Start in the center ch of one corner and end in the center ch of the next corner. Start each seam at the end opposite the start of the last seam to prevent the ends of the afghan from tapering.

7. Afghan Edging, Rnd 1: From the right side, attach yarn with sl st in the upper right corner sp, ch 6, dc in same sp, working across top edge, * (ch 1, dc in next dc) 9 times; ch 1, dec over next 2 corners as follows: Yo, insert hook in the center corner ch of the same strip, yo and draw up a lp, yo and through first lp on hook, yo and through next 2 lps on hook, yo, insert hook in the center corner ch of the next strip, yo and draw up a lp, yo and through first lp on hook, yo and through next 2 lps on hook, yo and through all 3 lps on hook; (ch 1, dc in next dc) 5 times; ch 1, dec over the center ch of the next 2 corners; rep from * across, end last rep with ch 1, (dc in next dc, ch 1) 8 times, dc in last dc, ch 1, work dc, ch 3, dc all in corner sp. Working across one long side, * ch 1, dc in next dc; rep from * across, end with dc in last dc, ch 1, work dc, ch 3, dc all in corner sp. Continue across the bottom edge the same as the top edge. Continue across the second long side the same as the first long side, end with ch-1, join with sl st to 3rd ch at beg. **Rnd 2:** ** Ch 2, sk next ch, sl st in next ch, * ch 2, sk next ch, sl st in next dc; rep from * across the first long side; rep from ** around the entire afghan, end with ch-2, join with sl st to first sl st. Fasten off. Steam the edging from the wrong side.

COUNTRY WAYS

COUNTRY WAYS

• Aran Knits •

The heavy white woolen sweaters we call fisherman's sweaters are more correctly known as Aran knits, named for the islands off the west coast of Ireland. They have been worn by generations of fishermen because of their warmth and sturdiness.

For our Irish knit afghans and pillows *(pages 187-193)*, we adapted some traditional Aran patterns. These projects are lovely to look at, and are even more interesting when you know their history.

Each textured pattern symbolizes something common to the life of an Aran fisherman. Cables represent fishing ropes, and diamonds represent the mesh on a fishing net. Here are some others:

Honeycomb—symbolizes the hard-
working bee

Moss Stitch—represents the local mosses

Trellis—symbolizes small fields fenced with stones

Zigzag—designates lightning, or jagged paths up an Aran cliff

Marriage Lines—depict the ups and downs of married life

Trinity, Tree of Life or Fern Stitch— symbolizes faith

Each Aran family had its own combination of patterns whose design was handed down through the generations via the sweaters themselves—it never was written down. Just looking at a sweater could help an Aran islander identify the wearer. This was a source of family pride, but also served a grim purpose—it helped to identify the fishermen lost at sea when their bodies washed ashore.

Better to be born lucky than rich.
—Irish proverb

ARAN ISLE AFGHAN
(photo, pages 188-189; about 68 x 70 inches, plus fringe)

What makes it country? Motifs direct from the Emerald Isle, brought over by our immigrant ancestors.

Average: For those with some experience in knitting.

Materials:
Lion Brand Sayelle 4-ply worsted weight yarn (4-ounce skein): 14 skeins of Eggshell; 1 pair size 7 knitting needles, OR ANY SIZE NEEDLES TO OBTAIN GAUGE BELOW; 1 double-pointed needle (dp); tapestry needle; crochet hook; 9-inch cardboard square.

Gauge: In Seed Stitch, 4½ sts = 1 inch; 6 rows = 1 inch. In Diamond Cable, 20 sts = 4 inches; 11 rows = 1 inch. In Ridge Cable, 44 sts = 9 inches; 6 rows = 1 inch.

Note: The afghan is worked in strips, which are sewn together. The strips are 70 inches long. The Seed Stitch strip is 7 inches wide. The Single Diamond Cable strip is 4 inches wide. The Center Diamond Cable strip is 12 inches wide. The Ridge Cable strip is 9 inches wide.

Diamond Cable Stitches, Cable Left (CL): Sl next 2 sts to dp needle, and hold in front of work; k next 2 sts, k 2 from dp needle. **Cross 2 Right (CR2R):** Sl next st to dp needle, and hold in back of work; k next 2 sts, p st from dp needle. **Cross 2 Left (CR2L):** Sl next 2 sts to dp needle, and hold in front of work; p next st, k 2 from dp needle.

Directions:
1. Seed Stitch Strip (make 2): Starting at a narrow end, cast on 31 sts. **Row 1:** K 1, p 1 across, ending with k 1. Repeat Row 1 for 70 inches. Bind off loosely in k 1, p 1.

2. Single Diamond Cable (make 2): Starting at a narrow end, cast on 20 sts. **Row 1:** P 8, k 4, p 8. **Row 2:** K 8, p 4, k 8. **Row 3:** P 8, CL, p 8. **Row 4:** K 8, p 4, k 8. **Row 5:** P 7, CR2R, CR2L, p 7. **Row 6:** K 7, p 2, p 1, k 1, p 2, k 7. **Row 7:** P 6, CR2R, k 1, p 1, CR2L, p 6. **Row 8:** K 6, p 2, k 1, p 1, k 1, p 1, p 2, k 6. **Row 9:** P 5, CR2R, p 1, k 1, p 1, k 1, CR2L, p 5. **Row 10:** K 5, p 2, p 1, k 1, p 1, k 1, p 1, k 1, p 2, k 5. **Row 11:** P 4, CR2R, k 1, p 1, k 1, p 1, k 1, p 1, CR2L, p 4. **Row 12:** K 4, p 2, k 1, p 1, k 1, p 1, k 1, p 1, k 1, p 1, p 2, k 4. **Row 13:** P 3, CR2R, p 1, k 1, p 1, k 1, p 1, k 1, p 1, k 1, CR2L, p 3. **Row 14:** K 3, p 2, p 1, k 1, p 1, k 1, p 1, k 1, p 1, k 1, p 1, k 1, p 2, k 3. There should be 10 seed sts on this row. **Row 15:** Repeat Row 13, crossing the stitches in the opposite direction: P 3, CR2L, p 1, k 1, p 1, k 1, p 1, k 1, p 1, k 1, CR2R, p 3.

(Continued on page 189)

Rows 16 to 24: Repeat Rows 12 to 4 *in reverse order* to complete the Single Diamond Cable pattern. When repeating the uneven rows, cross the stitches in the opposite direction as in Row 15. Work the Single Diamond Cable pattern until the strip is 70 inches long.

3. Center Diamond Cable Strip (make 1): Starting at a narrow end, cast on 60 sts. Work three patterns of Single Diamond Cable across as follows: **Row 1:** * P 8, k 4, p 8; rep from * 2 more times. **Row 2:** * K 8, p 4, k 8; rep from * 2 more times. **Row 3:** * P 8, CL, p 8; rep from * 2 more times. Continue working three patterns of Single Diamond Cable across until the strip is 70 inches long.

4. Ridge Cable Strip (make 2): Starting at a narrow end, cast on 44 sts. **Row 1:** P 17, k 2, p 6, k 2, p 17. **Row 2 (right side):** K 17, p 2, k 6, p 2, k 17. **Row 3:** P 17, k 2, p 6, k 2, p 17. **Row 4 (cable twist row):** P 17 for ridge, p 2, *sl next 3 sts onto dp needle, and hold in back of work; k next 3 sts, k 3 sts from dp needle—**cable twist made;** p 2, p 17 for ridge. **Row 5:** Repeat Row 1. **Rows 6 and 8:** Repeat Row 2. **Row 7:** Repeat Row 3. Repeat Rows 1 to 8 for the Ridge Cable pattern until the strip is 70 inches long. Bind off on the right side.

(Continued on page 190)

O, Ireland, isn't it grand you look —
Like a bride in her rich adornin'?
And with the pent-up love of my heart
I bid you top o' the mornin'!
—John Locke

Aran Isle Afghan (directions, page 187); Ridge Pattern Pillow and Seed Stitch Pillow (directions, page 193)

5. *Blocking:* Pin each strip to the finished measurements on a padded, flat surface. Cover the strips with a damp cloth, and let them dry; do not press the strips.

6. *Assembling:* Starting at the lower right corner of the afghan, from the right side, pin the strips together as follows: Seed Stitch, Single Diamond Cable, Ridge Cable, Center Diamond Cable, Ridge Cable, Single Diamond Cable, Seed Stitch. With yarn and the tapestry needle, from the right side of the work, sew the strips together taking a small running stitch at the edge of one strip, then taking a small stitch at the matching edge of the adjoining strip. Repeat, working back and forth until the entire seam is joined. Join the other strips in the same way.

7. *Fringe:* Wind the yarn 6 times around the cardboard. Clip the yarn at one end to make 18-inch-long strands. Holding the strands together, fold them in half to make a loop. With the right side of the afghan facing you, working along a narrow edge of the afghan, insert the crochet hook from the back to the front in the corner st of the Seed Stitch strip and draw the loop through. Draw the strands' loose ends through the loop, and pull tightly to knot the fringe. Repeat along the narrow edge, evenly spacing 5 fringes on each Seed Stitch strip, 3 fringes on each Single Diamond Cable strip, 5 fringes on each Ridge Cable Strip, and 9 fringes on the Center Diamond Cable strip. Repeat on the opposite narrow edge. Trim the fringe ends evenly.

COUNTRY WAYS

• Knitting •

Like many of the crafts we enjoy today, knitting is an ancient art. Believe it or not, people wore knitted woolen socks in ancient Egypt!

Historians believe the art of knitting was developed to knit grasses together into fishing nets, mats and baskets. We know that knitting was introduced to Europe sometime in the Middle Ages, probably from the Middle East. The technique caught on quickly, and by 1589, an English clergyman had invented the first knitting machine.

SAMPLE STITCH
ARAN AFGHAN
(about 50 x 70 inches, plus fringe)

What makes it country? A practical and pretty way to practice patterned stitches, much like the embroidery samplers of days gone by.

Average: For those with some experience in knitting.

Materials:
Materials for Aran Isle Afghan *(page 187)*.
Gauge: In Stockinette Stitch (st st), 4½ sts = 1 inch; 6 rows = 1 inch; each square = 10 inches.
Note: *The afghan is made of 35 squares, which are sewn together.*

Directions:
1. *Trinity Pattern Squares (make 8):* Starting at the lower edge of the square, cast on 58 sts. ***Row 1:*** P across. ***Row 2:*** P 1, * p 3 tog; in next st k 1, p 1, k 1 (3 sts worked in one st); rep from * across to last st, p 1. ***Row 3:*** P across. ***Row 4:*** P 1, * in next st k 1, p 1, k 1, p 3 tog; rep from * across to last st, p 1. Rep Rows 1 to 4 for Trinity pat until the square measures 10 inches. Bind off loosely.

2. *Ridge Pattern Squares (make 17):* Starting at the lower edge of the square, cast on 45 sts. ***Row 1:*** K across. ***Row 2:*** P across. ***Row 3:*** K across. ***Row 4:*** P across. ***Row 5:*** P across to form ridge. ***Row 6:*** P across. Rep Rows 1 to 6 until the square measures 10 inches. Bind off loosely.

3. *Diamond Cable Squares (make 10):* Three diamond cables are worked across. Starting at the lower edge of the square, cast on 50 sts. ***Row 1:*** P 7, k 4 to start cable, p 12, k 4 to start cable, p 12, k 4 to start cable, p 7. ***Row 2:*** K 7, p 4, k 12, p 4, k 12, p 4, k 7. ***Row 3:*** P 7, CL *(see Diamond Cable Stitches in Aran Isle Afghan, page 187)*, p 12, CL, p 12, CL, p 7. ***Row 4:*** K 7, p 4, k 12, p 4, k 12, p 4, k 7. ***Row 5:*** P 6, CR2R, CR2L, p 10, CR2R, CR2L, p 10, CR2R, CR2L, p 6. ***Row 6:*** K 6, (p 2, p 1, k 1, p 2, k 10) 2 times; p 2, p 1, k 1, p 2, k 6. ***Row 7:*** P 5, (CR2R, k 1, p 1, CR2L, p 8) 2 times; CR2R, k 1, p 1, CR2L, p 5. ***Row 8:*** K 5, (p 2, k 1, p 1, k 1, p 1, p 2, k 8) 2 times; p 2, k 1, p 1, k 1, p 1, p 2, k 5. ***Row 9:*** P 4, (CR2R, p 1, k 1, p 1, k 1, CR2L, p 6) 2 times; CR2R, p 1, k 1, p 1, k 1, CR2L, p 4. ***Row 10:*** K 4, (p 2, p 1, k 1, p 1, k 1, p 1, k 1, p 2, k 6) 2 times; p 2, p 1, k 1, p 1, k 1, p 1, k 1, p 2, k 4.

(Continued on page 192)

*Sample Stitch Aran Afghan; Trinity Pattern Pillow and
Cable Pillow (directions, page 193)*

*Sleeping is no mean art.
For its sake
one must stay awake all day.*
—Friedrich Nietzsche

Row 11: P 3, (CR2R, k 1, p 1, k 1, p 1, k 1, p 1, CR2L, p 4) 2 times; CR2R, k 1, p 1, k 1, p 1, k 1, p 1, CR2L, p 3. ***Row 12:*** K 3, (p 2, k 1, p 1, k 1, p 1, k 1, p 1, k 1, p 2, k 4) 2 times; p 2, k 1, p 1, k 1, p 1, k 1, p 1, k 1, p 2, k 3. ***Row 13:*** P 2, (CR2R, p 1, k 1, p 1, k 1, p 1, k 1, p 1, k 1, CR2L, p 2) 2 times; CR2R, p 1, k 1, p 1, k 1, p 1, k 1, p 1, k 1, CR2L, p 2. ***Row 14:*** K 2, (p 2, p 1, k 1, p 1, k 1, p 1, k 1, p 1, k 1, p 1, k 1, p 2, k 2) 2 times; p 2, p 1, k 1, p 1, k 1, p 1, k 1, p 1, k 1, p 1, k 1, p 2, k 2. There should be 10 seed sts on this row. ***Row 15:*** Repeat Row 13, crossing the stitches in the opposite direction: P 2, (CR2L, p 1, k 1, p 1, k 1, p 1, k 1, p 1, k 1, CR2R, p 2) 2 times; CR2L, p 1, k 1, p 1, k 1, p 1, k 1, p 1, k 1, CR2R, p 2. ***Rows 16 to 24:*** Repeat Rows 12 to 4 *in reverse order* to complete the Diamond Cable pattern. When repeating the uneven rows, cross the stitches in the opposite direction as in Row 15. Work the Diamond Cable pattern until the square is 3 diamonds long. Bind off loosely.

4. *Blocking:* Pin each square to the finished measurements on a padded, flat surface. Cover the squares with a damp cloth, and let them dry; do not press the squares.

5. *Assembling:* Join 7 rows of 5 squares each. Starting at the lower right corner of the afghan, pin the squares as follows. ***Row 1:*** Trinity, Ridge, Diamond Cable, Ridge, Trinity. ***Row 2:*** Ridge, Diamond Cable, Ridge, Diamond Cable, Ridge. ***Row 3:*** Same as Row 1. Repeat Rows 2 and 3 two more times until all 7 rows have been pinned. With yarn and the tapestry needle, from the right side of the work, take a small running stitch at the edge of one square, then take a small stitch at the matching edge of the adjoining square. Repeat, working back and forth until the entire seam is joined. Join the other squares in the same way.

6. *Fringe:* Make the fringe following the directions in Aran Isle Afghan, Step 7 *(page 190),* working along both narrow edges of the afghan and tying 9 fringes evenly spaced across each square.

COUNTRY WAYS

• *St. Patrick's Day* •

On March 17 we celebrate St. Patrick, the patron saint of Ireland, with parades, revelry and, of course, the wearin' of the green. The first St. Patrick's Day celebration in America took place in Boston in the 1700's, and it's been a tradition ever since.

There are only a few details about the life of St. Patrick that we know for sure. He was born around the year 385, when Britain was ruled by the Romans. Some say he came from what is now Wales, others say he came from Scotland.

When Patrick was 16, he was captured by a band of marauders and sold into slavery in pagan Ireland. He worked as a herdsman and, alone in the fields, became increasingly aware of God. Eventually, Patrick escaped and fled to his homeland, but heard voices that told him to return to Ireland and bring faith to the pagans. He spent the rest of his life traveling and teaching in Ireland. He died on March 17.

Although the best known legend about St. Patrick involves his driving the snakes out of Ireland, there is another, more saintly tale concerning him. It seems that the pagan Druids of Ireland could not comprehend the Holy Trinity of the Christian faith — how could three entities exist as one? St. Patrick used a shamrock to show how three leaves existed in unity on one stem. The shamrock has been a symbol of faith in Ireland ever since.

ARAN PILLOWS
(14 x 16 inches)

Average: For those with some experience in knitting.

Materials for One Pillow:
Lion Brand Bulky Knit 3-ply yarn (3½-ounce skein): 2 skeins of Eggshell; matching sewing thread; 1 pair size 10 knitting needles, OR ANY SIZE NEEDLES TO OBTAIN GAUGE BELOW; 1 double-pointed needle (dp); darner needle; crochet hook; 15 x 17 inches of fabric for back; 14 x 16-inch pillow form; 5-inch cardboard square.

TRINITY PATTERN PILLOW
(photo, page 191)

Gauge: 4 sts = 1 inch; 8 rows = 1 inch.

Directions:
1. Pillow Top: Starting at the lower edge of the pillow top, cast on 66 sts. Work in Trinity pattern, following the directions in Sample Stitch Aran Afghan, Step 1 *(page 190)*, until the pillow top is 14 inches long. Bind off loosely.

2. Blocking: Pin the pillow top to the finished measurements on a padded, flat surface. Cover the pillow top with a damp cloth, and let the top dry; do not press the pillow top.

3. Assembling: Pin the knitted pillow top to the fabric pillow back right sides together, with the knitted edges ½ inch from the fabric edges. Using the darner needle and sewing thread, stitch just inside the knitted edges around three sides and four corners. Turn the pillow right side out, and insert the pillow form. Turn in the open edges, and slipstitch the opening closed *(see Stitch Guide, page 214)*.

4. Fringe: Wind the yarn 4 times around the cardboard. Clip the yarn at one edge to make 10-inch-long strands. Holding the strands together, fold them in half to make a loop. Insert the crochet hook from the back to the front in a corner st at a narrow side edge of the pillow top, and draw the loop through. Draw the strands' loose ends through the loop, and pull tightly to knot the fringe. Repeat in every other st along the side edge of the pillow top. Repeat on the opposite side edge. Trim the fringe ends evenly.

RIDGE PATTERN PILLOW
(photo, pages 188-189)

Gauge: In Stockinette Stitch (st st), 3½ sts = 1 inch; 4 rows = 1 inch.

Directions:
1. Pillow Top: Starting at the lower edge of the pillow top, cast on 56 sts. Work in Ridge pattern, following the directions in Sample Stitch Aran Afghan, Step 2 *(page 190)*, until the top is 14 inches long. Bind off loosely.

2. Finishing: Finish the pillow following the directions in Trinity Pattern Pillow, Steps 2 to 4.

SEED STITCH PILLOW
(photo, pages 188-189)

Gauge: 3½ sts = 1 inch; 5 rows = 1 inch.

Directions:
1. Pillow Top: Starting at the lower edge of the pillow top, cast on 57 sts. Work in Seed st as follows. **Row 1:** K 1, p 1 across, ending with k 1. Repeat Row 1 until the pillow top is 14 inches long. Bind off loosely in k 1, p 1.

2. Finishing: Finish the pillow following the directions in Trinity Pattern Pillow, Steps 2 to 4.

CABLE PILLOW
(photo, page 191)

Gauge: In Stockinette Stitch (st st) 3½ sts = 1 inch; 4 rows = 1 inch.

Directions:
1. Pillow Top: Three 6-stitch cables are worked across. Starting at the lower edge, cast on 56 sts. **Row 1:** K 13, p 2, k 6, p 4, k 6, p 4, k 6, p 2, k 13. **Row 2:** P 13, k 2, p 6, k 4, p 6, k 4, p 6, k 2, p 13. **Row 3:** K 13, p 2, k 6, p 4, k 6, p 4, k 6, p 2, k 13. **Rows 4 to 6:** Rep Rows 2 and 3. **Row 7 (cable twist row):** P 13 for ridge, p 2, *slip next 3 sts onto dp needle, and hold in back of work; k next 3 sts, k 3 sts from dp needle—**cable twist made;** p 4, cable twist, p 4, cable twist, p 2, p 13 for ridge. Repeat Rows 2 to 7 until the pillow top is 14 inches long. Bind off loosely.

2. Finishing: Finish the pillow following the directions in Trinity Pattern Pillow, Steps 2 to 4.

> *When a task is once begun, never leave it until it is done.*
> — New England saying

BE MY
V·A·L·E·N·T·I·N·E

Make one of these country-style Valentine's Day projects, and show someone just how much you love him or her.

HEARTS & CHECKERS QUILT
(about 46 x 64 inches)

A beautiful quilt to thrill the heart of any little girl.

Average: For those with some experience in quilting.

Materials:
45-inch-wide fabric: 5½ yards of white calico, ½ yard of green calico, and 1¼ yards of solid red; white and red sewing threads; white quilting thread; safety pins, or quilter's pins and darner or milliner's needle; between needle; synthetic batting; quilting frame or hoop; brown paper; masking tape; hard pencil.
Note: *The quilt is assembled from eight patchwork Blocks A and seven appliquéd heart Blocks B (see* FIGS. *IV, 8B and 8C, page 196). Borders are added (see* FIG. *IV, 8D, page 196), with a sawtooth edging of folded squares enclosed in the outside seam. The seams are machine sewn; the heart appliqués and quilting are hand sewn.*

Directions (¼-inch seams allowed):
1. Pattern: Trace the small and large heart patterns in FIG. IV, 8A onto folded brown paper, placing the broken line on the fold. Unfold for the full patterns; the large heart (solid line) is the quilting design, the small heart (dotted line) is the appliqué.
2. Cutting: From the white fabric, cut two 36 x 52-inch pieces for the quilt back, two 9 x 52-inch borders, one 7 x 49-inch border, one 9 x 49-inch border, seven 10½ x 6½-inch rectangles, fourteen 2½ x 6½-inch rectangles, thirty-two 2½-inch squares for quilt blocks A, and one hundred sixty 2½-inch squares for the sawtooth edging. **From the green fabric**, cut seventy-two 2½-inch squares. **From the red fabric**, cut one hundred twenty-four 2½-inch squares. Also trace, without cutting, seven small (dotted line) hearts ½ inch apart.

3. Block A: Following the diagram in FIG. IV, 8B, sew the 2½-inch squares side by side to make five horizontal rows. Sew the rows from top to bottom, seams matching, to make the block. Make eight blocks.
4. Block B: Sew a red square at each end of a 2½ x 6½-inch white rectangle *(see* FIG. IV, 8C). Sew this row to one long edge of a 10½ x 6½-inch white rectangle. Repeat at the opposite edge. Make seven B blocks.
5. Assembling: Following the diagram in FIG. IV, 8D, sew five horizontal rows of three blocks each. Sew the rows one below the other, seams matching.
6. Borders: Sew a 52-inch-long border at each side of the assembly *(see* FIG. IV, 8D), and trim the ends flush. Sew the 7-inch-wide border to the top and the 9-inch-wide border to the bottom of the assembly.
7. Sawtooth Edging: Fold each 2½-inch white square in half diagonally, then in half again, raw edges even, to make a triangle; press. Repeat. Lap one triangle 1¼ inches over another, with the single folds at the top and raw edges even *(see* FIG. IV, 8E). Repeat to make 33 points. Stitch the points together a scant ¼ inch from the raw edges to make the top edging. Make a second row of 33 points the same way for the bottom edging. Make two rows of 47 points each for the side edgings. With right sides together and raw edges even, stitch the sawtooth strips to the top and bottom edges of the quilt top, then to each side edge; remove excess triangles if necessary. Press the edging outward.
8. Quilt Back: Sew the two quilt back pieces together along a long edge, and press the seam to one side. Spread out the quilt back, wrong side up, on a clean, flat surface, and tape down the corners. Cut a piece of batting to fit the quilt back. Spread the batting and then the quilt top, right side up and centered, on top of the quilt back. Using safety pins, pin-baste the quilt layers together from the center straight out to each edge, and diagonally out to each corner. Add more rows of pins

HEARTS & CHECKERS QUILT

FIG. IV, 8A HEART PATTERNS

FULL SIZE PATTERN

FOLD

· · · · SMALL (for appliqué)
——— LARGE

FIG. IV, 8B QUILT BLOCK A

■ GREEN   ▨ RED   □ WHITE

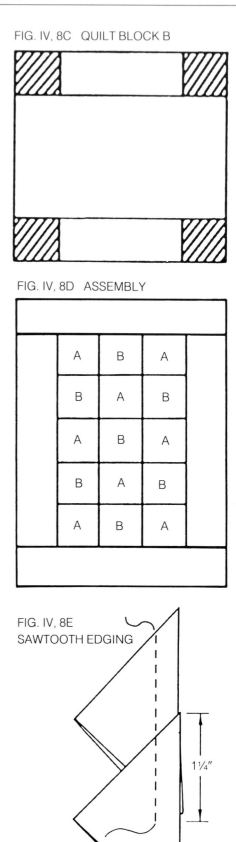

FIG. IV, 8C QUILT BLOCK B

FIG. IV, 8D ASSEMBLY

A	B	A
B	A	B
A	B	A
B	A	B
A	B	A

FIG. IV, 8E
SAWTOOTH EDGING

1¼″

about 6 inches apart. Or pin the quilt layers with quilter's pins, and then use a darner or milliner's needle, single lengths of white sewing thread and long stitches to baste through the quilt layers in the same way you pinned.

9. *Quilting:* Place the quilt in the quilting frame or hoop; work from the center outward if you use a hoop. Using the between needle and quilting thread, quilt about ¼ inch from each seam *(see Stitch Guide, page 214).* At the inner edge of the borders, quilt ½ inch outside the seam.

10. *Appliquéing:* Spread a piece of batting on the back of the red fabric on which the appliqué hearts are traced. Machine-stitch over the traced heart outlines. Cut out the hearts ¼ inch *outside the stitchlines.* Trim the batting close to the stitching. Pin a heart to the center of each Block B, all points toward the bottom. Turn under the appliqué edges on the stitchlines, clipping the curves, and slipstitch each heart in place through all the layers *(see Stitch Guide).* Quilt a smaller heart about an inch inside each appliqué heart.

11. *Border Quilting:* Using the hard pencil, trace a large heart diagonally at each corner. Trace more large hearts, spaced evenly, along the border, points toward the quilt edges *(see photo, page 194).* Quilt over the traced lines, and again about an inch inside them to make smaller hearts. Baste through the quilt ½ inch inside the sawtooth edging.

12. *Quilt Back Edges:* Turn the quilt wrong side up. Trim the batting flush with the outside seamline. Trim the quilt back ½ inch beyond the outside seamline. Turn under ½ inch at each quilt back edge, and slipstitch the fold to the seamline all around the quilt.

The heart speaks in many ways.
— Racine

BABY LOVE KNIT CARDIGAN & CAP

What makes it country? It's a classic cardigan style that's perfect for your littlest Valentine.

Average: For those with some experience in knitting.

Directions are given for Size 12 Months.

Materials:

Coats & Clark Red Heart 2-ply sport yarn (2-ounce skein): 2 skeins of Eggshell (A), and 1 skein of Pink (B); 1 pair each size 2 and size 4 knitting needles, OR ANY SIZE NEEDLES TO OBTAIN GAUGE BELOW; stitch holders; size E crochet hook; tapestry needle; 7 small buttons; two 3-inch-diameter cardboard circles.

Gauge: On size 4 needles, 6 sts = 1 inch; 17 rows = 2 inches.

CARDIGAN

Notes: *The cardigan is worked in one piece up to the underarms. The heart pattern is worked in Stockinette Stitch (St st; k 1 row, p 1 row).*

When changing colors, twist the color previously used once around the new color to prevent holes in the work; carry the unused color loosely on the wrong side unless otherwise noted. If the unused color is to be carried over 4 or more sts, twist it around the color being used every 2nd or 3rd st to hold it in place.

MEASUREMENTS:	
SIZE:	12 MONTHS
CHEST:	21¼"
FINISHED MEASUREMENTS:	
WIDTH ACROSS BACK AT UNDERARMS:	10½"
WIDTH ACROSS EACH FRONT AT UNDERARM (EXCLUDING BAND):	5"
WIDTH ACROSS SLEEVE AT UPPER ARM:	7½"

Directions:

1. Body: Starting at the lower edge of the Back and Fronts combined, with size 2 needles and A, cast on 123 sts. **Row 1 (wrong side):** K 1, * p 1, k 1; rep from * across. **Row 2:** P 1, * k 1, p 1; rep from * across. Rep Rows 1 and 2 until the ribbing measures 1½ inches, ending with a wrong side row. Change to size 4 needles, and work in Heart pat as follows. **Row 1:** K across. **Row 2:** P across. **Row 3:** With A k 5; drop A; attach B, * with B k 1; with A k 7; rep from * across to within last 6 sts, with B k 1, with A k 5. **Row 4:** With A p 4, * with B p 3, with A p 5; rep from * across to within last 7 sts, with B p 3, with A p 4. **Row 5:** With A k 3, * with B k 5, with A k 3; rep from * across to end of row. **Row 6:** With A p 3, * with B p 5, with A p 3; rep from * across to end of row. **Row 7:** With A k 3, * with B k 2, with A k 1, with B k 2, with A k 3; rep from * across to end of row. **Rows 8 to 10:** With A only, p 1 row, k 1 row, p 1 row. **Row 11:** With A k 5, with B k 1, drop B, with A k across to within last 6 sts, attach another strand of B and with this B strand k 1, with A k 5. **Row 12:** With A p 4, with B p 3, drop B, with A p across to within last 7 sts, with B dropped below p 3, with A p 4. **Row 13:** With A k 3, with B k 5, with A k to within last 8 sts, with B k 5, with A k 3. **Row 14:** Working the colors as established on the previous row, p across. **Row 15:** With A k 3, with B k 2, with A k 1, with B k 2, with A k to within last 8 sts, k 2 B, k 1 A, k 2 B, k 3 A. Rep Rows 8 to 15 for Heart pat until the total length is 6½ inches from beg, ending with a p row.

2. Dividing Sts for Upper Back and Fronts, Next Row: Continuing to work in Heart pat throughout, work across first 27 sts, place sts just worked on a st holder for Right Front; bind off next 6 sts for underarm; k until there are 57 sts on right-hand needle, place these 57 sts on another st holder for Back; bind off next 6 sts for underarm; work in Heart pat across to the end of the row—27 sts on needle.

3. Upper Left Front, Row 1: Working over the sts on the needle only, continue to work Heart pat along the front edge, decreasing one st at the armhole edge on the next row, then every other row 3 times in all—24 sts. Work even until 6 Heart patterns along the entire front edge have been completed. Then with A only, continue to work even in St st until the length from the bound-off sts at the underarm is 2¼ inches, ending at the front edge. **Neck Shaping:** Continuing with A only in St st, bind off 5 sts at the neck edge at beg of the next row. Dec one st at the neck edge every other row until 15 sts rem. Work even until the length from the bound-off sts at the underarm is 4 inches, ending at the armhole edge. Bind off all sts for the shoulder.

4. Upper Right Front: Slip the Right Front sts from the holder onto a size 4 needle; attach A strand at the armhole edge and complete to correspond with the Upper Left Front.

5. Upper Back: Slip the Back sts from the holder onto a size 4 needle; attach A strand at the left armhole edge. Working in St st, dec one st at each end every other row 3 times—51 sts. Work even until the length of the armholes is the same as on the Fronts, ending with a p row. **Shoulder Shaping:** Bind off 15 sts at beg of each of the next 2 rows. Place rem 21 sts on st holder for the back of the neck.

6. Sleeves: Starting at the lower edge with size 2 needles and A, cast on 30 sts. Work in k 1, p 1 ribbing for 7 rows, increasing 6 sts evenly spaced on last row—36 sts. Change to size 4 needles. Work in Stripe pat as follows: Drop A; attach B. **Rows 1 and 2:** With B, work 2 rows in St st. Drop B; pick up A. Carry the unused color loosely along the side edge of the Sleeve. **Rows 3 and 4:** With A, work 2 rows in St st. Drop A; pick up B. The first 4 rows form Stripe pat. Working in Stripe pat throughout Sleeve, inc one st at each end on next row, then every 6th row 5 times in all—46 sts. Work even until the total length is 6½ inches from beg, ending with a p row. **Top Shaping:** Continuing in Stripe pat, bind off 3 sts at beg of each of the next 2 rows. Dec one st at each end every other row 7 times. Bind off 3 sts at beg of each of the next 4 rows. Bind off rem sts.

7. Blocking: Pin each cardigan piece to the finished measurements on a padded surface. Cover the pieces with a damp cloth, and let dry. Sew the Shoulder seams.

8. Neckband: With the right side facing, using size 2 needles and A, pick up and k 18 sts along the Right Front neck edge, slip sts from Back st holder onto the free size 2 needle and k these sts, pick up and k 18 sts along the Left Front neck edge—57 sts. Work in k 1, p 1 ribbing the same as for the Body ribbing for 5 rows. Bind off in ribbing.

9. Buttonband: With the right side facing, using the crochet hook, attach A to the top corner of the Neckband on the Left Front edge. **Row 1:** Keeping the work flat, sc evenly along the entire Left Front edge. Ch 1, turn. **Row 2:** Sc in each sc across. Ch 1, turn. Repeat the last row 3 more times. At the end of the last row, break off and fasten.

10. Buttonhole Band: With the right side facing, attach A to the lower corner on the Right Front edge. **Rows 1 and 2:** Work the same as Rows 1 and 2 of Buttonband. Ch 1, turn. With pins, mark the position of 7 buttonholes evenly spaced along the last row, with the first pin ¼ inch above the lower edge and the last pin in line with the center of the Neckband.

Row 3: Sc in each sc to first pin, * ch 1, sk next sc, sc in each sc to next pin; rep from * 5 more times; ch 1, sk next sc, sc in each rem sc. Ch 1, turn. **Row 4:** Sc in each sc and in each ch across. Ch 1, turn. **Row 5:** Sc in each sc across. Break off and fasten. Sew the Sleeve seams. Sew on the Sleeves. Sew on the buttons.

CAP
(not shown)

Directions:
1. Starting at the lower edge with size 2 needles and A, cast on 90 sts. Work in k 1, p 1 ribbing for 7 rows. Change to size 4 needles, and work in Stripe pat the same as for the Cardigan Sleeves until the total length is 5 inches, or the desired length, allowing 1 inch for top shaping; end with a p row.

2. *Top Shaping, Row 1:* Continuing in Stripe pat throughout, * k 4, k 2 tog; rep from * across—75 sts. *Row 2 and All Wrong Side Rows:* P across. *Row 3:* * K 3, k 2 tog; rep from * across—60 sts. *Row 5:* * K 2, k 2 tog; rep from * across—45 sts. *Row 7:* * K 1, k 2 tog; rep from * across—30 sts. *Row 9:* (K 2 tog) 15 times. Leaving a 24-inch length, break off the yarn. Thread the tapestry needle with this length of yarn, and draw through the rem sts on the needle. Pull sts tightly tog and secure on the wrong side. Sew the back seam, matching stripes.

3. *Pompon:* Cut a ¾-inch-diameter hole in the center of each cardboard circle. Place the cardboard circles together. Cut four 1-yard-long strands of B. Holding the strands together, wind them around the double cardboard circle, drawing the strands through the center opening and over the edge until the center hole is filled. Clip the yarn around the outer edge between the circles. Cut a ½-yard length of B, and fold it in half. Slip the doubled strand between the cardboard circles, and tie the doubled strand securely around the pompon strands. Remove the cardboard circles, and trim the pompon ends evenly. Sew the pompon to the top of the cap.

BEAUTIFUL BEADED BOXES

Easy: Achievable by anyone.

Materials:
Heart-shaped wooden boxes; bag of tiny pink beads; bag of pearl beads; pearls by the yard; beaded bridal motifs in pieces, and by the yard; heart-shaped rhinestones; ten 1-inch-wide plastic doves; small artificial flowers; selection of satin ribbons in coordinating colors and various widths, including ⅛- and ⅜-inch widths; tacky glue; small flat brush; glue stick; hair clips.

Directions:
1. Using the photo as a guide, draw each design loosely on a box lid. Trace the bottom edge of the lid lightly onto the side of the box; apply trims to the side of the box only below the line.

2. *White Flight of Doves Box:* Brush a curved path of glue on the box lid. Sprinkle pink beads to cover the glue. Cover the rest of the lid, and the side of the box, with pearls by the yard. Glue eight doves to the pink bead path.

3. *White Flower Box:* Brush the top of the box lid with glue. Press bunches of small flowers on the lid, twisting their stems toward the lid's center. Glue additional flower bunches over the stems of the first bunches, twisting the additional stems to create a mound. Using the glue stick, glue satin ribbon around the side of the lid. Glue coordinating color satin ribbon around the side of the box. Tie two lengths of ⅜-inch-wide satin ribbon into a double bow with streamers. Glue a small flower to each streamer, and glue the bow to the box lid at the top of the heart *(see photo)*.

4. *White Love Dove Box:* Glue a beaded bridal motif to the top of the box lid; if necessary, cut the motif apart and rearrange it to fit the shape of the lid. Fill in spaces with loose pearl beads and heart-shaped rhinestones. Glue beaded bridal motif by the yard to the side of the lid; hold the motif in place with hair clips until the glue dries. Glue two doves to the top of the box lid. Glue a length of ⅛-inch-wide satin ribbon to the box lid, allowing the ribbon to cascade. Using the glue stick, glue the cascades to the lid in various places. Brush glue on the side of the box in a wave-like pattern. Sprinkle on pearl beads, or attach bridal motif fragments. Repeat until the side of the box is covered.

How do I love thee?
Let me count the ways.
I love thee to the depth
and breadth and height
My soul can reach,
when feeling out of sight
For the ends of Being
and ideal Grace.
—Elizabeth Barrett Browning

place. Trim off the excess canvas. Cut a circle from the colored paper or illustration board to fit inside the inner ring of the hoop. Place the circle against the back of the canvas inside the inner ring, and tape the circle to the hoop.

"THE HEART THAT LOVES" CROSS STITCH KEEPSAKE
(10 inches in diameter)

What makes it country? A wise and charming saying, simply expressed in a beloved crafting style.

Average: For those with some experience in counted cross stitch.

Materials:
14-inch square of 16-threads-to-the-inch single-thread tan canvas; embroidery floss: 1 skein of White; tapestry needle; 10-inch-diameter embroidery hoop; tacky glue; colored paper or illustration board; masking tape.

Directions:
1. Place the canvas in the embroidery hoop, making sure the threads are squared and straight.
2. Using all six strands of floss in the needle, and starting at the center, work the design in Fig. IV, 9 in half cross stitch *(see Stitch Guide, page 214)*. Avoid carrying the floss long distances between letters, or the floss will show behind the canvas. Weave floss ends under the backs of the stitches.
3. Turn the hoop wrong side up. Spread glue over the back of the hoop to hold the edge of the canvas in

FIG. IV, 9 "THE HEART THAT LOVES"
CROSS STITCH KEEPSAKE   CENTER

CENTER

Love is, above all, the gift of oneself.
—Jean Anouilh

C·R·A·F·T·S B·A·S·I·C·S &
A·B·B·R·E·V·I·A·T·I·O·N·S

HOW TO KNIT

THE BASIC STITCHES

Get out your needles and yarn, and slowly read your way through this special section. Practice the basic stitches illustrated here as you go along. Once you know them, you're ready to start knitting.

CASTING ON: This puts the first row of stitches on the needle. Measure off about two yards of yarn (or about an inch for each stitch you are going to cast on). Make a slip knot at this point by making a medium-size loop of yarn; then pull another small loop through it. Place the slip knot on one needle and pull one end gently to tighten (FIG. 1).

FIG. 1

• Hold the needle in your right hand. Hold both strands of yarn in the palm of your left hand securely but not rigidly. Slide your left thumb and forefinger between the two strands and spread these two fingers out so that you have formed a triangle of yarn.
• Your left thumb should hold the free end of yarn, your forefinger the yarn from the ball. The needle in your right hand holds the first stitch (FIG. 2).

FIG. 2

You are now in position to cast on.
• Bring the needle in your right hand toward you; slip the tip of the needle under the front strand of the loop on your left thumb (FIG. 3).

FIG. 3

• Now, with the needle, catch the strand of yarn that is on your left forefinger (FIG. 4).

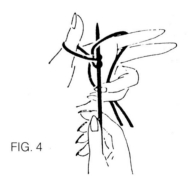

FIG. 4

• Draw it through the thumb loop to form a stitch on the needle (FIG. 5).

FIG. 5

KNITTING ABBREVIATIONS AND SYMBOLS

Knitting directions are always written in standard abbreviations. Although they may look confusing, with practice you'll soon know them:

beg — beginning; **bet** — between; **bl** — block; **ch** — chain; **CC** — contrasting color; **dec(s)** — decrease(s); **dp** — double-pointed; ″ or **in(s)** — inch(es); **incl** — inclusive; **inc(s)** — increase(s); **k** — knit; **lp(s)** — loop(s); **MC** — main color; **oz(s)** — ounces(s); **psso** — pass slipped stitch over last stitch worked; **pat(s)** — pattern(s); **p** — purl; **rem** — remaining; **rpt** — repeat; **rnd(s)** — round(s); **sk** — skip; **sl** — slip; **sl st** — slip stitch; **sp(s),** — space(s); **st(s)** — stitch(es); **st st** — stockinette stitch; **tog** — together, **yo** — yarn over; **pc** — popcorn stitch.

* (asterisk) — directions immediately following * are to be repeated the specified number of times indicated in addition to the first time — i.e. "repeat from * 3 times more" means 4 times in all.

( ) (parentheses) — directions should be worked as often as specified — i.e., "(k 1, k 2 tog, k 3) 5 times" means to work what is in ( ) 5 times in all.

• Holding the stitch on the needle with your right index finger, slip the loop off your left thumb (FIG. 6). Tighten up the stitch on the needle by pulling the freed strand back with your left thumb, bringing the yarn back into position for casting on more stitches (FIG. 2).

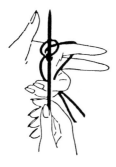

FIG. 6

• **_Do not cast on too tightly._** Stitches should slide easily on the needle. Repeat from * until you have cast on the number of stitches specified in your instructions.

KNIT STITCH (k): Hold the needle with the cast-on stitches in your left hand (FIG. 7).

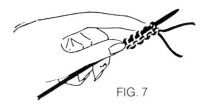

FIG. 7

• Pick up the other needle in your right hand. With yarn from the ball in **_back_** of the work, insert the tip of the right-hand needle from **_left to right_** through the front loop of the first stitch on the left-hand needle (FIG. 8).

FIG. 8

• Holding both needles in this position with your left hand, wrap the yarn over your little finger, under your two middle fingers and over the forefinger of your right hand. Hold the yarn firmly, but loosely enough so that it will slide through your fingers as you knit. Return the right-hand needle to your right hand.

• With your right forefinger, pass the yarn under (from right to left) and then over (from left to right) the tip of the right-hand needle, forming a loop on the needle (FIG. 9).

FIG. 9

• Now draw this loop through the stitch on the left-hand needle (FIG. 10).

FIG. 10

• Slip the original stitch off the left-hand needle, leaving the new stitch on right-hand needle (FIG. 11).

FIG. 11

Note: *Keep the stitches loose enough to slide along the needles, but tight enough to maintain their position on the needles until you want them to slide.* Continue until you have knitted all the stitches from the left-hand needle onto the right-hand needle.

• To start the next row, pass the needle with stitches on it to your left hand, reversing it, so that it is now the left-hand needle.

PURL STITCH (p): Purling is the reverse of knitting. Again, keep the stitches loose enough to slide, but firm enough to work with. To purl, hold the needle with the stitches in your left hand, with the yarn in ***front*** of your work. Insert the tip of the right-hand needle from ***right to left*** through the front loop of the first stitch on the left-hand needle (FIG. 12).

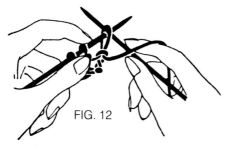

FIG. 12

• With your right hand holding the yarn as you would to knit, but in ***front*** of the needles, pass the yarn over the tip of the right-hand needle, then under it, forming a loop on the needle (FIG. 13).

FIG. 13

• Holding the yarn firmly so that it won't slip off, draw this loop through the stitch on the left-hand needle (FIG. 14).

FIG. 14

• Slip the original stitch off of the left-hand needle, leaving the new stitch on the right-hand needle (FIG. 15).

FIG. 15

SLIPSTITCH (sl st): Insert the tip of the right-hand needle into the next stitch on the left-hand needle, as if to purl, unless otherwise directed. Slip this stitch off the left-hand needle onto the right, but ***do not*** work the stitch (FIG. 16).

FIG. 16

BINDING OFF: This makes a finished edge and locks the stitches securely in place. Knit (or purl) two stitches. Then, with the tip of the left-hand needle, lift the first of these two stitches over the second stitch and drop it off the tip of the right-hand needle (FIG. 17).

FIG. 17

One stitch remains on the right-hand needle, and one stitch has been bound off.

• Knit (or purl) the next stitch; lift the first stitch over the last stitch and off the tip of the needle. Again, one stitch remains on the right-hand needle, and another stitch has been bound off. Repeat from * until the required number of stitches have been bound off.

• Remember that you work two stitches to bind off one stitch. If, for example, the directions read, "k 6, bind off the next 4 sts, k 6 . . ." you must knit six stitches, then knit **two more** stitches before starting to bind off. Bind off four times. After the four stitches have been bound off, count the last stitch remaining on the right-hand needle as the first stitch of the next six stitches. When binding off, always knit the knitted stitches and purl the purled stitches.

• Be careful not to bind off too tightly or too loosely. The tension should be the same as the rest of the knitting.

• To end off the last stitch on the bound-off edge, if you are ending this piece of work here, cut the yarn leaving a 6-inch end; pass the cut end through the remaining loop on the right-hand needle and pull snugly (FIG. 18).

FIG. 18

SHAPING TECHNIQUES

Now that you are familiar with the basic stitches, you are ready to learn the techniques for shaping your knitting projects.

INCREASING (inc): This means adding stitches in a given area to shape your work. There are several ways to increase.

1. To increase by knitting twice into the same stitch: Knit the stitch in the usual way through the front loop (FIG. 19), but **before** dropping the stitch from the left-hand needle, knit **another** stitch on the same loop by placing the needle into the back of the stitch (FIG. 20). Slip the original stitch off your left hand needle. You now have made two stitches from one stitch.

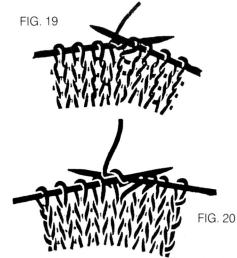

FIG. 19

FIG. 20

2. To increase by knitting between stitches: Insert the tip of the right-hand needle under the strand of yarn **between** the stitch you've just worked and the following stitch; slip it onto the tip of the left-hand needle (FIG. 21).

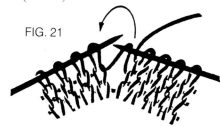

FIG. 21

Now knit into the back of the loop (FIG. 22).

FIG. 22

3. To increase by "yarn-over" (yo): Pass the yarn **over** the right-hand needle after finishing one stitch and before starting the next stitch, making an extra stitch (see the arrow in Fig. 23). If you are knitting, bring the yarn **under** the needle to the back. If you are purling, wind the yarn **around** the needle once. On the next row, work all yarn-overs as stitches.

FIG. 23

DECREASING (dec): This means reducing the number of stitches in a given area to shape your work. Two methods for decreasing are:

1. To decrease by knitting (Fig. 24) **or purling** (Fig. 25) **two stitches together:**

FIG. 24

FIG. 25

Insert the right-hand needle through the loops of two stitches on the left-hand needle at the same time. Complete the stitch. This is written as "k 2 tog" or "p 2 tog."

• If you work through the **front** loops of the stitches, your decreasing stitch will slant to the right. If you work through the **back** loops of the stitches, your decreasing stitch will slant to the left.

2. Slip 1 stitch, knit 1 and psso: Insert the right-hand needle through the stitch on the left-hand needle, but instead of working it, just slip it off onto the right-hand needle (see Fig. 16). Work the next stitch in the usual way. With the tip of the left-hand

needle, lift the slipped stitch over the last stitch worked and off the tip of the right-hand needle (Fig. 26). Your decreasing stitch will slant to the left. This is written as "sl 1, k 1, psso."

FIG. 26

Pass Slipped Stitch Over (psso): Slip one stitch from the left-hand needle to the right hand needle and, being careful to keep it in position, work the next stitch. Then, with the tip of the left-hand needle, lift the slipped stitch over the last stitch and off the tip of the right-hand needle (Fig. 26).

ATTACHING YARN

When you finish one ball of yarn, or if you wish to change colors, attach the new ball of yarn at the start of a row. Tie the new yarn to an end of the previous yarn, making a secure knot to join the two yarns. Continue to work (Fig. 27).

FIG. 27

HOW TO CROCHET

THE BASIC STITCHES

Most crochet stitches are started from a base of chain stitches. However, our stitches are started from a row of single crochet stitches which gives body to the sample swatches and makes practice work easier to handle. When making a specific item, follow the stitch directions as given.

• Holding the crochet hook properly (FIG. 1), start by practicing the slip knot (FIG. 2 through FIG. 2C) and base chain (FIG. 3 through FIG. 3B).

FIG. 1   HOLDING THE HOOK

FIG. 2   THE SLIP KNOT
(BASIS FOR CHAIN STITCH)

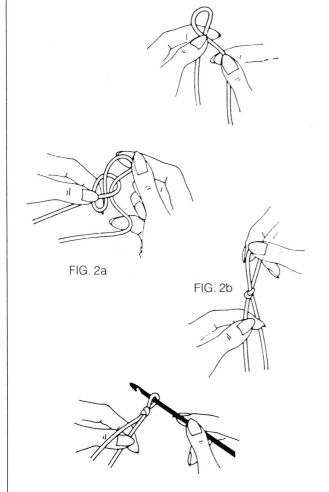

FIG. 2a

FIG. 2b

FIG. 2c

FIG. 3   CHAIN STITCH (CH)

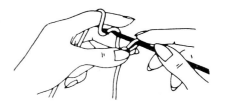

YARN OVER (YO)

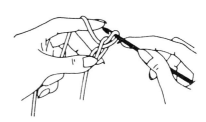

FIG. 3a

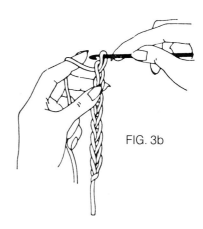

FIG. 3b

CHAIN STITCH (cb): Follow the steps in FIG. 3 through FIG. 3B. As you make the chain stitch loops, the yarn should slide easily between your index and middle fingers. Make about 15 loops. If they are all the same size, you have maintained even tension. If the stitches are uneven, rip them out by pulling on the long end of the yarn. Practice the chain stitch until you can crochet a perfect chain.

From here on, we won't be showing hands — just the hook and the stitches. ***Note:*** *Left-handed crocheters can use the illustrations for right-handed crocheting by turning the book upside down in front of a free-standing mirror. The reflected illustrations will provide left-handed instructions.*

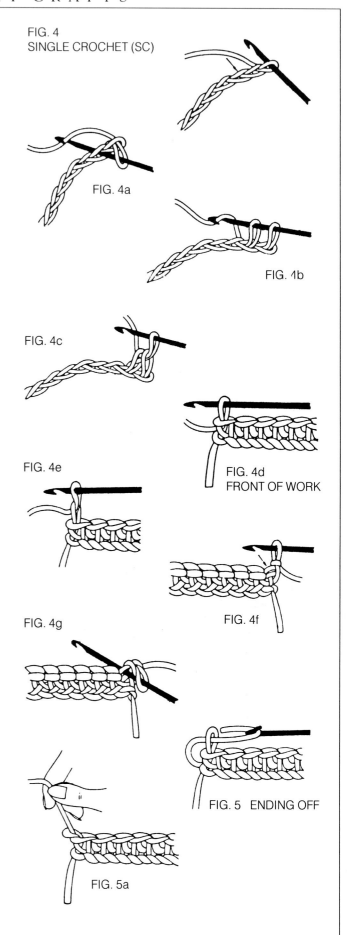

FIG. 4
SINGLE CROCHET (SC)

FIG. 4a

FIG. 4b

FIG. 4c

FIG. 4e

FIG. 4d
FRONT OF WORK

FIG. 4g

FIG. 4f

FIG. 5   ENDING OFF

FIG. 5a

CROCHET ABBREVIATIONS AND SYMBOLS

The following is a list of standard crochet abbreviations with definitions of the terms given. To help you become accustomed to the abbreviations used, we have repeated them throughout our instructions.

beg—begin, beginning; **ch**—chain; **dc**—double crochet; **dec**—decrease; **dtr**—double treble crochet; **hdc**—half double crochet; **in(s)** or **″**—inch(es); **inc**—increase; **oz(s)**—ounce(s); **pat**—pattern; **pc**—picot; **rem**—remaining; **rnd**—round; **rpt**—repeat; **sc**—single crochet; **skn(s)**—skein(s); **sk**—skip; **sl st**—slip stitch; **sp**—space; **st(s)**—stitch(es); **tog**—together; **tr**—triple crochet; **work even**—continue without further increase or decrease; **yo**—yarn over.
* (asterisk)—directions immediately following * are to be repeated the specified number of times indicated in addition to the first time.
( ) (parentheses)—directions should be worked as often as specified.

SINGLE CROCHET (sc): Follow the steps in FIG. 4. To practice, make a 20-loop chain (this means 20 loops in addition to the slip knot). Turn the chain, as shown, and insert the hook in the second chain from the hook (see arrow) to make the first sc stitch. Yarn over (yo); for the second stitch, see the next arrow. Repeat to the end of the chain. Because you started in the second chain from the hook, you end up with only 19 sc. To add the 20th stitch, ch 1 (called a turning chain) and pull the yarn through. Now turn your work around (the "back" is now facing you) and start the second row of sc in the first stitch of the previous row (at the arrow). Make sure your hook goes under both of the strands at the top of the stitch. Don't forget to make a ch 1 turning chain at the end before turning your work. Keep practicing until your rows are perfect.

ENDING OFF: Follow the steps in FIG. 5. To finish off your crochet, cut off all but 6-inches of yarn and end off as shown. (To "break off and fasten," follow the same procedure.)

DOUBLE CROCHET (dc): Follow the steps in FIG. 6. To practice, ch 20, then make a row of 20 sc. Now, instead of a ch 1, you will make a ch 3. Turn your work, yo and insert the hook in the second stitch of the previous row (at the arrow), going under both strands at the top of the stitch. Pull the yarn through. You now have three loops on the hook. Yo and pull through the first two, then yo and pull through the remaining two—one double crochet (dc) made. Continue across the row, making a dc in each stitch (st) across. Dc in the top of the turning chain (see arrow in FIG. 7). Ch 3. Turn work. Dc in second stitch on the previous row and continue as before.

FIG. 7

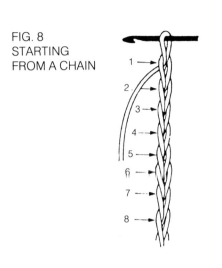

FIG. 8
STARTING
FROM A CHAIN

Note: *You may also start a row of dc on a base chain (omitting the sc row). In this case, insert the hook in the fourth chain from the hook, instead of the second (FIG. 8).*

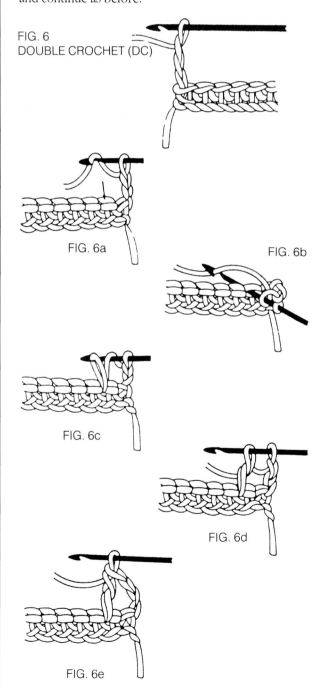

FIG. 6
DOUBLE CROCHET (DC)

FIG. 6a

FIG. 6b

FIG. 6c

FIG. 6d

FIG. 6e

SLIP STITCH (sl st): Follow the steps in FIG. 9. This is the stitch you will use for joining, shaping and ending off. After you chain and turn, **do not** yo. Just insert the hook into the **first** stitch of the previous row (see FIG. 9A), and pull the yarn through the stitch, then through the loop on the hook—the sl st is made.

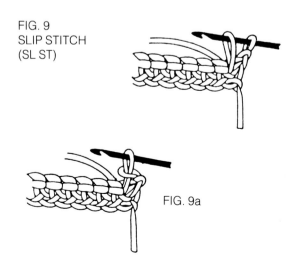

FIG. 9
SLIP STITCH
(SL ST)

FIG. 9a

HALF DOUBLE CROCHET (hdc): Follow the steps in FIGS. 10 and 10A.

To practice, make a chain and a row of sc. Ch 2 and turn; yo. Insert the hook in the second stitch, as shown; yo and pull through to make three loops on the hook. Yo and pull the yarn through *all* three loops at the same time—hdc made. This stitch primarily is used as a transitional stitch from an sc to a dc. Try it and see— starting with sc's, then an hdc and then dc's.

FIG. 10
HALF DOUBLE CROCHET

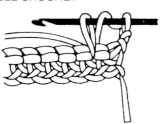

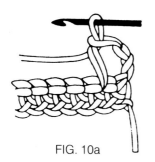

FIG. 10a

SHAPING TECHNIQUES FOR CROCHETING

Now that you have practiced and made sample squares of all the basic stitches, you are ready to learn the adding and subtracting stitches that will shape your project by changing the length of a row as per the instructions. This is done by increasing (inc) and decreasing (dec).

To increase (inc): Just make two stitches in the same stitch in the previous row (see arrow in FIG. 11). The technique is the same for any kind of stitch.

FIG. 11   INCREASING (INC) FOR SINGLE CROCHET

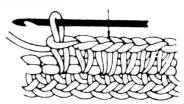

To decrease (dec) for single-crochet (sc): Yo and pull the yarn through two stitches to make three loops on the hook (see steps in FIG. 12). Pull the yarn through all the loops at once—dec made. Continue in the stitches called for in the instructions.

FIG. 12   DECREASING (DEC)

FOR SINGLE CROCHET   FIG. 12

To decrease for double crochet (dc): In a dc row, make the next stitch and stop when you have two loops on the hook. Now yo and make a dc in the next stitch. At the point where you have three loops on the hook, pull yarn through all loops at the same time. Finish the row with regular dc.

HOW TO BLOCK LIKE A PRO

These step-by-step instructions for blocking will insure that your needlework has a professional finished look.

MATERIALS:

• **A Blocking Board** An absolute *must* for professional-looking blocking. You can usually buy a blocking board at craft and sewing centers.
• **Rustproof T-pins and Staples** Used to hold the needlework pieces in place.
• **Undyed Cotton Cloth** A dampened cloth covers the needlework while it is being pressed.
• **Iron** With a dry setting.
• **Yellow Soap** Dels Naptha or Kirkman. For blocking needlepoint. Restores natural sizing to canvas and helps prevent infestations of insects.

KNITTED OR CROCHETED WORK:

The purpose of blocking is to align the stitches, loft the yarn and straighten the knitted or crocheted pieces.
• Pin the work or the pieces, right side down, to the blocking board with the T-pins. Place the pins close together to avoid ripples in the work.
• Dampen a cotton cloth with water and wring it out; the cloth should be moist, not dripping wet. Place the cloth over the work on the board.
• Set the iron on "dry" and select a temperature setting suited to the fibers in the work.
• Gently iron over the cloth in the direction of the stitches. **Do not** apply pressure to the iron or iron against the grain. You may need to remoisten the cloth and iron the work several times, until it is moist and warm to the touch.
• Carefully remove the cloth. If the cloth clings, leaving the work damp and rippled, don't panic. This occurs when a synthetic fiber is pressed with steam that is too hot. No permanent damage can be done unless pressure is used and the stitches are flattened. To restore the work to the desired shape, pat the pieces gently with your hands.
• Allow the work to dry on the board in a flat position for at least 24 hours.
• When the work is completely dry, remove the pins; the pieces are ready to be assembled.

Note: You can ease or stretch pieces a bit to achieve the desired size, but you can't turn a size 10 sweater into a size 16, or shrink a size 40 vest into a size 34.

NEEDLEPOINT PROJECTS:

Blocking needlepoint realigns the threads of the canvas, lofts the yarn and naturally sets each stitch.
*Note: Check for yarn color fastness before you begin to needlepoint. If you've completed a work, and are unsure of the color fastness, **do not block.** Press the work on the wrong side with a warm iron. This won't yield the same results, but avoids color streaking.*
• Place a bar of yellow soap *(see Materials)* in a bowl of warm water and let it stand until the water becomes slick to the touch.
• Place the needlepoint, right side down, on the blocking board.
• Dip a cotton cloth into the soapy water and wring it out. Place the damp cloth over the needlepoint.
• Set an iron on "dry" and select a temperature suited to the fibers in the work. Lightly pass the iron over the cloth; **do not** apply pressure.
• Repeat dampening the cloth and pressing until the canvas is very soft and flexible; moist, but not wet.
• Turn the needlepoint right side up on the board.
• Keeping the threads of the canvas parallel to the grid on the blocking board, staple the canvas to the board leaving 1 inch between the staples and the edge of the needlepoint. (Remove tape or selvages before stapling.) The staples should be fairly close together (staples are preferable to pins because they maintain a straight line and even tension across the work).
• Staple along the bottom edge of the canvas, again, maintaining an even tension across the work. Gently pull one side of the canvas to align the fabric grain with the grid lines on the board, and staple along this edge. Repeat on the other side of the canvas. (**Do not** stretch the canvas; just pull it gently into its original size.) As you are aligning the third and fourth sides, wrinkles may appear in the center of the work; as the fourth side is eased into alignment, these should disappear. If the canvas is pulled off the grain while being blocked, remove the staples and realign the sides. When the grain of the work is perfectly square, the stitching should be aligned; remember, you are not straightening the stitching, you are squaring the threads of the canvas.
• Allow the needlepoint to dry on the board for at least 24 hours.
• When the needlepoint is completely dry, gently pull it up from the board; the staples will pull out easily. Your needlepoint is now ready to be finished.

Note: If the design becomes distorted, reblock the piece. This can be avoided if you use enough soapy steam on the canvas and staple it carefully into a perfect square.

S·T·I·T·C·H
G·U·I·D·E

QUILTING STITCH (RUNNING STITCH)

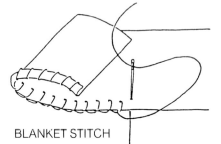

BLANKET STITCH

CHAIN STITCH

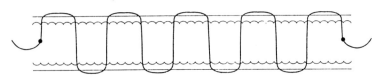

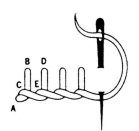

BUTTONHOLE STITCH

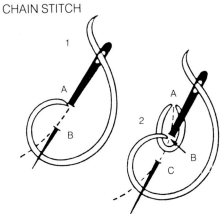

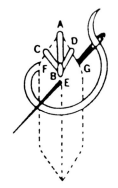

FISHBONE STITCH

BACKSTITCH

CROSS STITCH

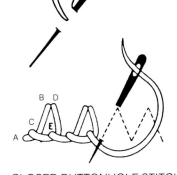

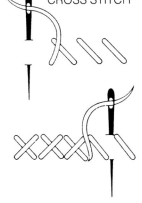

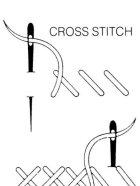

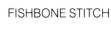

SATIN STITCH

CLOSED BUTTONHOLE STITCH

HALF CROSS STITCH

STRAIGHT STITCH

CONTINENTAL
STITCH

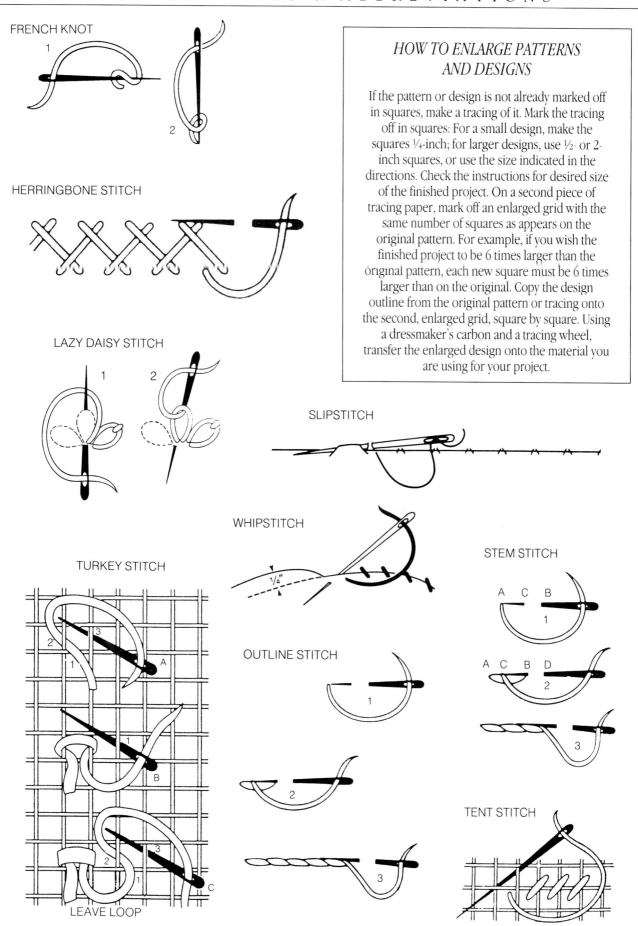

FRENCH KNOT

1

2

HERRINGBONE STITCH

LAZY DAISY STITCH

1   2

TURKEY STITCH

LEAVE LOOP

SLIPSTITCH

WHIPSTITCH

¼"

OUTLINE STITCH

1

2

3

HOW TO ENLARGE PATTERNS AND DESIGNS

If the pattern or design is not already marked off in squares, make a tracing of it. Mark the tracing off in squares: For a small design, make the squares ¼-inch; for larger designs, use ½- or 2-inch squares, or use the size indicated in the directions. Check the instructions for desired size of the finished project. On a second piece of tracing paper, mark off an enlarged grid with the same number of squares as appears on the original pattern. For example, if you wish the finished project to be 6 times larger than the original pattern, each new square must be 6 times larger than on the original. Copy the design outline from the original pattern or tracing onto the second, enlarged grid, square by square. Using a dressmaker's carbon and a tracing wheel, transfer the enlarged design onto the material you are using for your project.

STEM STITCH

A   C   B

1

A   C   B   D

2

3

TENT STITCH

INDEX

PHOTOGRAPHY CREDITS

David Bishop: Pages 19, 158, 165. **Ralph Bogertman:** Pages 13, 60, 89, 135.
Scott Dorrance: Pages 42, 53. **David Glomb:** Pages 68, 71.
Kari Haavisto: Page 180. **Richard Jeffrey:** Pages 188-189. **Elyse Lewin:** Pages 62, 65.
Virginia Liberatore: Page 114. **Mort Mace:** Pages 87, 128, 183, 185.
Bill McGinn: Pages 9, 13, 16, 29, 31, 38, 45, 47, 76, 78, 79, 101, 104, 107, 109, 117, 118, 119, 145, 149, 152-153, 170, 175, 178. **Rudy Muller:** Page 84. **Allan Newman:** Page 125.
Jeff Niki: Pages 130, 142, 167. **Leonard Nones:** Page 194.
Frances Pellegrini: Pages 16, 96, 145, 152-153, 198. **David Phelps:** Page 4.
Dean Powell: Pages 22, 23, 32, 115, 132. **Carin Riley:** Cover Photo, Page 112.
Gordon E. Smith: Page 35. **William Stites:** Pages 120-121, 122.
Bob Stoller: Pages 24, 134, 140. **Theo:** Page 109.
Rene Velez: Pages 13, 16, 45, 47, 81, 96, 101, 104, 107, 109, 145, 149, 152-153, 191, 201, 202.
Ken Whitmore: Pages 9, 38, 76, 78.

CRAFT DESIGNER CREDITS

Amy Albert: Page 96. **Bob Anderson:** Page 132-133. **Elaine Bass:** Page 60.
Joanne Beretta: Page 79, 115. **Shirley Botsford:** Page 38.
Donald Bowman, AIA: Page 62, 65. **Creative Cabinetry:** Page 71.
Jennifer Cecere: Page 81. **Lucy Ciancia:** Page 104. **Coats & Clark:** Page 128, 185.
Camilla Crist: Page 130. **Diana Dahlem:** Page 125. **Dane Danner:** Page 164.
Gail Diven: Page 183. **Gail Diven/Lurdes Mortagna:** Page 9.
Rosemary Drysdale: Page 42, 53, 87, 188-189, 191. **Alexandra Eames:** Page 13.
Lynne Gordon: Page 19. **Blake Hampton:** Page 167. **Millie Hines:** Pages 34-35.
Margot Hotchkiss/Barbara Brooks: Page 22.
Lawrence Kane/Bruce Murphy: Page 134, 140. **Ann Leggiero Kelly:** Page 109.
Lee Lindeman for Coats & Clark: Page 107. **Judy Martin**, Placid Paint Co. : Page 23.
Suzanne McNeil: Page 89 Designs Originals (817) 625-1910.
Cathy Miller: Page 117, 118-119. **Jeff Milstein:** Page 149. **Maryanne Moreck:** Page 47.
Bruce Murphy: Page 145. **Courtesy of Winterthur Museum:** Page 84.
Barbara O'Connor: Page 160, 163. **Howard Pedersen:** Page 45.
Bob Pfreundschuh: Page 152-153. **Lynne Rukowicz:** Page 198.
Darrell Russ: Page 120-122. **Julienne Marie Scanlon:** Page 4.
Cherry Schacher: Page 170, 175, 178. **Constance Spates:** Page 101.
Tom Tavernor: Page 142. **John Teeple:** Page 202. **Louise Tucker:** Page 32.
Twigs Inc: Page 112. **Rene Velez:** Page 135, 147. **Elizabeth Wilder:** Page 194.
Jean Wilkinson: Page 24, 29, 31. **Bernat Yarn:** Page 180.